VIRTUAL JUSTICE

VIRTUAL JUSTICE

the new laws of online worlds

[F. Gregory]
greg lastowka

Yale UNIVERSITY PRESS / new haven and london

Portions of this work are adapted, with substantial revisions, from my prior writings on virtual worlds, including "The Laws of the Virtual Worlds" (with Dan Hunter), 92 *California Law Review* 1 (2004); "Virtual Crimes" (with Dan Hunter), 49 *New York Law School Law Review* 293 (2004); "Amateur-to-Amateur" (with Dan Hunter), 46 *William & Mary Law Review* 951 (2004); "Against Cyberproperty" (with Michael Carrier), 22 *Berkeley Technology Law Journal* 1485 (2007); "Decoding Cyberproperty", 40 *Indiana Law Review* 23 (2007); "User-Generated Content & Virtual Worlds," 10 *Vanderbilt J. Entertainment & Technology Law* 893 (2008); "Planes of Power: EverQuest as Text, Game and Community," 9 *Game Studies* 1 (2009); and "Rules of Play," 4 *Games & Culture* 379 (2009).

Yale University Press books may be purchased in quantity for educational, business, or promotional use. For information, please e-mail sales.press@yale.edu (U. S. office) or sales@yaleup.co.uk (U. K. office).

Set in Minion type by Westchester Book Services

Library of Congress Control Number: 2010926458

ISBN 978-0-300-14120-7

A catalogue record for this book is available from the British Library.

This paper meets the requirements of ANSI/NISO Z39.48-1992 (Permanence of Paper).

10 9 8 7 6 5 4 3 2 1

for Carol

If you have built castles in the air, your work need not be lost; that is where they should be. Now put the foundations under them.

—*Henry David Thoreau*

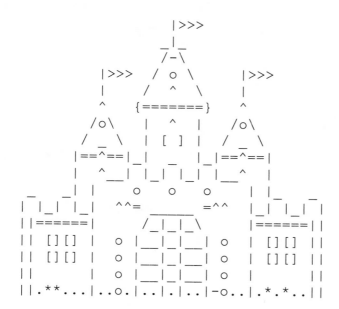

CONTENTS

ACKNOWLEDGMENTS

This book would not have been possible without the help of many people.

First and foremost, I want to thank Carol Chase Lastowka, for providing me with the encouragement, inspiration, support, and time that I needed to complete this project. I also thank Adam and Daniel Lastowka, who were my primary research assistants, and who certainly taught me far more about virtual worlds than I taught them.

My professional colleagues at Rutgers were essential to this project as well, especially Ray Solomon, dean of the law school at the Camden campus. Ray is an ideal dean in so many ways. He has consistently and cheerfully encouraged me to pursue a topic that even I can find, at times, both bizarre and baffling.

In many ways, the wellspring of this project was the enthusiasm of Mike O'Malley, my editor at Yale University Press, who believed there was a place for a book about law and virtual worlds and actually thought I could write it. My friend and co-author on this topic, Dan Hunter, also deserves a full share of the credit for anything original and valuable herein. Dan deserves special thanks for persuading me to write the book I wanted to write, not the one I thought I *ought* to write.

For very constructive comments on early drafts, I thank Mia Consolvo, Nate Combs, James Grimmelmann, Carol Lastowka, Paul Ohm, Michael Risch, and Dmitri Williams. Particular thanks for extensive editorial help go to Richard Bartle, Julian Dibbell, and Josh Fairfield. All these reviewers went far beyond the call of duty in trying to set me straight.

Though I can't hope to offer a comprehensive list of all the people who have helped me in significant ways, I feel obliged to at least make an attempt. So I want to thank: Chara Armon, Jack Balkin, Richard Bartle, Tom Boelstorff, Ian Bogost, Betsy Book, Greg Boyd, Fran Brigandi, Tim Burke, Bryan Camp, Debbie Carr, Michael Carrier, John Carter McKnight, Ted Castronova, Florence Chee, Nate Combs, Bruce Damer, Julian Dibbell, Joost van Dreunen, Benjamin Duranske, Josh Fairfield, Randy Farmer, Jay Feinman, Kim Ferzan, Andres Gadamuz, Alexander Galloway,

Jane Ginsburg, Eric Goldman, Ellen Goodman, Sara Grimes, James Grimmelmann, Andrew Herman, Brian Hirsch, Sal Humphreys, Dan Hunter, Joi Ito, Peter Jenkins, Scott Jennings, Jesper Juul, Avery Katz, Raph Koster, Carol Lastowka, Liz Lawley, Vili Lehdonvirta, Mark Lemley, Will Leverett, Yee Fen Lim, Mike Madison, Thomas Malaby, Viktor Mayer-Schönberger, Kyle McCormick, Shane McGee, John Carter McKnight, Matt Mihaly, Nick Montfort, Juliet Moringiello, Torill Mortensen, Ulf Müller, Jessica Mulligan, Dave Myers, Mira Burri Nenova, Prokofy Neva, Rich Newsome, Beth Noveck, John Oberdiek, Paul Ohm, Cory Ondrejka, Celia Pearce, Jon Penney, Marc Pincus, Juan Carlos Pineiro, David Post, Joel Reidenberg, Ren Reynolds, Dave Rickey, Michael Risch, Alice Robinson, Bonnie Ruberg, Ralph Schroeder, Wolfgang Schulz, Mike Sellers, Bart Simon, Constance Steinkuehler, Nic Suzor, Rick Swedloff, Frank Taney, T. L. Taylor, Dan Terdiman, Mark Terrano, David Thomas, Kevin Werbach, Nick Yee, Unggi Yoon, Andy Zaffron, and Jon Zittrain.

My research assistants also helped me with the text, offering insightful comments and much-needed proofreading. They include Joseph Hickson, Candidus Dougherty, Sidharth Uberoi, Gus Sara, Victoria Mercer, Ryan Strauss, Sang-Eun Kim, Joe Blowers, Carly Karlberg, Danielle Reiss, Melissa Briggs, and Scott Amitrano. I also had the pleasure of teaching thirty-odd students in two virtual law seminars at Rutgers and Columbia Law School. Those students taught me a great deal about virtual worlds. They wrote various papers about the intersection of law and virtual worlds and recounted their experiences touring new realms as penguins, pirates, orcs, ogres, and manga maidens.

This book would never have existed without the authors and the online community at the Terra Nova weblog, where much of my education took place in a public and open forum, via the tutelage of sages with much lengthier virtual world résumés. You can visit the weblog (and search the archives of seven years of discussions) currently at terranova.blogs.com.

Finally, my parents deserve considerable credit for this book. In particular, thirty years ago, with my best interests at heart, they took my Dungeons and Dragons books away from me. Then, a couple weeks later, they gave them back. Things turned out okay, I think.

As a former English professor told me, one's formal writing is no place for a mea culpa. However, I feel obliged to note that this is a book about law that strays fairly far afield from my professional comfort zone. I make extended forays into medieval history, airplanes, and professional sports simply because I could find no better way to say certain things about virtual worlds. I am not a licensed guide to much of this terrain, and perhaps I should have studied the maps more closely.

I will steal some words from Johan Huizinga, since they so aptly describe the dilemma: "I had to write now or not at all. And I wanted to write."

INTRODUCTION

The house of everyone is to him as his castle and fortress.

—Sir Edward Coke

I want to begin not with law or virtual worlds exactly, but with a study of three castles. One castle is real, one is sort of real, and one is arguably unreal, insofar as it exists primarily in a virtual world. All three share the common name of "castle," however. And all three can serve to introduce some basic observations about power, technology, artifice, and law.

CARDIFF CASTLE

Cardiff Castle, with its Norman Keep portion pictured below, sits at the center of the Welsh city from which it derives its name. During their heyday, stone castles like Cardiff Castle were abundant in Europe and served multiple purposes. They were military strongholds, governmental centers, and sites of cultural prominence.[1] Their outward appearance, however, is evidence of their military function. High and heavy stone walls, towers, parapets, gates, and moats are all features that insulate those inside the castle from attacks by outsiders. Though castles are rightly understood as defensive structures, they often served offensive purposes as well, providing a visible base for the occupation and military domination of the local community.

When the first full-fledged stone castles started to appear in the ninth century, European governments recognized them as potential threats to central control. Charles the Bald, who claimed dominion over much of the territory of modern France, even issued an order that required the destruction of unauthorized castles.[2] However, his Edict of Pistres failed to stop castle proliferation. Instead, the Carolingian Empire that Charles ruled was swept away by Viking raiders. Castles grew in importance as a result. They provided local protection against invaders and soon occupied a central position in the post-Carolingian system.[3] Their lords were recognized as local governors, levying taxes and dispensing their own style of justice from castle courts.[4] Some scholars of the medieval era have even

1

Cardiff Castle *Photo credit: John Oyston*

suggested that during the eleventh century the castle became the "fundamental element in judicial organization."[5]

The central authorities' struggle against the power of castles continued, however. For instance, during the fourteenth century and afterward, the English Crown issued "licenses to crenellate." These were, essentially, official permissions to erect castles.[6] Yet many castles were erected in the absence of these licenses. What ended the challenge to central government posed by the castle was another technological shift: gunpowder. By the beginning of the sixteenth century, the cannon had rendered stone castles out of tune with military needs. The castle lost its centrality to legal authority.

Yet echoes of the castle-centered society have persisted in law. Like all technologies of power, the castle allowed the interests of its owners to become intertwined with the workings of law. As Max Weber explained, governments are social institutions that possess a monopoly on the legitimate use of violent force. It should be no surprise that those who control the modalities through which force is exerted shape the law with their ideologies.[7]

The age of the castle court was an era of rule by soldiers. Military leaders were, essentially, political authorities. During the era of "feudalism," as some historians have termed it, this military culture was made part of the law of the land, quite literally.[8] Land was commonly owned subject to an ongoing military and personal relationship between the possessor of the land and a lord. The lord's vassal could possess and profit from the land, but this legal right was contingent on the performance of military (and later, economic) obligations for the benefit of the lord.[9] The failure to serve the lord in battle would result in the forfeiture of the land.[10]

Feudal law did not suddenly cease to exist but rather was gradually trimmed and rewritten by various statutes and judicial decisions into something more fitting to modern sensibilities. Traces of feudalism, however, linger today in the law of property in the West, including the law of the United States, where there are no native castles.[11] The United States owes its property law primarily to England, and England owes its feudal logic to the Norman framework imposed upon it by William the Conqueror. So the law in the United States today reflects a feudal heritage. Lawyers use terms such as "landlords," "tenants," and "estates in fee," none of which would have seemed very strange to the ear of the medieval lawyer. Supreme Court Justice Oliver Wendell Holmes Jr. once remarked in an essay, "It is revolting to have no better reason for a rule of law than that so it was laid down in the time of Henry IV."[12] Yet this seems a fair characterization of much of property law.

Feudal law is hard to divorce from the culture that created it, and that culture is hard to disaggregate, causally, from the medieval technology of the castle. Castles were new sorts of places that gave rise to new sorts of social and legal ordering. They were a new and important technology that left a lasting imprint on law and society.

Today, we might look around at the technologies shaping our lives and ask what sorts of new social places, analogous to the castle, are being created. One particular place I'd like to examine is another castle, located in a Magic Kingdom in the southeastern United States.

CINDERELLA CASTLE

Cinderella Castle is a central feature of Disney World, the largest and most popular theme park in the world, owned by one of the largest media and entertainment companies in the world.[13] Most people would put Cinderella Castle at the heart of Disney World, since it is reportedly the most heavily photographed feature there (and in Florida more generally).[14]

Cinderella Castle in Disney World *Photo credit: Jason Pratt*

Disney's web site says that Cinderella Castle is "the iconic fairy-tale fortress that serves as the gateway to Fantasyland in Magic Kingdom theme park. It is not only one of the central icons of Walt Disney World Resort, but its romantic beauty has also come to represent all of the Walt Disney Company."[15]

Cinderella Castle looks like Cardiff Castle in many ways. It has high, heavy stone walls, towers, parapets, gates, and a defensive moat. Its appearance is clearly intended to say "castle" to the viewer. Perhaps, to the eyes of some modern American viewers, Cinderella Castle looks even *more* castle-like than Cardiff Castle. Yet arguably, it is not a real castle at all.

For instance, the walls are not made of stone or brick, but of decorated plaster bolted onto a steel frame. The upper spires are beautiful and tall (stretching skyward over 180 feet), but they also decrease in scale as they rise; they are built to appear taller than they actually are. The moat around the castle serves no military purpose. It does not frustrate armed attackers; it just looks pretty. So Cinderella Castle's form is not explained by its castle function. Instead, its function is to stir the mind of the viewer with a visible depiction of what a fairy-tale castle should look like.

To be precise, the visual depiction of Cinderella Castle presents a structure based on a film that was borrowed from a folk story. The folk tale of Cinderella has written origins in the seventeenth century, though the story likely dates back earlier. The Cinderella story offers a wondrous inversion of feudal social hierarchy. A cinder-maid vaults from the lowest rung of menial servitude to a royal life.

This Cinderella story, while well known and captivating, is a fairy tale, a constructed illusion just like Cinderella Castle. There may be a person acting the role of Cinderella in Disney World at any given moment, but most people older than six understand that she is not a real princess, and her face probably changes from day to day. Disney's Cinderella does not threaten the authority of the Florida government. Rather, the Florida government recognizes that a greater power, Disney, employs the actress, and that Disney is a profitable business that operates in compliance with the laws of Florida and benefits the state by providing employment opportunities and significant tax revenues.

What many people don't know is that Disney's powers within its Magic Kingdom go a bit beyond those enjoyed by other businesses and theme parks in their jurisdictions. Special Florida legislation, passed at the request of Disney, actually makes Disney World a true local government, with municipal powers over the regulation of the land on which its park is situated.[16] So, for instance, Disney has the legal authority to set and enforce its own building codes and zoning laws.[17] According to Richard Foglesong, Disney achieved this power through negotiations with lawmakers and a promise that Disney World would actually *be* a political community, populated by twenty thousand full-time residents.[18] However, it failed to deliver on that promise, instead providing the theme park of Epcot, something "more like a permanent world's fair."[19]

In addition to its municipal powers, Disney also enjoys the standard powers of any private theme park. For instance, if you flaunt the dress or speech code, you risk being ejected from the park. Its ownership of the land entitles it to set certain rules restricting public admission, and these are rules that the law will recognize and enforce.

None of these powers, however, give it the sort of control that we would associate with a medieval lord or a sovereign state. The Magic Kingdom is a private domain, but it must comply with the rules of state and federal government. As just one example, Disney is required by federal law to provide reasonable accommodations for those who are disabled, such as ramps for those who use wheelchairs. As another example, if Disney were to injure, confine, or defraud those who visit its parks, it would risk civil lawsuits and criminal prosecutions. Its ownership of land does not entitle it to violate criminal and tort laws. And as one more example, if you buy something in a Disney gift shop, the laws of property and contract would dictate that Disney cannot simply reclaim legal ownership of your T-shirt or coffee mug while keeping your payment. So while Disney's private ownership of its land gives it the power to make some rules, the law places significant limits on the extent of that rule-making authority.

In the realm of fantasy, however, the Magic Kingdom has much greater autonomy. Sometimes Cinderella shares her fantastic court at her castle with other Disney princesses, and no one questions Disney's power to change its fiction in this way, even though some visitors might prefer their version of Cinderella to be independent of, say, mermaids and talking fish. The exact nature of the illusions that Disney provides is very important to its visitors—tens of millions come to Disney World each year to partake in them—yet there are few limits on how Disney shapes its fictions.[20] At the level of the Magic Kingdom fantasy, entering Disney World is like entering a zone of fairly absolute private control.[21]

I offer Disney World as an intermediate step toward the final castle I want to discuss, the one that plays a central role in the rest of this book. In this third castle, the structure, the land, and even the bodies of the actors are all part of an elaborate fantasy much like Disney's fantasy of Cinderella and her castle. That fantasy is built, like Disney World, on a form of private property. However, given its peculiar characteristics, it is subject to the authority of a ruler that is even more fantastic, and much more magically potent.

Dagger Isle Castle *Copyright Electronic Arts*

THE DAGGER ISLE CASTLE

The castle shown here is not a tangible structure at all but a representation of a castle that exists, to the extent it exists at all, in the fictional location of Dagger Isle. Dagger Isle is a snow- and ice-crusted landmass located in the northern oceans of a world called Britannia. Britannia is the imaginary world of a multi-player "game" called Ultima Online.[22] Despite its frigid and bleak climate, Dagger Isle is a fairly busy place. Among its many inhabitants are polar bears, snow leopards, orcs, and frost trolls, all of which are hazards for wandering travelers. But the Frozen Mountains at the center of the island are its main attraction. By exploring them, one can find the entrance to the Dungeon of Deceit, a tomb filled with all manner of undead creatures such as ghouls, mummies, wraiths, and zombies. Many people who visit Britannia seek out this place—they are eager to find and destroy the undead (and other beasts and monsters as well).

The name Britannia and the appearance of the castle are, much like Cinderella Castle, intended to evoke pleasing fantasies of medieval times. Like Disney's Cinderella, Britannia combines a romantic repackaging of medieval Europe with a strong dose of magic and mythology borrowed from folklore.[23] But because Britannia is not a tangible structure in the physical world, it is a much more flexible stage than Disney World. The magic in Britannia is made of exactly the same stuff as the castles. Bricks, zombies, and fire-breathing dragons are all simply lines of computer code.

While the Dagger Isle castle is not "real" in the sense that it is not tangible, it is quite real in another sense. I originally encountered the castle, displayed as the picture above, on eBay. On October 28, 2003, the seller was offering it for $999.88. This castle was hardly the only virtual property from Britannia that was being sold on eBay at the time. Various other listings were posted, including Britannian real estate, currency, and sundry other items (including some people).

You might be asking at this point, "Why would anyone pay a thousand dollars (minus twelve cents) for a virtual castle?"

At one point, I wondered the same thing. On further consideration, however, it does not seem so strange. The best way to understand it, I think, is to ask the same question about someone paying a thousand dollars for a week of strolling among the dreams and illusions provided by Disney World. There is nothing tangible about that purchase. If you are in the market for an intangible experience, for about the same price, you could rule over your own castle in Britannia for a much longer time. And when you own the Dagger Isle castle, you get to *be* a ruler, not just take a picture of Cinderella from a distance. You can become the lord of a castle, using your power as you please, in a dreamlike society where your social status actually means something to those around you.

This is where property law comes into play. The actress who plays Cinderella in Disney World has no legal title to her namesake castle. She might enjoy her job, but she must hang up her tiara at closing time. She gets paid to rule the castle in fiction, but she has no legal rights in fact. So, we might ask, is the same true of the Dagger Isle castle in Britannia? Say you were to buy the Dagger Isle castle (or something like it) on eBay. Would you really own it? At what point does the fantasy of your castle in Britannia become a legal reality?

1

law

And no man putteth new wine into old bottles: else the new wine doth burst the bottles.

—Mark 2:22 1:9 (KJV)

This book explores the way law relates to places like Britannia. Britannia is a virtual world.[1] Virtual worlds come in many shapes and sizes. Some have medieval themes, like World of Warcraft. Some are set in outer space, like Eve Online. Some are more eclectic and malleable dream spaces, like Second Life. Some are geared toward children, like the (Disney-owned) land of snow, ice, and flightless birds called Club Penguin.

All virtual worlds, however, are Internet-based simulated environments that feature software-animated objects and events.[2] Users are represented in virtual worlds by "avatars," digital alter egos that both embody and enable users within the simulated space.[3] The social and interactive complexity of virtual worlds can be substantial, making users feel like they are truly "present" somewhere else. This is why virtual worlds are called "worlds."

In 2009, by conservative estimates, about 100 million people were interacting in some sort of virtual world. A 2008 survey conduct by the Pew Internet and American Life Project suggests that about 20 percent of teens and about 10 percent of adults in the United States have participated in some kind of virtual world.[4]

Virtual worlds are something different from traditional forms of media, which generally offer consumers the role of a passive audience. People may care deeply about what happens in the halls of Harry Potter's Hogwarts,

9

and they may dress up as Harry Potter characters on Halloween or spend their time writing fan fiction about Harry Potter on the Web.[5] But they are essentially powerless observers when it comes to the canonical Harry Potter universe. They are not participants with the power to shape the world created by J. K. Rowling.

The canonical text of a virtual world, however, is the very stage on which the community performs. The most compelling element of virtual worlds, it turns out, is not the powerful graphic technologies they employ but the very real social interactions that occur through that technology.[6] Virtual worlds are fundamentally new sorts of *places*, like the castles discussed in the introduction. As books by journalists, anthropologists, sociologists, and others have explained, because virtual worlds are places, they are also sites of culture.[7]

Like Disney World, virtual worlds are communities that are premised on an escape to fantasy. Those who visit virtual worlds seem to bring with them a desire to experience a new sort of freedom to step outside conventional rules.[8] Virtual worlds often promise, quite explicitly, this sort of freedom. The following marketing pitch, for instance, was used to promote Britannia:

> What if you could take on a new persona? One that you could make into anything you wanted. That wasn't limited by physical, economic, or social restraints. That could be anything and everything you ever imagined. If you've ever felt like you wanted to step out of yourself, your life, into one that was full of fantasy and adventure—virtual worlds offer you this opportunity.[9]

Another well-known virtual world today is Second Life, a name that seems designed, once again, to sell the possibility of an alternative existence, a chance to "be" something different in a different sort of place.[10]

But a virtual alter ego, however different it may be in some ways, is never truly separate from the "real" identity of the user. Instead, as Sherry Turkle, T. L. Taylor, and Tom Boellstorff have documented in their studies, what users of virtual worlds often seem to be doing is experimenting, both playfully and seriously, with the boundaries of their true identities. This is part of the reason that sociologist T. L. Taylor calls virtual worlds border or boundary spaces. The societies that use them tend to be communities at play between two worlds: crossing back and forth between fiction and reality.[11] In this book, I will be exploring how legal institutions are handling these sorts of crossings between the virtual and the real, detailing the various problems that are arising at the borders.

THE LAW OF LORD BRITISH

The primary force drawing legal attention to virtual worlds today is the new wealth they are creating, exemplified by the Dagger Isle castle. Simply put, when disputes arise over the disposition of significant amounts of valuable property, the law can usually be called upon to sort things out. As the Britannian castle demonstrates, during the last decade or so, virtual worlds have given rise to significant "virtual economies."[12] Researchers today estimate that over two billion dollars changed hands in 2009 in exchange for items that exist only within virtual worlds.[13] When tens of millions of people start spending billions of dollars on virtual objects, there will inevitably be disputes that lead to lawsuits. The questions that these lawsuits raise seem unusual enough to warrant a separate field of legal analysis. The generic term for this new field is "virtual law."[14]

Though there are at least two hundred legal publications and many court cases dealing with the interplay of law and virtual worlds, there is no authoritative body of virtual law today, or even much of a consensus that this field should really exist as a separate arena of legal doctrine. To the extent that virtual law does exist, it seems to be a field characterized by questions rather than answers.

To get a sense of these questions, consider again the Dagger Isle castle. Imagine you own (or your avatar owns) that castle. The reason we might say you "own" the castle is that, when you log on to the world of Britannia, the software interacts with you in a way that makes you feel as if your avatar actually controls the castle and enjoys a right to possess it. You can also exclude other avatars from intruding on your right of possession. In other words, your avatar can go inside the virtual castle and keep other avatars out. You also have the power to, without much trouble, transfer the castle to another user so that another avatar "owns" the castle. Selling the castle for real money is therefore quite simple: you post a listing via eBay and receive payment for it from the buyer. Then you hand over the "keys" within the virtual world of Britannia.

But if you think you own the castle, and you can, as a practical matter, sell it to someone else for a thousand dollars, does that mean you legally own the castle? Would the government be willing to recognize the castle as a thing that you own? Would the government be willing to enforce your rights of ownership?

Before you say yes, think of the legal implications of recognizing the castle as a form of property. Do you want to see Britannian castles listed as assets in divorce proceedings? Should Britannian castles be disposed of by will as part of an estate? Do you want to pay taxes on your castle?[15] If your castle is *really* legal property, these are just the sort of things you might expect to happen. At the same time, how can your castle *not* be legal property, given that it is valuable to you, you seem to control it, and you seem to enjoy the practical ability to sell the castle to someone else for real money?

Putting aside what the law of your jurisdiction might say about your property interest in the castle, you might wonder if the ownership of the castle is properly a matter for "real law" in the first place. Perhaps there might be a separate law that is applicable in Britannia? It turns out that even though Britannia is not a physical space like Disney World, it has a similar sort of private government. In fact, in Britannia, there is even a fictional ruler, Lord British, who, much like Cinderella, presides fictionally over Britannia's fictional domain. At one time, Richard Garriott, the creator of the Ultima series of single-player computer games, controlled the tiny royal avatar of Lord British.[16]

As is befitting his elevated social status, the avatar of Lord British, ruler of Britannia, is unlike common avatars. He is exceedingly powerful and almost invulnerable to attack. One day when Lord British was taking a stroll, he spotted a thief stealing from one of his loyal subjects. The victim was dismayed, but Lord British came to the rescue, using one of his many magical powers to apprehend the villain. He forced the thief to return the stolen property to the victim. The thief then pleaded for mercy, promising Lord British that he would not steal again. Lord British, in a show of mercy, let the thief go.

A moment later, the thief was back, stealing from the same victim, right under the nose of the lord. Richard Garriott lost his temper. Stepping outside the role of Lord British, he threatened to cancel the account of the player who controlled the thief, banning him from the world of Britannia forever.

In response, the player stepped out of his role as a thief and became indignant himself, perhaps as you might in Disney World if Cinderella were to have you chained and dragged to the dungeon. The thief explained to Garriott that the justice meted out by Lord British was a matter of fantasy and not anything like the justice meted out by the owner of the virtual world. The gist of his argument was this: If thievery were truly wrong (if it were something that the owner of the virtual world actually thought should not occur within Britannia), then the software of the world should have made it impossible for thievery to occur. In other words, if stealing was so wrong in Britannia, why did avatars have the ability to steal? The virtual thief reasoned that because theft of virtual property was *possible* in Britannia, theft of virtual property must be *legal* in Britannia.

Swayed by this argument—or at least sufficiently confused by it—Lord British let the thief go.[17] Today, the owner of Britannia, Electronic Arts (EA), clearly announces on its web page that the thievery of virtual objects is simply a "play style" that is legitimate under Britannian law. Theft of virtual property is something for avatars to deal with through whatever powers the technology grants them. If the innocent are robbed by villains within Britannia, they cannot come to EA petitioning for redress.[18]

Allowing thievery to exist in Britannia might seem like common sense if you think of Ultima Online as just another computer game. After all, simulated murder and mayhem is common in many video games, and petty virtual theft really pales by comparison. If stealing virtual things is a way people can have fun online, then what is the problem with letting people have fun this way in Britannia?

Yet recall that the Britannian castle was selling for one thousand dollars on eBay. Suppose the thief that Lord British apprehended had in fact stolen from the victim a deed to a castle on Dagger Isle. In the physical world, it is impossible to steal a person's home by taking a deed from her pocket. However, in the early days of Ultima Online, the deed to a virtual castle could be stolen in exactly this way. If a thief stole a virtual castle, the victim would not have lost a trinket, but a virtual asset with a significant amount of market value.

Now return to the earlier question: Is a Britannian castle a form of legal property? If the answer is yes, shouldn't it be characterized as theft if you steal something worth a thousand dollars from another person? Because if you cannot steal a watch worth a thousand dollars from another person on the street, why should you be able to steal the equivalent of that watch in Britannia? On the other hand, if stealing is fine in Britannia, then should we understand Britannia as a different legal society with its own special rules that govern the ownership and loss of property?

As another example of the social impact of virtual worlds on standard legal expectations, consider the story of Peter Ludlow.[19] In 2003, Ludlow was an active participant in The Sims Online, a virtual world owned and operated by EA, the same company that owns and operates Britannia.

Peter Ludlow, for whatever reason, enjoyed posting muckraking online journalism about the seedy side of The Sims Online. His journalism included stories about virtual prostitution, virtual currency scams, and other unseemly virtual activities. For obvious reasons, EA did not like what Ludlow was doing. It e-mailed Ludlow to demand that he cease promoting his brand of online journalism within the virtual world.[20] When Ludlow did not comply, he was summarily banned for violating the EA terms of service. Ludlow cried censorship, and the *New York Times* actually ran a story on Ludlow's virtual exile.[21] But EA did not relent, and Ludlow remained banned from the virtual world.

When interviewed by a reporter, an executive from Electronic Arts suggested that both the account termination and Ludlow's journalistic activities were no big deal. Regarding the virtual prostitution and other misconduct, he said: "If someone says that is going on in cyberspace, is it lost on anybody that it's not actually happening? No law was violated. It's a game."[22] Rather than pursue a lawsuit demanding re-admittance to the virtual world of The Sims Online, Ludlow simply relocated his journalistic practices to a competing virtual world: Second Life.[23]

These two stories suggest that Electronic Arts effectively enjoys the power to shape the rules of both property and free speech within its virtual worlds. If the law affords the owners of virtual worlds this sort of freedom, will virtual worlds, like the medieval castle, become new sites for the emergence of new forms of law?

This book is not so much about understanding how the law, set in stone somewhere, applies to these sorts of situations. Instead, I am asking you to consider what *should* be the proper rules for these novel places. In order to explore that question, however, we should start with how courts and law enforcement officers are already dealing with disputes arising in virtual worlds. At this point, there are many cases where "real law" has been called into play to resolve disputes arising in virtual worlds.

"HOMES" IN SECOND LIFE

The first case I want to discuss concerns land in the virtual world of Second Life, the virtual world where Peter Ludlow settled down after his exile from The Sims Online. Second Life is created and maintained by a San Francisco company called Linden Lab. Just as people buy and sell virtual castles in Britannia for real money, so people buy and sell virtual land in Second Life. However, Second Life has received far more media attention in recent years than many other virtual worlds. Part of this is due to the fact that Second

Life is a newer and more populous virtual world than Britannia and many other older virtual worlds. But a larger factor is probably that Second Life has, more so than almost any other virtual world, embraced the concept of a virtual economy. While the dollar trade for virtual castles and currency in the aging world of Britannia has been treated, by and large, with benign neglect by EA, the trade of virtual land and currency in Second Life is intentionally promoted by the software design decisions of Linden Lab.[24]

Second Life presents the user with a robust in-world virtual economy, where users around the world are constantly buying and selling virtual land and goods and services in exchange for the virtual currency (Linden dollars, or "Lindens"). Linden dollars can be earned by working for other users, but they can also be purchased from other users via the Second Life web site in exchange for real cash. They can also be converted (again via an exchange provided by Linden Lab) back into real dollars.[25] Additionally, Linden Lab has a web site that facilitates transactions in virtual land between users, called "residents" in Second Life parlance.

Unlike EA, Linden Lab also sells and rents portions of the world's simulated "land" directly to users. "Private islands" generally cost about twice as much as a Britannian castle, but they become the exclusive virtual domains of their purchasers and can be shaped into whatever form the purchaser desires. Many prominent companies (such as IBM and Sun Microsystems) and educational institutions (such as Harvard, Princeton, and Rutgers) have created their own virtual outposts in Second Life.

Linden Lab has encouraged users of Second Life to build real businesses in its virtual world and make real money through their virtual activities.[26] In 2007 and 2008 the Second Life economy featured daily trades of Linden dollars worth over a million real dollars.[27] According to statistics posted to the Linden Lab web site, in 2007, at least fifty users of Second Life were making more than $8,000 a month working in the Second Life economy.[28] Thousands of users were making in excess of $1,000 a month. One woman even held a press conference where she stated that her avatar had acquired virtual landholdings in Second Life worth a million real dollars.[29]

This virtual land boom in Second Life did not go unnoticed in the *real* real estate industry. In 2007, the brokerage firm Coldwell Banker issued a press release titled "Company Leads Real Estate Industry into Virtual Future." The first few sentences of that press release stated:

With the 3-D virtual world of Second Life® having become an online phenomenon, Coldwell Banker Real Estate Corporation today announced that it is the first national real estate company to sell homes within the community. Offering houses in a variety of architectural styles and the ability to tour neighborhoods with a real estate professional, Coldwell Banker is reinforcing its mission to ensure that everyone can achieve the dream of home ownership, whether on Main Street or in the metaverse.[30]

When I first read this press release, I thought it was a joke.[31] While many users enjoy having their own parcels of simulated space in Second Life, a "home" in Second Life is much more like a dollhouse than it is like real estate. A virtual home does not provide shelter or even a place for the avatar to sleep, since avatars in Second Life don't need shelter or sleep. (Avatars in virtual worlds do sometimes "sleep," but only as a humorous indication that their users have "gone AFK" or spent too long away from the keyboard.) So given that Coldwell Banker's expertise in home sales was only tenuously related to the form of Second Life homes, what possible expertise could its agents offer?

Yet, as it turned out, this press release was not a joke. Coldwell Banker had actually commissioned the construction of over five hundred virtual homes and a virtual sales office in Second Life.[32] A few months later, an article in the *Newark Star-Ledger* reported that more than one hundred of these virtual homes had been sold and that more than one hundred thousand people had visited Coldwell Banker's virtual properties.[33] The company also began offering Second Life visitors a walkthrough of a simulated version of a multimillion-dollar (real) home they were offering for sale.

Charlie Young, an executive vice president at Coldwell Banker, touted the company's experience in an interview: "Rather than having to negotiate for top dollar with Second Life 'land barons,' users can visit our virtual office and interact with our virtual sales associate to buy homes from Coldwell Banker at reasonable rates." The primary goal of Coldwell Banker, he stated, was to "give residents the opportunity to participate in fair and reasonable real estate transactions."[34]

At about the same time that Coldwell Banker was promoting its "dream of home ownership," a lawsuit in Pennsylvania was raising the question of whether this sort of home ownership was legally real. The first major case in the United States that concerned virtual property was *Bragg v. Linden Research*, and it was a dispute over the ownership of land in Second Life.[35]

Marc Bragg, an attorney from Pennsylvania, was a resident of Second Life and a virtual home owner. In fact, Bragg had paid several thousand dollars for various parcels of Second Life land. However, on April 30, 2006, something went wrong.

Linden Lab claimed that Bragg had used a forbidden technique to purchase land that was not officially listed for public sale. To punish Bragg, Linden Lab did exactly what Lord British had threatened to do to the thief in Britannia and what EA had done to Peter Ludlow. It banned Bragg permanently from Second Life, canceling his account. After doing so, it put up all of Bragg's virtual land for resale. In essence, Bragg was forcibly evicted from the virtual world, and his feudal fief was subject to forfeiture. A medieval vassal might have suffered the same fate for disloyalty to his lord. Bragg had lost access not only to the land he had purchased in the disputed auction, but to *all* of his virtual property, worth thousands of real dollars.

Bragg felt he was entitled to something, either the return of his purchase money or the return of his account. Given that he was a lawyer, he filed a complaint in a Pennsylvania state court, seeking reimbursement for his property losses. He also issued a short press release on his law firm's web site promoting the novelty of his legal claim and asserting that this was a "first-of-its-kind" lawsuit about rights in virtual land.[36]

As the Bragg case played out in the court system, Linden Lab was required to justify its actions. Gene Yoon, Linden Lab's lawyer at the time, did not deny that Linden Lab had kept both Bragg's money and his virtual land. But in language much like EA used with regard to Peter Ludlow's journalism, he pointed out that the "land" in this case was not real land. He explained to one news reporter, "The term 'virtual' may not have a strict legal interpretation, but if anything it means that the thing being described is NOT whatever comes after the word 'virtual.'"[37]

This response didn't resolve the dispute, though. Yoon was certainly right that virtual land is not the same as tangible land. But what exactly is it? According to the court papers filed by Linden Lab, they claimed that virtual land could not be defined as something that users of Second Life actually owned, at least vis-à-vis Linden Lab in the event of a violation of their rules. Instead, they claimed, "land" in Second Life was a service that Linden Lab provided and was free to cancel at any time.

Linden Lab claimed that Bragg should have known this because he had been explicitly informed of the nature of his purchase. When Bragg first downloaded the software that ran Second Life, he had been required to click on a box in a software form that indicated his consent to the rules that governed his use of the Second Life software. Linden Lab argued that this set of rules limited Bragg's legal rights in Second Life. Among those rules was a statement that Linden Lab was free to ban Bragg permanently from using the Second Life software:

> Linden Lab has the right at any time for any reason or no reason to suspend or terminate your Account, terminate this Agreement, and/ or refuse any and all current or future use of the Service without no-tice or liability to you.[38]

Other provisions in the contract contained the same message: use of Second Life was permitted only to those who were in the good graces of the company. So even if someone like Bragg had paid thousands of dollars for something that he and Linden Lab described as "land," the rules writ-ten by Linden Lab said that Bragg's practical ownership of that "land" could vanish and that Bragg would have no cause to complain.

Of course, the fact of the matter is that very few people (including lawyers) actually read the detailed and often vaguely worded terms and conditions of online contracts. One recent study suggests that the fraction of those who even skim such language may be about two in every one thousand.[39] Instead, most people, not keen on scanning ten or twenty pages of legalese, tend to click "agree" and move on. Yet even if Marc Bragg read and understood the terms above that were written by Linden Lab, he likely never thought Linden Lab would actually do what that agreement said it could: exercise its right to ban him from Second Life for "no reason." However, "I had no idea you were actually going to do what you said you might do" is not a particularly effective legal argument. So Bragg argued in his court case that, among other things, public policy did not permit Linden Lab to enforce the terms of the agreement.

Bragg argued that the contract was so lopsided and unfair in favor of Linden Lab that it was legally "unconscionable" and the court should not enforce it. He also claimed that Linden Lab was promising one thing to its users in its advertising but delivering another thing in its terms of service. In particular, he pointed out how Linden Lab had promised users on its web site that they could "own virtual land." But what did this ownership mean, he argued, if the land could be taken away at any time for no rea-son?

In May 2007 in Philadelphia, Judge Eduardo Robreno issued an opinion on some preliminary issues in Bragg's case. In the first paragraph of Robreno's opinion, he summarized the dispute as follows:

> Bragg contends that Defendants, the operators of the virtual world, unlawfully confiscated his virtual property and denied him access to their virtual world. Ultimately at issue in this case are the novel questions of what rights and obligations grow out of the relationship between the owner and creator of a virtual world and its resident-customers. While the property and the world where it is found are "virtual," the dispute is real.[40]

However, though the court in the *Bragg* case suggested that it might ultimately explore the novel questions of the mutual rights and obligations of virtual world owners and users, the legal issue it decided that day was more narrow: whether the arbitration clause in the terms of service was enforceable. Linden Lab claimed that before he could file suit, the terms of service required Marc Bragg to travel to California and meet with an arbitration board in an effort to resolve the dispute without litigation.

Bragg had claimed that this provision, like the rest of the contract, was "unconscionable" and could not be enforced against him. Judge Robreno agreed with Bragg. Applying the existing law, Judge Robreno ruled that Bragg could not be required to travel to California for the expensive arbitration the terms required. The online contract was too one-sided to be enforced by the court, and therefore it would not be the final word on the rights of Marc Bragg.

Bragg v. Linden ended there. Soon after Judge Robreno's opinion was issued, the dispute was settled. The parties kept the terms of the settlement confidential. As a matter of law, the fundamental question raised by the lawsuit—the legal status of virtual property interests—remains unanswered.

Meanwhile, on the other side of the world, a more tragic tale of virtual property and law had already come to its conclusion.

QIU CHENGWEI

In 2005, at about the same time that Marc Bragg started buying land in Second Life, a forty-one-year-old man in Shanghai came into possession of another piece of virtual property. Though there are some virtual worlds in China, such as HiPiHi, that resemble Second Life, the virtual world of choice for Qiu Chengwei was Legend of Mir. Legend of Mir offers its users a fantasy world similar to Ultima Online. It is part of the larger class of virtual worlds known as massively multiplayer online role-playing games, or MMORPGs. In 2005, millions of Chinese players were spending countless hours in the simulated world of Legend of Mir, published by Shanda Interactive.[41]

Qiu's most valuable virtual property in Legend of Mir was neither land nor a castle, but a powerful magical sword called a Dragon Saber. The Dragon Saber, like other virtual property, was essentially an image on a screen. It was a potent weapon within the virtual world, but also a sort of trophy, making its owner the envy of other players. Qiu had acquired it through long and grueling hours of play. Yet just as people pay real money for virtual land and castles, they also pay money for Dragon Sabers and other fantasy items in Legend of Mir.

The Dragon Saber was so rare and powerful that it had a market price in China of almost one thousand U.S. dollars. Given that the average annual income in China at the time was about two thousand dollars, Qiu Chengwei probably regarded the Dragon Saber as a significant financial asset. But he ultimately valued the Dragon Saber too much. Rather than bringing a civil lawsuit like Marc Bragg did, Qiu Chengwei killed the person who stole his property from him.

According to news accounts, Zhu Caoyuan was a friend of Qiu Chengwei's who also played Legend of Mir. Zhu asked Qiu if his avatar could borrow the Dragon Saber from Qiu's avatar.[42] Qiu trusted Zhu and lent the virtual sword to him. Zhu never gave it back. Instead, he sold the Dragon Saber to another player (for cash) and pocketed the money.

Qiu's initial reaction was reasonable. He went to the police to report the theft. The Chinese police, however, were of the opinion that a Dragon Saber in Legend of Mir was not legal property. While a person might commit theft by stealing a real, valuable, and tangible sword, the theft of a virtual sword, in the opinion of the police, was simply playing a video game. So the police told Qiu Chengwei that Zhu could not be prosecuted.

Qiu brooded over the loss of the Dragon Saber for days. Finally, he went to Zhu's real home, taking with him a real knife. After a short argument, Qiu stabbed Zhu, killing him. Two hours later, he turned himself over to the police, confessing to the murder. The court that considered Qiu's case imposed a sentence of death. However, it suspended that sentence due to his voluntary surrender and admission of guilt.

It is shocking that anyone might respond to a virtual theft with an act of murder. While the law in some jurisdictions will sometimes permit individuals to use force to defend property rights, no modern legal system would condone Qiu Chengwei's actions. Instead, if Qiu's property were stolen, he should have reported it to the police so he could enlist the help of the state in securing its return. But of course, that is what he did, and the police did nothing. If Zhu had stolen a thousand dollars of Qiu's money, or a ring valued at that price, the police would probably have intervened. But since this was virtual property in a virtual world, they did nothing.

Many people today are suffering similar losses at the hands of some other known virtual property thief. In 2008, Geoff Luurs, a twenty-year-old from Blaine, Minnesota, lost virtual property reportedly worth about $3,800. Luurs, like Qiu Chengwei, knew who the thief was. "Ayri" had robbed Luurs's avatar in the virtual world of Final Fantasy XI, stripping him of his virtual possessions. Through online auction sites, Ayri could easily convert those virtual items into real cash.

Talking with police in Minnesota, Luurs got the same response that Qiu Chengwei received in China. The police turned him away, saying that there was nothing they could do. They stated that they could not "validate any actual dollar loss."[43] Luurs was upset, but he told a reporter that he was resigned to the outcome. He said he had never expected the police to be able to help him.

Law professor Susan Brenner, writing about the incident, has argued that virtual property theft represents a problematic disconnection in criminal law that will soon be fixed: "The officers clearly did not understand, or were simply unfamiliar with, the concept of virtual property with equivalent value in the real world. In time, that will most certainly change in Blaine, Minnesota as well as elsewhere."[44]

The policy argument for the law's recognition of virtual property is fairly straightforward. As a general matter, when governments enforce ownership rights to private property, we live in a less violent society. Where states fail to recognize private property, those who claim it must hide it or defend it with their own force. The absence of property rights would return us to what Hobbes called the "state of nature," where life is "nasty, brutish, and short." If we fail to recognize rights in virtual property, will the state of nature be the state of virtual worlds?

If so, that state will likely spill into the non-virtual world as well. The case of Qiu Chengwei suggests that at least some people are willing to resort to offline violence in response to virtual deprivations. Additionally, where the law turns a blind eye to virtual property theft, it becomes more lucrative to engage in this sort of behavior. For instance, a 2001 *Time* magazine article describes a series of crimes involving a young boy in South Korea:

> A 14-year-old runaway . . . recently defrauded gamers out of about $10,000 by promising to sell them virtual weapons but not delivering the goods after he was paid. The boy, who often slept in the PC café where he played Lineage, pulled off 128 fraudulent deals over a year before he was captured.[45]

This account also describes how quasi-criminal businesses in Korea at the time were doing "a brisk side business trading in virtual weapons." In the ensuing years, these sorts of businesses have expanded, raising the economic stakes and the competitive market for those acquiring and selling virtual property. Indeed, for over one hundred thousand users of virtual worlds today, acquiring virtual property is not simply part of a game. It is a full-time job.[46]

GOLD FARMERS

In virtual worlds, users want things for their avatars: castles, land, Dragon Sabers, and other goods. The most popular sort of property, though, is money. In this case, "money" means some sort of virtual currency. By standard conventions in virtual worlds, wealth tends to be represented as gold coins, though other forms of currency, such as acorns, are used in some cases. In most virtual worlds, gold can be acquired by engaging in simple and repetitive activities. This ensures that all users have the potential to climb the virtual ladder toward status, wealth, and "winning." However, the fact that virtual property can be transferred for cash means that one user can pay another user for the fruits of the arduous process of virtual wealth acquisition. When virtual currency is harvested expressly for resale to other players, this is called "gold farming."[47]

In many countries around the world, thousands of individuals—perhaps even hundreds of thousands—are farming virtual gold. If a hundred million people are using virtual worlds, it is perhaps not so surprising that this would sustain a substantial market for gold farming. In some cases, gold farmers operate as solo ventures. For instance, high school and university students in the United States will sometimes play in virtual worlds in order to acquire and sell virtual property as a new variant of summer employment. The "job" of playing a game might not pay as well as landscaping or waiting tables, but it may compete favorably in terms of its intrinsic rewards.

In countries where the wage expectations are lower, the relative value of the financial rewards of gold farming are higher, while the intrinsic appeal is constant. So the profession of gold farming becomes more popular. Several journalists and researchers have written about gold farming operations in China, a country generally identified as a leader in gold farming operations.[48] In 2005, a reporter for the *New York Times* interviewed a gold farmer in one Chinese business. The twenty-three-year-old worker described his profession:

> For 12 hours a day, 7 days a week, my colleagues and I are killing monsters. I make about $250 a month, which is pretty good compared with the other jobs I've had. And I can play games all day.[49]

Working for eighty-four hours a week for less than a dollar an hour may not seem like playing games. But often the line between what is called play and what is called work in this space is blurry. When journalist Julian Dibbell visited one Chinese gold farm, he observed some workers, journalist after their shifts had ended, actually continuing to work "off the clock."[50] The workers were still doing, for fun, pretty much what they had been doing all day.

Given the value associated with virtual property, it is not surprising that larger companies have moved into the market for virtual goods and attempted to build economies of scale by branding themselves as reputable middlemen in the virtual property trade. Perhaps the most well-known company to have operated in this industry to date is the Hong Kong–based Internet Gaming Entertainment, or IGE for short. In 2006, IGE reportedly made $250 million by buying and selling virtual property.[51] As early as 2004, an IGE officer, Steve Salyer, estimated the value of the global virtual property trade at $880 million.[52]

Richard Heeks, a researcher at the University of Manchester, recently made a similar rough estimate that, in 2007, the revenues from professional gold farming exceeded one billion dollars.[53] By comparison, other researchers estimate that trades in virtual property, including land purchases in Second Life, amounted to two billion dollars in 2007.[54] Heeks also estimated that about half a million people are engaged in the gold farming business worldwide, with the largest numbers of these people in China and other developing countries.[55]

Though the "sweatshop" conditions of gold farming are often described in journalistic reports, these circumstances are hardly unique to gold farming.[56] In much of the world, people labor long hours under burdensome conditions and receive low wages for their efforts. Yet gold farming is often viewed as troubling for an additional reason. The "land" that is farmed is inevitably "owned" by a virtual landlord, and the landlords are not always supportive of the efforts of the farmers. While some companies seem largely indifferent to gold farming, others see gold farmers as unfairly extracting value from property that they do not own. Gold farming is often described as a parasitic business practice that undermines the stability of virtual economies.

Since virtual world owners control the machines at the center of the simulation, they have the technological power to ban the accounts of those they suspect of farming gold. In short, they can, by punching a few buttons, delete the virtual treasuries of gold farmers. Virtual worlds like World of Warcraft have banned tens of thousands of game accounts in attempts to eradicate gold farming.[57] This places gold farmers in a position of substantial risk. Thousands of hours of invested labor can be wiped out in massive account bans.

Gold farming presents an interesting variant on the legal claims of Qiu Chengwei and Marc Bragg. Both Bragg and Qiu Chengwei felt that they had a legal right to keep the virtual property that they had acquired. If we recognize a legal right to the possession of virtual property, does this necessarily entail a right to sell one's virtual property to others? What if the owner of that virtual world—and the majority of the community that uses it—object to the practice of gold farming? Can real economies be kept separate, either practically or legally, from virtual economies?

USERS

In the upcoming chapters, I will consider some of the questions above. However, before exploring the legal issues raised by virtual worlds, I want to provide a better picture of what virtual worlds are today. I want to explain where they come from, how they operate as businesses, and how their technology functions.

Before I start down that path, however, I want to confront an issue that may already be on the minds of some readers. To put the question bluntly (as many people have put it to me), "Are these people crazy?"

The short answer is no.

After giving that short answer many times, however, I think a slightly longer explanation is necessary. Many people, quite honestly, find the whole phenomenon of virtual worlds bizarre. I have spoken with several reasonable people who seem firmly convinced, for some reason, that anyone who spends much time in any virtual world must be socially maladjusted or out of touch with reality.

I am not sure of the source of this conviction, but I think it might be attributed, at least in part, to a powerful stereotype found in the media. As Dmitri Williams has observed, the stereotypical "gamer" is often presented to the public as "male and young, pale from too much time spent indoors, and socially inept."[58] You can probably visualize the image now of the adolescent boy in his parents' basement, gazing into the world of the computer screen.

The problem with this stereotype is not that there are no socially inept, pale young boys exploring virtual worlds today—the problem is that the community that uses virtual worlds goes far beyond this. Though not everyone plays video games, they are certainly a mainstream form of media. Surveys in recent years suggest that almost 90 percent of teenagers are playing video games today, and about half of adults do so as well. Women are actually slightly more likely to play games online than men. Among those adults who play games, the average time spent per week is about seven hours, making it a fairly significant hobby.[59]

Of course, multi-user virtual worlds move a step beyond video games, so the demographic of gamers, whatever that happens to be, is not necessarily the same as the demographic of Britannian society or Second Life. Though not many virtual world demographic surveys exist, a recent survey of Everquest II did provide a great deal of information.[60] Like Ultima Online and Legend of Mir, Everquest II is a fantasy-themed virtual world that features castles, magic, and dragons. Perhaps this is just the sort of place one might expect to find the stereotypical gamer.

Yet the survey data paints a different picture. It indicates that the average Everquest II player is about thirty years old. Fewer than 20 percent of Everquest II players are college age or younger. The average salary of an Everquest II player is $84,000, meaning that this person is probably fairly well educated and is probably not lingering in a parent's basement. Additionally, Everquest II players seem to be more physically fit and get more exercise than their peers in the general population. One demographic fact does hold true to the gamer stereotype, though: there are significantly more men than women in Everquest II. However, about 20 percent of Everquest II players are female, which means the game is not exclusively a men's club. And it turns out that those women who play Everquest II tend to play for longer, on average, than men.

The Everquest II survey does not describe the universe of virtual worlds generally, but it should help the skeptical reader realize that virtual worlds today have demographics that go beyond the universe of basement-bound teenage boys. Not all virtual worlds have older demographics, of course. Disney's Pixie Hollow virtual world and Mattel's BarbieGirls are targeted at young girls. Given the thousands of virtual worlds that are in existence, there are plenty of other groups that can be targeted. As Mia Consalvo says, each virtual world can provide a unique subculture.[61]

One factor that seems to unite users of virtual worlds is their passion for the medium. Virtual worlds can take up a substantial amount of time in the lives of those who use them. For instance, the survey of Everquest II players found that average users spent about twenty-five hours each week playing. This type of intense usage is fairly common in other virtual worlds as well. So how do these mostly adult players of Everquest II—who are also holding down jobs—find the time for this level of online involvement?

It turns out that Everquest II players spend significantly less time than their peers watching television. The typical American spends about twenty-eight hours a week in front of a television, whereas users of Everquest II reportedly watch about eighteen hours of television. So while Everquest II users do spend more total time with screens, they cut back significantly on more passive forms of media.[62]

This shift from largely passive media to networked and interactive media is culturally significant, but at this point there are differing views, and inconclusive findings, about its ultimate societal effects. Some might argue that replacing passive media time with more interactive and participatory virtual worlds will be a positive development because it will lead to richer forms of community. In many ways, a group of eight or twelve people talking, creating, and playing together through the medium of a virtual world seems like an improvement over the same group sitting and watching *American Idol*. Likewise, for children, exploring a virtual world like Club Penguin with friends is probably better, in some ways, than much of what today's commercial-laden television offers.

Ideally, we might all be better off spending less time with television and computer screens and more time with real-world pursuits. Our social world today, many people would claim, is too caught up in technology and electronic networks. Also troubling are frequent stories about addiction to online games, pointing at situations in which people find virtual worlds so alluring that they abandon important professional and social commitments to engage in them. Anyone who is more than superficially familiar with virtual worlds probably has a story of a friend who claimed to be "addicted" at some point. Yet some people claim to be addicted to the Internet generally, and the colloquial usage of the term, while it may point to a significant psychological problem, may also simply be a way of expressing passionate enthusiasm. There is certainly no evidence that the majority of people who enjoy virtual worlds are either psychologically unstable or suffering personal harms as a result of their involvement.

My point here is fairly simple: the person who buys a castle in Ultima Online or a plot of land in Second Life is, in all likelihood, not in need of professional psychological help. We should accept that people who are healthy and sane can be passionate participants in virtual worlds. Not everyone will want to own a virtual castle in the future, just as not everyone today wants to visit Disney World, attend a NASCAR race, collect baseball cards, ride horses, or purchase a luxury handbag. But even if we think that owners of horses and handbags are spending money on things we would not purchase, we do not think of them as people without legal rights. Is there any reason we should think differently about the rights of those who invest time, money, and creative energy in virtual worlds?

OVERVIEW

This chapter, I hope, has explained why virtual worlds present an interesting set of legal problems worth the extended consideration I provide in this book. In the following chapters, I will try to explore the intersection of virtual worlds and law by focusing on specific questions. I begin with the facts. Chapter 2 explores the origins of avatars and virtual worlds. Chapter 3 provides an overview of the various sorts of virtual worlds in use today.

Because the law of virtual worlds is at such an early stage of development, chapter 4 opens the discussion on the topic by providing two brief historical examples of the creation of new law by new technologies, spending some time on the law of the Internet, which provides the "traditional" positive law of virtual worlds. The following chapters move into more specific legal issues. Chapter 5 considers the laws of jurisdiction and contract as applied to virtual worlds. Chapter 6 considers the interaction of law and games, and how this might affect virtual worlds designed as games. Chapter 7 returns to the questions raised here, with a fuller investigation of the nature of legal property and how that doctrine might apply to virtual objects. Chapter 8 focuses on the laws that forbid computer hacking and unauthorized access, exploring how these laws apply in virtual worlds. And finally, chapter 9 looks at the intersection of virtual worlds and the laws of intellectual property.

While I make arguments and offer opinions at various points in the following chapters, I should stress, again, that virtual worlds are novel, and the law has only begun to adapt to this new technology. I am not really setting out to provide a comprehensive account of how today's laws apply to today's virtual worlds. In the coming years, the law will need to change. Given that, I want to give the reader a basis for forming opinions about how the law should apply to virtual worlds in the future. And to do that, we will need to start with the past.

2

history

Upon this point, a page of history is worth a volume of logic.

—Justice Oliver Wendell Holmes Jr.

In 1998, when the Internet still seemed new and strange to most people, the Hollywood romantic comedy *You've Got Mail* featured Tom Hanks and Meg Ryan falling in love with each other anonymously via e-mail. The interesting twist was that offline, the characters of Hanks and Ryan were bitter rivals, oblivious to their growing romance in cyberspace. While the premise was high-tech, the film was actually based on a movie created over fifty years earlier, *The Shop Around the Corner*. The film starred Jimmy Stewart and Margaret Sullivan as two antagonistic co-workers who were, unwittingly, amorous pen pals. *You've Got Mail* was merely an updated version of epistolary romance, replacing mail with e-mail.

News stories about virtual worlds can be similar to *You've Got Mail*. Romance, unsurprisingly, can blossom in virtual worlds. To the extent that virtual worlds add something new, it is a richer context for disembodied communication. Virtual worlds allow for a new form of embodiment, the avatar. The technology of the avatar is not all that recent. In the late 1990s, psychologist Sherry Turkle explained how simulated sexual contact between avatars was taking place in text-based virtual worlds.[1] In 1998, Julian Dibbell described in greater detail how "cybersex" occurred in one particular text-based virtual world, LambdaMOO. Those who practiced cybersex, essentially a form of collaborative real-time erotic authorship, employed special avatars coded for that purpose, capable of scripted responses and various stages of undress. Dibbell dabbled in cybersex

29

practices, but ultimately concluded that his adventures with avatar love were detrimental to his real marriage.[2]

Cybersex has been upgraded in recent years to entail more explicit and visual simulations of sexual interactions between avatars. In February 2007, newspapers across the world featured a story about an unusual divorce suit in England.[3] Amy Taylor had initially met David Pollard in an online chat room of the sort featured in *You've Got Mail*. It turned out they were both fans of Second Life. Taylor and Pollard were soon married in real life, and they also became "married avatars" in Second Life. One day, Taylor came home to find her husband logged on to Second Life, watching a screen where his avatar was engaged in simulated sex with a female avatar controlled by another user.

At first Pollard denied that his avatar's philandering was anything significant, but he ultimately admitted that he had fallen in love with the other woman, whose avatar went by the name of Modesty McDonnell. Taylor sued for a fault-based divorce based on her husband's "unreasonable behavior," and a court in England dissolved the marriage.

Many people found the story fascinating and strange, since the divorce decree seemed premised on avatar infidelity. Given the popularity of the story, it was no surprise when, a few months later, a British tabloid, *The News of the World*, featured another tale of Second Life divorce. This time, the wife discovered the husband with his avatar engaged in simulated gay sex and bondage.[4]

Cybersex infidelity may indeed raise some novel legal questions. Given that some courts receive and consider evidence of "cruelty" and egregious actions by one party, exactly how close does avatar-based infidelity come to its real-life counterpart? Is it just a matter of words and images flickering on screens, or is there something more meaningful taking place?

At a deeper level, however, we might ask whether it is truly all that novel. Those who sell tabloids are understandably interested in titillating stories about sexual misconduct in any new technological wrapper, yet the heart of the plot is just the age-old tale of romance and betrayal. Likewise, I think that much of what interests the media about virtual worlds today is simply a repetition, with some minor twists, of very old practices.

To separate the novelty in today's virtual worlds from the timeless questions they rephrase, it is important to get a sense of how virtual worlds developed historically. For a long time, people have been struggling with the social impact of new technologies and tools of simulation. A sense of history can help us better understand what is happening today. Often, reporters (and some researchers) give a reader the impression that virtual worlds are a phenomenon that began last year. In fact, they are at least thirty years old, and in some ways, much older than that.

This chapter offers a brief overview of the history of virtual worlds in several dimensions, including the evolution of relevant technologies, business models, platforms, subcultures, and formative ideas.[5]

VIRTUAL PLACES

Any history of virtual worlds, even a brief one, should begin with a definition of what they are. There is no fixed definition of virtual worlds at present, but here is one that I think reflects the rough consensus among contemporary researchers who use the term:

> Virtual worlds are persistent, interactive, simulated social places where users employ avatars.[6]

If we accept this definition, there are several key components needed to have a virtual world. A virtual world should be *persistent*, meaning that actions taken and investments made in the simulation are expected by users to last for some time. It should be an *interactive simulation*, meaning that it offers an imitation of reality and allows users to affect the reality represented. It should be a *social place*, meaning that users interact with each other and with the changes in the simulation that they collectively create. And finally, a virtual world should employ the technology of avatars.

This definition excludes certain things that might, colloquially, fall within the scope of the term "virtual world." The Internet and the current incarnation of Facebook, for instance, are sometimes described as virtual worlds. Yet neither simulates a place and features the interaction of avatars with that simulation. Applications that run on the Internet (and Facebook) are needed to create virtual worlds. Video games offer avatars and simulated places, yet they are often neither social nor persistent media: a "game over" screen regularly resets the world to an initial condition.

The various components of virtual worlds evolved along different paths. I believe there are two key components that benefit from historical perspective: simulated places and avatars.

The art of simulation has a very long history and has always been seen as a potentially disruptive technology. For instance, the Greek writer Pliny told the story of the painter Zeuxis, who painted grapes so realistically that birds flew down from the sky and tried to feast on them.[7] The power of simulation to deceive creates a sort of anxiety. Perhaps the most famous expression of simulation anxiety is in Book 7 of Plato's *Republic*. There, the character of Socrates provides an allegory about a cave in which a society of prisoners is chained in darkness.[8] The darkness is broken by a bright light that shines from behind them, allowing puppeteers to cast moving shadows on the wall in front of the prisoners. The character of Socrates explains that the chained prisoners could become so engrossed in the shadow play that they might confuse it with reality. If a prisoner were to escape from the cave and report back to the other prisoners about the world outside, those committed to the fantasy of the shadow play would refuse to accept the truth. They would even persecute and belittle those who denied the false truth of the shadow play. The story suggests that entire societies, like Zeuxis's birds, can be deluded by false representations. To scholars of new media, Plato's cave seems like a prescient vision of media saturation: a society absorbed in a world of flickering symbols projected on screens.[9]

For Plato, the shadows in the cave represented what many scientists today would call reality, as opposed to the truth of philosophy. At the same time, Plato was certainly worried about the social power of artistry. For Plato, an artist's imitations of the visible world simply provided shadows of the truth. Worse yet, art and poetry were crafted to manipulate the irrational instincts of the viewer. For this reason, in Book 2 of *The Republic*, Socrates famously bans poetry (or, more accurately, regulates it) within the ideal city.

Plato's anxiety about the gap between representation and truth has persisted over the subsequent millennia. One modern example can be found in the short story "Tlön, Uqbar, Orbis Tertius," written by Jorge Luis Borges during the early twentieth century. The story twists the allegory of the cave to adapt it to a more modern context and worldview.[10] In the story, Borges (the first-person narrator) hears a friend mention the country of Uqbar. A reference book is consulted which presents Uqbar as a real country, but as Borges learns, it is a country that shares no geographic borders with any other. As the story progresses, it is revealed that the fictional country of Uqbar was created as part of an organized plot to replace fact with fiction. At the story's end, the conspiracy is triumphant: many in the "real" world have adopted the language, culture, and philosophy of Uqbar. Borges's story of Uqbar forces the reader to wonder how much of what we know as "real" is simply blind faith in symbols.

Many of today's virtual worlds, like Ultima Online and World of Warcraft, pay tribute, directly or indirectly, to the sort of fantastic literature that Borges wrote. Literature often creates new and fictional worlds. Though the roots of such worlds date back to mythology, the more modern fantasy protagonists are often not heroes, but ordinary people who find strange portals to fantasy realms. For instance, Gulliver is shipwrecked, Alice falls down a rabbit hole, and Harry Potter discovers that he is the son of powerful wizards. This sort of escapist fantasy clearly has something in common with the escape offered by virtual worlds.

At the same time, writers of fantastic literature anticipated long ago the development of virtual world technologies. With the dawn of various forms of mechanical simulation in the industrial age, fantasy writers began to consider how science and technology could create portals (other than rabbit holes) to the worlds they sought to describe. No doubt, these sorts of fictions inspired some of the inventors of virtual worlds.[11] As Thomas Disch has said, science fiction is "the dreams our stuff is made of."[12]

Ray Bradbury created one of the earliest fictions of a virtual world in his short story "The Veldt."[13] The setting of Bradbury's story is a technological utopia where a family, the Hadleys, has just acquired an automated home. In addition to cooking dinner, the home bathes the children and ties their shoes. The highlight of the home, though, is its most expensive technology, a "nursery" with crystal walls that responds automatically to fulfill the desires of those who enter it. While the two Hadley parents grow increasingly anxious about the home's technological control over their lives, their children grow obsessed with the nursery. One day, the Hadley parents visit the room and discover that their children are spending their time in an African veldt:

> Now, as George and Lydia Hadley stood in the center of the room, the walls began to purr and recede into crystalline distance, it seemed, and presently an African veldt appeared, in three dimensions, on all sides, in color reproduced to the final pebble and bit of straw. The ceiling above them became a deep sky with a hot yellow sun.

In the course of the story, the parents, fearing that the technology has turned their children into monsters, seek to shut down the nursery. The spoiled children are opposed, and they cleverly trap the parents in the room with the virtual lions, who kill the parents.

Bradbury's story can be read as a commentary on the new technologies affecting the world of the early 1950s, reflecting the social transformation of television and modern consumer convenience culture. But for a certain subset of readers, the key appeal of the story is the nursery's technology. Bradbury's nursery features not only amazing imagery, but sound, smell, and temperature as well. It is an early vision of "virtual reality."

At the time Bradbury published the story, computing was in its infancy. It did not take long, however, for other writers to envision how Plato's cave might be crafted from silicon chips.[14] Perhaps the most well known and celebrated of these writers was Vernor Vinge, who wrote the novella *True Names*, published in 1981.[15] Vinge taught computer science, and his writing reflected this. The protagonist in Vinge's story is an author of "participation novels," as well as one of the first stereotypical hacker protagonists. "Mr. Slippery" owns racks of "optical memory" and CPUs buried under his home. By using his "Other World" portal (consisting of electrodes that attach to the scalp), he can enter a virtual world of high-tech warlocks, a society that meets and confers within a well-guarded virtual castle.

In addition to *True Names*, two other early fictional works are generally considered required reading on virtual worlds. In 1984, William Gibson published *Neuromancer*, a novel featuring another antisocial hacker addicted to the exploration of virtual reality.[16] Gibson's book popularized many familiar terms applied to the Internet today, such as "cyberspace," "the matrix," and "the Net," to describe a virtual world of data. Like Vinge's Mr. Slippery, Gibson's antihero uses neural connections to enter cyberspace.

Finally, Neal Stephenson's *Snow Crash*, published in 1992, is the latest of the early fictions about virtual worlds.[17] Mixing humor with technology and Sumerian mythology, Stephenson images a "Metaverse" that is essentially a mirror version of Earth. His protagonist, Hiro Protagonist, is a hacker/samurai/pizza delivery man.

By the time *Snow Crash* arrived in bookstores, film and television had already mapped out a visual terrain of virtual reality. In 1982, Disney popularized the notion of a world inside a computer with the film *Tron*, which drew on the booming culture of video arcades, featuring a hacker/arcade owner who becomes trapped inside a computer and is forced to combat evil programs threatening to take over the world.

However, Paramount's *Star Trek* probably popularized virtual reality more than anything that came before it. In 1987, *Star Trek: The Next Generation* introduced a new *Enterprise* equipped with a state-of-the-art recreational contraption called the Holodeck.[18] Like Bradbury's nursery, the four walls of the Holodeck magically (and without neural connections) brought visitors into an immersive computer simulation. Like the nursery, the Holodeck seemed to malfunction in a malevolent way more often than not.[19]

By the 1990s, virtual reality was almost a cliché. Popular films like *Total Recall* (1990), *Lawnmower Man* (1992), *Virtuosity* (1995), *Existenz* (1999), and *The Thirteenth Floor* (1999) were essentially variations on familiar themes. However, the flagship version of virtual reality is probably *The Matrix* (1999), which spawned two sequels as well as its own licensed virtual world. *The Matrix* might be understood as a sequel to *Tron* in which the evil machines actually take over. Keanu Reeves discovers that his life—as a skilled hacker—is just an illusion fed into his mind by cranial implants. In reality, machine overlords are farming humanity in vats of clear goo. An elite class of philosopher-hackers rescues Reeves from his shadow play and introduces him to the real world: metal monsters, big guns, fashionable clothes, and superhuman kung fu.

AVATAR TECHNOLOGIES

The various fictions of virtual reality have always outpaced the facts, but the facts have often caught up, given sufficient time. It took about forty years for Ray Bradbury's fiction to arrive. In 1992, the first Cave Automatic Virtual Environment (CAVE for short) was developed at the University of Illinois.[20] This early virtual reality system was a room with animated and interactive walls that immersed users (equipped with stereoscopic glasses) in a three-dimensional artificial virtual environment. CAVE environments, though expensive, now exist in many universities around the world. They are not exactly what Bradbury had in mind, but they are similar enough.

Other expensive and immersive technologies offer similar experiences of "virtual reality" today. Due to the popular fictions, most people have the idea that virtual reality involves helmets and gloves. The graphics, presumably, must provide convincing illusions: something like the Holodeck or Bradbury's nursery.

Yet that sort of technology is not popularly available today. The "virtual worlds" I discuss in this book are certainly not much like the Matrix.[21] Instead, they resemble video games. Indeed, many virtual worlds *are* video games, since they are marketed under that designation. And even if they are a somewhat different medium, they share certain formal characteristics with video games. Users of both virtual worlds and video games grapple with interactive digital texts, struggling to produce certain effects from fields of symbols.[22] A key element is the avatar, which represents the agency of the user on the screen.

As Julian Dibbell has noted, the avatars of both video games and virtual worlds can be traced back to older social and symbolic practices, and in particular, the board game.[23] In ancient games like Senet and the Royal Game of Ur, players interacted with game pieces that represented their agency in a simulated space. Actions within that space were dictated by specific rules—a sort of constructed physics of movement and interaction. We can see, I think, in the constellation of pieces spread out on a chessboard, the ancestors of the avatar.

Although board games have always been associated with leisure, they were eventually recognized as tools for strategic training. For instance, in the mid-1600s, Christopher Weikhmann adapted chess to create a game he described as "a compendium of the most useful military and political principles."[24] In the early nineteenth century, a Prussian lieutenant, Georg von Reisswitz, reinvented Weikhmann's game as Instructions for the Representation of Tactical Maneuvers under the Guise of a Wargame. These early military simulations took fairly simple games and adapted them to military purposes. Likewise, some virtual worlds today, like There.com, have been adapted to serve as training instruments for the modern military.[25]

The interchange between leisure games and military simulation has been a two-way street. For many people, war simulations are fascinating and enjoyable, much the opposite of actual war. This was certainly how science fiction author H. G. Wells saw things. Although Wells was an ardent pacifist, in 1913 he published a book of rules called *Little Wars* for a game conducted on lawns and floors utilizing toy metal soldiers.[26]

Miniatures-based gaming had enthusiastic adherents throughout the rest of the twentieth century. In the early 1970s, two fans of military wargames, Gary Gygax and Jeff Peren, combined traditional rules of simulated combat with the fantasy fiction of swords and sorcery.[27] Their game was called Chainmail. Subsequently, Gygax collaborated with Dave Arneson to revise Chainmail so that the game centered on individual heroes rather than the complex dynamics of fantasy battlefields. Rather than control armies, each player was represented by his own tiny lead tabletop figure. The new game was called Dungeons and Dragons, or D&D for short. Its original subtitle reflected its roots in wargaming: Rules for Fantastical Medieval Wargames.

D&D was described as a "role-playing game," because players controlled heroic alter egos who were classified as warriors, clerics, and magic-users. The referee of D&D was referred to as the dungeon master. While dungeon masters enforced the rules of the game, they were very strange referees. They did not arbitrate disputes between players, since players generally cooperated. The dungeon master instead authored the story, provided challenges, and ensured that puzzles, traps, and villains were not so weak that players overcame them easily, but also not so strong as to make victory impossible. In essence, the dungeon master was the ringleader of a rule-based form of improvisational fantasy.

Many of today's virtual worlds, especially games like Ultima Online and World of Warcraft, feature tropes, structures, and systems that originated (or at least were popularized) in Dungeons and Dragons. The crucial step was transforming a machine into a dungeon master, allowing electronics to handle the complex business of depicting worlds, presenting opponents, enforcing rules, and giving praise to the victor.[28] The history of this particular technology is essentially the history of video games.

The invention of contemporary video games is usually traced back to Ralph Baer, the inventor of Pong, the crude digital equivalent of table tennis.[29] However, the popularization of video games is better traced to Steve Russell, a graduate student who studied at MIT in the early 1960s. Russell is commonly credited for creating Spacewar with the help of collaborators.[30] In Spacewar, each competitor controlled a spaceship. The players navigated the ships on a flat plane around a central sun (with simulated gravity) and attempted to destroy each other with missiles. In an interview with a reporter from *Rolling Stone* magazine, Russell described Spacewar not as a game, but as a way to "simulate a reasonably complicated physical system and actually see what is going on."[31]

What made Spacewar so memorable, however, was not its success as a real-time simulation. It became a craze because people could not stop playing it. The novelty of competing with another person *within* a computer simulation was so much fun (at least for computer science students) that Spacewar often took precedence over sleep. The code of the game was freely copied and it swept up graduate students in computer science departments across the United States.

In 1971, a Californian entrepreneur named Nolan Bushnell decided to deliver Spacewar to the masses. Computer Space—essentially Spacewar repackaged—was the first modern coin-operated arcade game. However, it was not a huge success. What fascinated computer science students may have been too complex as an alternative to pinball.[32] So Bushnell formed a new company, Atari, and borrowed Ralph Baer's idea of electronic table tennis, which he christened with the name of Pong. After a lawsuit based on Baer's patent was settled, the Pong craze spread.[33]

Computer graphics evolved slowly, however. As a result, some of the most interesting virtual environments of the 1970s were built out of text. The most important advance was made by Will Crowther, a computer programmer at Bolt, Beranek, and Newman. Crowther's program, Colossal Cave Adventure, commonly known as "ADVENT" or Adventure for short, was written as a pet project for his two young daughters. After Crowther released the program on the early Internet, Don Woods, a computer scientist at Stanford University, improved and re-released Adventure, adding many more game-like elements.[34]

Adventure was reminiscent of Dungeons and Dragons (which Crowther played). The game spoke to the player much like a dungeon master would. After asking the user if instructions were needed, the program explained the scenario:

> You are standing at the end of a road before a small brick building. Around you is a forest. A small stream flows out of the building and down a gulley.

There were no images and no joysticks. To play Adventure, you needed to "talk" back, just as you might speak to a dungeon master, by typing, for instance, "go south" or "enter building." Exploring this way would eventually lead you to the entrance of Colossal Cave. However, a locked grate barred entry. To get past the grate, you needed to enter the small brick building. If you did this, the game responded:

You are inside a building, a well house for a large spring.
There are some keys on the ground here.
There is a shiny brass lamp nearby.
There is food here.
There is a bottle of water here.

The keys could be acquired by typing, "get keys." And you needed to get the keys, because the keys unlocked the grate. Though the game recognized many commands, "go" and "get" were crucial. At its core, Adventure was a game about going places and getting things. The acquisitive and exploratory goals were made clear in the instructions, which stated: "Somewhere nearby is Colossal Cave, where others have found fortunes in treasure and gold."

MMORPGs today are really not all that much different from the game that Will Crowther and Don Woods wrote in the 1970s. They simulate going to new places, solving problems, acquiring treasures, and trying to stay alive. Countless computer games have been written that follow this same trajectory—today they constitute an "adventure" genre. However, virtual worlds needed something more. The first virtual worlds arrived when the game of role-play and acquisition merged with the social interactions made possible by networked computing.

MUD

Spacewar and Pong, though they were hardly virtual worlds, were both two-player games. They established the point that playing with others within simulated spaces was fun and feasible. Even during the late 1960s, before the advent of Pong, distant competitors were playing Spacewar over a computer network. This network was aptly named PLATO, and it was developed as a research project at the University of Illinois.[35] In the mid- to late 1970s, PLATO provided what might be described as the earliest set of virtual worlds. Many multi-player environments existed on PLATO. Though the audience was limited, games like Oubliette apparently offered multi-player groups the chance to explore a simulated environment and collaborate together in real time.

However, for many reasons, most histories of virtual worlds begin with MUD (short for Multi-User Dungeon), a virtual world developed at the University of Essex in England. Like Adventure, MUD was a text-based game program written by two authors. Roy Trubshaw created the basic code of MUD and worked out how to simulate multi-player interaction in a series of rooms. However, Trubshaw eventually graduated and transferred control of MUD to another student, Richard Bartle. Bartle developed a much larger world with more entertaining game play.[36]

Like Adventure, the original MUD was a textual simulation that described locations and objects. The key advance it offered was that multiple users could interact with the environment and each other. So if a user named Alice was in a room with one named Neo, the program would inform Neo not only about the features of the room, but also that "Alice is here." Neo could speak to Alice by typing "Alice hi," which would display "Neo says hi" on Alice's computer. Trubshaw's version of MUD was not much more than this. It was a simulated setting that allowed for interactive communication. It was not much of a game.

Bartle fixed that, adding fantasy tropes: combat, monsters, and the hard-won accumulation of objects and powers. In Bartle's version, Alice could now type "Kill Neo." If she succeeded in combat, she might gain some experience points, while Neo would need to start the game over with a new avatar. The ultimate goal of MUD was to reach the coveted rank of wizard, which ended the game (and actually granted the player quasi-administrative powers over the environment).

The original MUD continued to be played on computers at the University of Essex until 1987, after Richard Bartle had left and started a commercialized version of the game. By that time, a variety of other text-based multi-player virtual worlds had appeared. After seeing MUD's code, computer science students were inspired to write their own virtual worlds (just as Trubshaw and Bartle were influenced by Adventure). Compared to contemporary virtual worlds, MUDs were relatively inexpensive to create, leading to a great degree of innovation in styles and forms.

In the 1980s and 1990s, and continuing to the present day, MUDs exploded into countless forms, leading to many open-ended and creative experiments in virtual community.[37] While MUD is the collective designation for all text-based worlds, a complicated genealogy of MOOs, MUSHes, MUCKs, and other such things soon arose, with the term indicating not just a specific type of software, but often a particular type of online community.[38] MUSHes, for instance, are MUDs that encourage or require active role-playing around a particular fictional theme. For instance, some MUSHes are based on the universe of *Star Trek* or the fictional world of Anne McCaffrey's *Dragonriders of Pern* books. Within these role-play worlds, game rules are less important than collaborative theater. Players are expected to hew to their alternative identities and behaviors in ways consistent with the fictional world.

Perhaps the most celebrated deviation from the MUD form was a project created by James Aspnes (now a professor of computer science at Yale University) who, in 1989, wrote TinyMUD.[39] TinyMUD reversed the course of Richard Bartle—it took away the game and offered users the ability to create their own world. In TinyMUD, players could (and did) create customized rooms and objects. This led to what Bartle describes as a "slash and burn" ecology.[40] TinyMUD worlds grew into wild and ungainly realms, as newcomers added more content compulsively. They eventually became so data-heavy and ponderous that they had to be shut down. Indeed, Aspnes closed the original TinyMUD within a year.

The most well-known MUD based on a TinyMUD-type model is LambdaMOO. It was initiated in 1990 by Pavel Curtis of the Xerox Palo Alto Research Center and is still running today. LambdaMOO has been the MUD of choice for journalists and scholars, and it is mentioned in hundreds of academic books and papers on the topic of MUDs.[41] In many ways, LambdaMOO resembles the non-game of Second Life in text, without the cash economy.

However, LambdaMOO is not to everyone's liking. As Lynn Cherny has explained, sets of LambdaMOO users often left to form their own MUDs with other models of virtual community.[42] Cherny studied one such spin-off, which she called ElseMOO (a pseudonym). Cherny describes ElseMOO as having a more realistic environment modeled after a town in Minnesota. ElseMOO also had a "humans only" rule (players were not allowed to use dragon avatars, for instance) that was thought to promote more civil exchanges. Generally, ElseMOO users seemed to reject the game-play of MUD, the role-play of MUSHes, and the lack of continuity found in LambdaMOO. They wanted something more uniform, genteel, and calm, so they moved to a virtual Minnesotan suburbia.

At the risk of simplifying the considerable diversity and social complexity of MUDs, the technology of virtual worlds led to major genre divergences at a fairly early point. Some users sought out games (Bartle-type MUDs), some sought out theater (MUSHes), some wanted creative tools (LambdaMOO), while others just wanted a space to socialize (ElseMOO). This same sort of diversity is found in virtual worlds today.

DESKTOP WORLDS

Like Spacewar before it, MUD was passionately played by a small subset of people while the rest of the world was oblivious to the phenomenon. MUDs were generally located on large mainframe computers at universities, making students the most likely participants. While some individuals could dial in to these computers, most did not have the needed equipment or were unaware that the software existed. However, as personal computers became popular, home users began to access virtual worlds. And as the market demand for virtual worlds formed, they became increasingly visual.

A first step toward visual virtual worlds was moving the world of video game graphics beyond the single screens featured in Spacewar and Pong. Nolan Bushnell again played a central role in this. Again following Ralph Baer, Bushnell created specialized computers that connected to televisions and played games. (Baer had done this earlier with the Magnavox Odyssey.) Bushnell, once again, was more successful, developing the Atari VCS (also known as the Atari 2600).

One of the earliest and most popular games for the Atari was Adventure, a variant of the Crowther/Woods Adventure game created by Warren

Robbinett.[43] Atari Adventure turned the "you" of Adventure into a very basic visual avatar: a dot resembling a Pong ball. The avatar moved through a rudimentary visual environment, departing from one edge of a television screen "room" and arriving from the opposite side of the screen at a new location. The virtual places in the game featured dragons, castles, and mazes. Like the original Adventure, the Atari version was all about going and getting. Keys unlocked castle gates, a sword was required to slay the multiple duck-like dragons, and the duck-dragons guarded treasures (such as a chalice and a magnet).

In exchange for its graphics, Atari Adventure provided a much more rudimentary world, with far fewer rooms and features than the text version. Complex visual environments really could not appear on the home console (which was limited by its hardware) or in the arcade (where complex games took too much time and too few quarters). The platform that worked best for visual virtual worlds was the personal computer.

The most well known early personal computer was the Apple, and its two founders had some interesting connections to the history of video games. Steve Jobs was an Atari employee, and his friend Steve Wozniak had written the code for Atari's Breakout. According to some reports, Jobs even offered the Apple computer prototype to Atari, but Nolan Bushnell wanted to focus on home consoles, not general-purpose computers.

According to Wozniak, the first Apple was built to play good visual games.[44] And in short order, it did. Richard Garriott, the controller of Lord British discussed in chapter 1, created the game Akalabeth for the Apple II when he was a teenager and sold it at local Texas stores in ziplock plastic bags. His next game was the first in the Ultima series, a line of single-player fantasy games featuring increasingly larger and more complex virtual worlds, with better graphics and richer stories. Other companies, like Sierra Online, were active in creating entertaining visual worlds for the Apple as well.

Yet the Apple was still primarily a textual machine, based on a command line interface. New Apple II systems were often shipped with free copies of a Space Invader clone and text Adventure. Infocom's Zork, which was largely a more humorous and complex variation on the model of Adventure, took advantage of the market for complex (though text-only) virtual environments. In the early years of home computing, these text-based games occupied a major slice of the market for virtual environments.

For owners of early personal computers, playing Adventure was an introduction to how computers operated. As Steve Levy has noted, "Adventure was a metaphor for computer programming."[45] The contents of a floppy disk needed to be navigated with textual commands. To know your computer, you needed to burrow down into subdirectories and make inventories of contents, which could be transferred from place to place. Working with files and programs on the Apple II was, like playing Adventure, a process of going and getting in a virtual space.[46]

However, as graphics technology advanced, home computers became just as visual as arcade games. Again, Apple was the pioneer, introducing the simulated visual desktop with the Macintosh. In the virtual world of the Macintosh desktop, files, directories, disks, and operations (such as deleting files), were represented by images rather than words. The world of the text cursor disappeared in favor of free-flying arrows, wands, and avatar-like hands.

As Brenda Laurel has described, the graphical user interface was a sort of digital theater, enacting visual events that stood for underlying logical operations.[47] As Sherry Turkle documented, many earlier computer users found the movement from text to graphics alienating, as a confusing layer of simulation obscured system transparency.[48] Graphical interfaces placed pretty illusions between the user and the machine, and were themselves a step toward virtual worlds.

This trend only accelerated with the advent of the World Wide Web, which presented a series of screens replete with images and hyperlinks. And, more importantly, as the Internet expanded, the simulated world on the desktop became social. Computer games followed this same trajectory, becoming increasingly visual and, ultimately, social.

MUDs gradually made their way to modems, though they featured crude graphics and expensive subscriptions at first. For instance, in 1985 the game Islands of Kesmai appeared on the Compuserve network and cost several dollars an hour to play. The "graphics" of a wall would consist of "=" symbols, and your avatar was a "V" if you faced south.[49]

A more appealing visual virtual world arrived in the later 1980s, when Lucasfilm released the virtual world of Habitat, which ran on the Commodore 64 personal computer and could be accessed via the early version of America Online.[50] Habitat consisted of around twenty thousand "rooms" and hosted several thousand users. In addition to being one of the first graphical virtual worlds, it was also the first virtual world that used the word "avatars" to describe the graphical agents of users. The graphics of Habitat were cartoonish. However, the social dynamics of the game were as complex as those found in MUDs. Habitat featured an in-game currency and formed the basis for player-created groups, games, and even churches.

As virtual environments, like MUDs and Habitat, became social, their designers came to realize that they could not be designed on the same terms as past computer games. During its early design stages, creators Chip Morningstar and Randy Farmer realized that Habitat defied attempts at top-down control. Morningstar and Farmer explained that when they struggled to provide a standard game goal for players, these activities were completed in hours or less. So they soon gave up on thinking of Habitat as a game and began managing it as an online virtual community.[51]

Multi-player games and virtual worlds of various sorts existed in the 1990s. The title of first MMORPG should probably go to a 1996 Korean game called Kingdom of the Winds, or to a 1996 U.S. game called Meridian 59. However, the game that cast the longest shadow in the U.S. market is the one mentioned in the introduction, Ultima Online. Released in 1997, it was based on Garriott's popular Ultima series of solo computer games and it garnered over one hundred thousand subscribers in its first year, making millions of dollars for its owners. The designers had extensive backgrounds with MUDs, and they sought to simulate a complete virtual world, with a balanced ecology and economy. There was more to the game than combat. Players could mine ingots, become blacksmiths, or bake bread.

Yet two years after Ultima Online was launched, another MMORPG, Everquest, quickly surpassed the popularity of Ultima Online by acquiring roughly half a million paying subscribers.[52] Everquest was styled as a combat-based MUD. It used a first-person perspective, allowing players to see through the eyes of their avatars or over their shoulders (Ultima Online offered a top-down view). Everquest set the standard for MMORPGs and contemporary virtual worlds generally. Today's leading virtual worlds, such as World of Warcraft and Second Life, tend to have interfaces that resemble the interface of Everquest.

THE SOCIAL AVATAR

As the history above should suggest, many events taking place in today's virtual worlds were anticipated by events that took place in virtual worlds like MUD or Habitat two or three decades ago. The popular notion that virtual worlds are computer games is not without basis. The advancement of virtual worlds from text to their modern form has been closely tied to the revenues amassed by companies manufacturing entertaining games.

In the next chapter, I will offer a short sketch of the virtual world landscape today, including how the current technology works and what constitutes the major genres of virtual worlds. Before doing so, however, I want to pause briefly to discuss the social avatar, which plays a key part in contemporary virtual worlds. At the beginning of this chapter, I suggested that avatar embodiment was one detail that made romance in Second Life slightly different from romance by mail or e-mail. Now that we have a thumbnail sketch of the development of the relevant technology, it is worth considering how people understand their relationships to their avatars.

The word "avatar" originally came from Sanskrit and means "divine incarnation." Its modern technological meaning came from Habitat and was independently popularized by Neal Stephenson's *Snow Crash*. The technology of the avatar originated in video games. In many software operations, a user needs some sort of agent on the screen to interact with the environment. On a contemporary computer desktop, the agent is the cursor or floating arrow. In video games, the avatar tends to be a person or creature. Video game avatars evolved from the rudimentary Pong paddle to Pac-Man, to Mario, to Lara Croft, and they continue onward today.

While the video game avatar is technically just a representation controlled by the user, it is hard to deny that players perceive it as an extension of their body. Anyone who has watched video game players in action can attest that, while only fingers may be needed, players often use their whole bodies to encourage the avatar to lean, dodge, jump, and duck. They also wince, sweat, and spasm in reaction to events on the screen. However, despite all this evidence of psychological embodiment, the video game avatar is not generally a social agent. In solo video games, all players use the same avatar. In virtual worlds, at a bare minimum, avatars have customized names so that other co-present users can recognize them.

Initial research on the social life of avatars has revealed that, in many ways, the same cognitive processes and shortcuts that guide the social use of our bodies in real space are projected and mapped onto social encounters between avatars in simulated spaces. As just one example, it appears that people will generally cluster their avatars together when talking in a virtual world, even if this has no effect on their ability to "hear" each other in the simulation. People place their avatars so that they stand a proper distance from each other, not too far or too close. Many other cultural norms about the physical body seem to extend to the social use of avatars in virtual worlds.[53]

The close psychological relationship between a user and her avatar is also revealed by language. When a person speaks of "you" in a virtual world, the word often refers to your avatar. Likewise, when most users of virtual worlds recount personal experiences, they use the word "I" to describe actions and events that might be attributed to their avatar. As anthropologist Tom Boellstorff puts it, the self and the avatar appear to be "isomorphic." He notes examples of users in Second Life saying things such as "I am wearing the dress she made" or "You have amazingly muscley muscles."[54] In both of these cases, the "I" and "you" refer to the avatar body, not the physical body of the user. The semantic confusion between the avatar and the controller is so common that acronyms such as IRL ("in real life") are needed to provide context for questions such as "Where are you, IRL?"

It is hard to find a fitting analogy in history for the social avatar. I used an analogy to chess pieces earlier in this chapter, but in most board games, players see each other in addition to the pieces that they control. Another analogy might be the marionette, though that object is rarely seen outside of the context of a staged and scripted performance. Because they are employed socially, masks and disguises might be similar to avatars, but masks are not usually active agents in their environment. Perhaps the most apt candidate for an avatar-like object is the prosthetic limb, a functional tool uniquely identified with the agency and body of its controller. The problem with this analogy is that prosthetics merge with the physical body, whereas the avatar stands socially on its own.

In short, the avatar is something new. Avatar bodies therefore provide new sources of confusion and a new sort of simulation anxiety. Just as anyone can "be" Lara Croft, so avatar bodies in virtual worlds often have little or no relation to the bodies of their controllers. Users generally have the ability to modify the hair, dress, skin color, and body shape of their avatars. MUD avatars are perhaps the most flexible, since they are garbed completely in language. Although the Internet is sometimes described as a zone of anonymity, avatars make virtual worlds zones of pseudonymity.

The body of the avatar may be artifice, but it still sends important social messages, just as the physical body, which can also be artificially modified, speaks about a person's social status and aspirations. In the non-virtual world, we rely on visual indicators of the body, such as age, gender, expression, and dress, to give us information about a person's nature. In virtual worlds, a person's avatar is "read" for these same sorts of messages—yet the avatar's appearance reveals not what that person is inherently, but what that person chooses to present to others.

It is no surprise that in Vinge's *True Names* and many other fictional works about virtual worlds, a common plot twist is a mismatch between the avatar's presentation and the controller's identity. As William Mitchell has noted, choosing an avatar is "like dressing up for a masked ball."

> And the irresistible thing is that you can experiment freely with shifts, slippages, and reversals in social and sexual roles and even try on entirely fantastic guises. You can discover how it *really* feels to be a complete unknown.[55]

The majority of avatar customization that takes place in virtual worlds today is a cosmetic process that bears no relation to avatar performance. Regardless of whether your avatar is tall or short, with white hair or blue, it will be able to do pretty much the same things. In MMORPGs, however, some choices about avatar appearance are strategically important. For instance, in World of Warcraft, users must choose a racial "type" of avatar that is allied with a particular faction of users and tied to certain abilities and performances. During play in World of Warcraft, when one sees another avatar, that avatar's body type acts as a signal indicating whether he or she should be treated as friend or foe.

Of all the choices made with respect to avatars, the free choice of gender is perhaps the most socially charged and frequently discussed. In almost all virtual worlds, the choice of gender, like the choice of hair color and height, is cosmetic. While gender is a socially charged category, it is functionally irrelevant in virtual worlds. (The Korean MMORPG MapleStory provides an interesting exception to this rule: user avatars are restricted to the gender indicated by the account holder and there are consequences that flow from the gender choice.)

Despite the functional and strategic inconsequentiality of gender in most virtual worlds, users have long been exploring virtual worlds in avatar drag, or "gender-bending" as it is sometimes called.[56] Somewhere around a quarter of users, when presented with this option, take advantage of it, with men being more inclined to gender-bend than women.

We might wonder why gender-bending is so popular. One common explanation, offered by MMORPG researcher Nick Yee, is that gender-bending actually *is* strategic, though it is coded to be inconsequential in terms of software operations. Female avatars are sometimes preferred because they receive more social attention, assistance, and gifts.[57] There is a significant downside to this, however, because that attention can also take the form of sexual harassment. In fact, some female users reportedly prefer to use male avatars just to avoid what they see as the undesirable work of countering the gender prejudices held by other users.[58]

Additionally, as T. L. Taylor has noted, women may prefer to pass as men because female avatar bodies are often designed as highly sexualized, forcing female players to question the nature of their virtual embodiment.[59] (The hyper-sexualized nature of female avatars may also explain why some male players choose them as their agents.) Curiously, even though more men than women gender-bend, when female avatar bodies are sold, they tend to fetch a lower market price than equivalent male avatar bodies.[60]

Avatar gender-bending also adds a new wrinkle to the questions of marital fidelity discussed at the beginning of this chapter. If we accept that some people take cybersex quite seriously, sometimes as flirtation and sometimes as a precursor to "real" offline romance, we can see why avatar gender fluidity often causes what Sherry Turkle described over a decade ago as "gender trouble."[61] There are, by now, numerous accounts of men falling in love with female avatars who turn out to be men. There are also stories of women attracted to male avatars who turned out to be women. There are accounts of gay and lesbian users attracted to users with avatars of the opposite sex, only to discover, happily, that the other user was engaged in gender-bending. And in some stories, users maintain long-term romantic relationships in virtual worlds with other avatars without knowing or caring about the offline gender of the other user.[62]

In addition to playing with gender, virtual world users also play with skin color, body shape, age, and other aspects of appearance. For some, these sorts of experiments give rise to eye-opening experiences of discrimination. It is also not uncommon to see claims by some users, such as disabled individuals, that the flexibility of the avatar allows them to enjoy the freedom to pass socially in bodies that do not set them visibly apart from the bodies of others.[63]

If the social avatar is unique to virtual worlds, it needs to be understood as an essential part of what draws people to these environments. The flexibility of avatar appearance often leads to confusion about the true identity of the avatar controller, but that very confusion may be a core attraction of virtual worlds.

3

landscape

While you're exploring the lands of Azeroth and Kalimdor, you'll be treated
to a multitude of different regions, each with its own visual style. . . . This
variety and detail can be seen in the lush forests in Ashenvale and Feralas,
the snowy mountains in Dun Morogh, the savannah of the Barrens, the
plains of Mulgore, and the deserts of Tanaris.

—World of Warcraft Guide

World of Warcraft is set in the world of Azeroth, a virtual environment
that currently spans three virtual continents. At the same time, the virtual world of Azeroth spans the non-virtual globe, with over ten million
players in Asia, North America, and Europe. While this book gives far
greater attention to the virtual worlds that are most popular in the United
States, the Asian market for virtual worlds is as large, if not larger, than
the Western market. In Asia, there are two leading nations in the business
of virtual worlds: China and the Republic of Korea.

China's prominence is a given in Asia today, but Korea's leading role
in the creation and use of virtual worlds deserves some explanation. Prior
to 1998, the Republic of Korea banned the import of many Japanese cultural products, including console video games. Personal computers became central to gaming in Korea due to this ban. Given the proliferation
of broadband Internet access in the heavily populated area around Seoul,
it was not hard for the Korean gaming culture to become networked. As a
result, Korea has emerged at the forefront of online games.[1] Before Facebook and MySpace use became common in the United States, one-third of
Koreans already had avatars in Cyworld, where many millions of dollars

have been spent on a virtual currency of "acorns," which can be used to buy popular songs as well as virtual furniture.[2]

The various geographic markets for virtual worlds are subject to intense competition among many large and small companies. Larger corporations include Electronic Arts, Disney, Blizzard-Activision, Sony, and NCsoft, which sell their virtual worlds in multiple countries, sometimes in multiple versions. However, in each geographic market, there are profitable virtual world companies that operate on a much smaller scale with much simpler technologies. For instance, some commercial text-based MUDs are still profitable today in many parts of the world.

As a result of this diversity, finding precise and reliable numbers to describe the shape of the virtual world market is difficult. The companies do not help much, since competitive pressures lead most to be tight-lipped about their business operations. When companies do issue press releases about their numbers, their claims are generally not subject to independent verification and may be substantially inflated.

Still, many people and many market research firms have tried to estimate popular participation in virtual worlds based on press releases, industry gossip, public polls, and other reports. Today the estimated range of virtual world users falls somewhere between fifty million and four hundred million. Having considered many of these estimates, my conservative guess is that, according to my definition of a virtual world, there are (as of 2010) about one hundred million adults and children using virtual worlds on a weekly basis. If I were to be less conservative, I might double that number.

Many analysts predict that whatever the number is in 2010, it should double or triple again within five or ten years. It does seem inevitable that as the information landscape becomes more interactive, immersive, data rich, and social, virtual worlds will become more common and will be more easily integrated into other forms of media.

To make sense of the complex contemporary landscape of virtual worlds, this chapter will examine the diversity of virtual worlds from multiple angles. I will begin by describing the basic technologies of virtual worlds.

TECHNOLOGY AND BUSINESS

From the user's perspective, the experience of using a virtual world is similar to the experience of using stand-alone computer software. Yet since virtual worlds are interactive and social simulations, they can only exist as a result of a complicated relationship between a wide array of digital machinery that coordinates the collective actions of multiple users. Understanding how these machines relate, who owns them, and how access to them is controlled is essential to understanding both the business and the law of virtual worlds.

Though the details of creating and maintaining a virtual world are exceedingly complex, the basic structure is simple: there are servers and clients. Servers are the machines that host virtual worlds and manage what happens within them. They are usually owned and controlled by the commercial firms that create and profit from virtual worlds. Client software, on the other hand, is what presents the virtual world to the user. Generally, clients are present on the machines in physical proximity to the user, which means the clients are often either purchased or downloaded by the users.

In America and Europe, clients are usually on the user's personal computer. In Asia, where many people gain access to virtual worlds at Internet cafés, the machines may be owned by a third party providing computing services. Virtual worlds can also be hosted on game consoles, though the standard user interface of game consoles is often more rudimentary. The most popular console-based virtual worlds today come from Sony, which produces the MMORPG Final Fantasy XI and the virtual world Home, both tied to Sony consoles. Final Fantasy XI reportedly has several hundred thousand subscribers,[3] while Home virtual world reportedly has over seven million users currently.[4]

To illustrate how the technology functions in practice, imagine that the avatars of two people, Neo and Alice, are meeting in a virtual castle courtyard. In real life, Neo is using a software client on an Internet-connected game console in Costa Rica, and Alice is using a client on her laptop in Scotland. The virtual world server is located in Fairfax, Virginia, though neither Alice nor Neo is aware of its exact location.

Sitting in a café in Edinburgh, Alice sees Neo's avatar on her screen standing over by the east tower in the courtyard. She types "hello" and clicks a button to make her avatar wave and approach. At this second, her client software in Scotland transmits a set of instructions to the server in Fairfax using the standard Internet protocol that handles e-mail, web pages, and online videos. To get to Fairfax, her command first passes through the network of the Edinburgh coffee shop to a local Internet service provider, across a transatlantic "backbone" cable, and ultimately ends up in a room full of large racks of climate-controlled computer servers in Virginia.

In Virginia, the particular server handling the interactions of Alice and Neo processes Alice's command alongside thousands of other simultaneous commands coming from all over the globe. It responds to these commands according to its programming, transmitting new information to all the connected clients. So, as a result of Alice's action, both Neo and Alice will see Alice's avatar wave and say "hello" while walking forward. Due to the speed of today's technology, the whole process of obtaining the signals, calculating their effect, and sending an updated "world state" back to the users will take a fraction of a second. For Alice, her commands seem to work instantly. She may have little idea that the other person in the virtual courtyard is physically in Costa Rica and that she has sent data via the United States. From her subjective perspective, everything is occurring on the screen.

This technology took some time to mature. The MUDs of the early 1980s were text-based and often used very advanced mainframes connected to very simple terminals. Yet despite the simplicity of text-only worlds, the advanced computers used at that time were sometimes strained by the processing tasks. The mainframes that hosted many MUDs would be overwhelmed by commands and would slow down, a phenomenon known as lag.

Most virtual worlds today still have lag problems. A laggy virtual world is one that takes noticeable time (for example, several seconds) to process user commands and inform the client of the new state of affairs. If an avatar is walking toward a cliff when the server starts lagging and refusing to process new commands, this can be a problem. The problem of lag was potentially disabling for the business of making and selling early virtual worlds. Commercially available mainframes in the 1980s were certainly incapable of quickly rendering customized graphic images for transmission back to thousands of PC users. Even if they could accomplish this, a screen of graphics might take many minutes to download via an old PC modem.

The answer to the lag dilemma, as the makers of Habitat explained, was to shift computational burdens from the server to the client. The user's PC could be tasked with handling graphics, audio, and animation.[5] The central mainframe would do only the most important task: maintain the authoritative world status. To do this, it did not need to render the virtual world visually. Instead, it could reduce the world to a numerical description of objects, identities, and actions.

The client/server distinction therefore creates the possibility of different modalities of virtual world "truth." Recalling Plato's ideal forms, the "truest" version of a virtual world is arguably the abstract logic maintained on the server, not the secondary visual depictions experienced by users via their clients. The "true" virtual world is simply dressed up by client software that fills in images, sounds, and animations. Conceivably, two people with different client software could interact in the same virtual world and see very different things. One might view lush graphics and the other might see a bare-bones description.

If a developer today wants to create a visually rich and immersive virtual world, the model used by Habitat is still the best strategy. Many of today's leading virtual worlds feature heavy clients that handle the processor-intensive tasks of creating graphics, audio, and animation. The richer the world, the larger the data required to depict it. For instance, installing World of Warcraft, the leading heavy-client MMORPG, can require uploading four DVDs full of data to a computer and spending several hours downloading additional data before play.

Creating four DVDs of animation, images, and sounds, however, requires a great deal of time and effort, especially if you add to that the task of making the virtual world socially dynamic. Making a rich virtual world requires hiring teams of industry specialists who know how to do various sorts of complicated programming work and how to make it fit together in a compelling way. There are programmers, artists, writers, game designers, and many others that can play a part. Some virtual worlds have even hired economists to optimize their virtual economies.

This means that developing a complex virtual world costs money, potentially as much money as is required to make a major Hollywood movie. Most industry commentators assume that World of Warcraft incurred over $50 million in early production costs and has added roughly $150 million above that in maintenance and further development. In the case of World of Warcraft (WoW), this was money well spent. Reportedly, the game has made over a billion dollars in profit from sales and subscriptions. This success has allowed WoW to be seen in places where few virtual worlds have gone before, such as car commercials, the television show *South Park*, and co-branded ad campaigns for Mountain Dew and Coca-Cola. This success has also made WoW a favored research arena for those with an academic interest in video and computer game studies.[6]

Like almost all heavy-client MMORPGs, WoW makes its money in American and European markets by charging a fee for the client software (up to fifty dollars, plus more for expansions) and also charges a monthly subscription free of about ten to fifteen dollars per month. Competitors that follow this same business model include Age of Conan, Aion, City of Heroes, EVE Online, EverQuest 2, Lord of the Rings Online, Star Wars Galaxies, and Warhammer Online. But none of these has an audience as large as WoW. While WoW is not the market leader in Asia, it is not clear when another company will topple WoW in the American and European high-end MMORPG market.

However, WoW is not the only model for virtual world businesses. The WoW model actually has some drawbacks. WoW and virtual worlds like it require that huge amounts be placed on the user's hard drive. This means that any attempt to change the virtual world entails changing the client software, which generally requires users to download gigabytes of additional data. These downloads, called patches, can occur several times a month and can take hours to complete.

There are many people who do not want to spend hours a month patching client software. Young children, in particular, are averse to that sort of thing. So an alternative model is to provide simpler virtual worlds that are less taxing on servers and clients. These are faster and cheaper to produce as well. Probably the most interesting recent example is Farmville, developed for the Facebook platform. Farmville is a free game that operates on Adobe Flash, a popular code for web page animation. Farmville is such a light piece of software that it is barely a virtual world. However, it does create a persistent space, rewards forms of social interaction, and uses social avatars. The most amazing thing about Farmville, by far, is its rate of growth. Farmville launched in June 2009. In October, four months later, over sixty million people—about a fifth of Facebook users—had avatars in Farmville.[7]

Club Penguin, designed by a Canadian company but now run by Disney, is another "light" virtual world. Like Farmville, it is offered for free and it runs on Flash, which makes it comparatively fast to load and run. It describes itself as "a snow-covered, virtual world where children play games and interact with friends in the guise of colorful penguin avatars." Club Penguin is reported to have over six million unique users.

The pressing question for many of these lightweight virtual worlds is how they can best make money. As a spokeswoman for Mattel has stated about BarbieGirls.com, the company's popular virtual world for girls, "It was a question of we had this network of users, but how do we monetize it?"[8]

While web sites currently look to advertising for money, many virtual worlds today look instead to subscriptions. For instance, about 10 percent

Farmville *Copyright Zynga, reproduced with permission*

of those children who use Club Penguin pay six dollars per month to own
an igloo, a place to show off one's virtual possessions. An igloo also provides
a more private place to socialize with friends.[9] Hundreds of thousands of
young subscribers paying for igloos translates into tens of millions of dollars a year in subscription fees for Disney.

Dofus, a French virtual world with millions of users, offers a world
somewhat like WoW with a business model like Club Penguin. Users of
Dofus can wander the fantastic and monster-filled landscape for free, yet
only paying subscribers can have pets, join the social guilds, and possess
the most powerful items. Runescape, another light MMORPG, claims to
have over eight million users and over one million paying subscribers.[10]

While subscriptions seem like a healthy market for some light virtual
worlds, there is an alternative to the "free plus subscriptions" (sometimes
called "freemium") model: the sale of virtual property. In the summer of
2009, my two familial research assistants (my sons) transitioned from
Disney's Club Penguin to Sony Online's Free Realms, the latest kid-targeted
MMORPG. Free Realms was launched in 2009 and soon garnered millions of registrations. It might be described as a somewhat simplified, teen-
oriented version of World of Warcraft, but it also includes various "mini
games," such as collecting cards, taking care of pets, and racing go-carts.
While my sons starting playing Free Realms for free, they were soon

Free Realms *Copyright Sony Online Entertainment, reproduced with permission*

enticed to subscribe to the game and be "members" so that they could do more interesting things.

Membership in Free Realms can be bought with a virtual currency called Sony Station Cash, which has to be paid for with real cash. As Free Realms constantly informs children, Station Cash can be purchased at stores like Target, Best Buy, and 7-Eleven at the exchange rate of a penny a point. After receiving several requests, I took my sons to the corner drugstore so they could spend their allowance money on Free Realms cards. The boys used their Station Cash to buy memberships, but they also wanted to purchase virtual pets. So, each plunked down virtual currency for virtual cats. One bought Zinx, a semi-transparent "ghost cat" that glows with a white aura ($3.50), and the other bought Lina, a calico that wears bionic boots ($2.00 for the cat, $0.50 for the boots).

My children are not alone. Many children and adults are purchasing virtual goods this way. Farmville reportedly makes millions selling virtual tractors and lawn gnomes to those willing to pay. An early leader in this business model was the cartoonish Korean MMORPG MapleStory. According to some news reports, over forty million people have registered to play MapleStory worldwide, and while the game is free, a substantial number are paying cash for virtual perks.[11] Another market leader is Finland-based Habbo Hotel, which claims over one hundred million registered users worldwide. According to the company, in 2009, this number translated to over ten million unique visitors a month.[12] Habbo sells "coins" at a rate of fifty dollars for three hundred coins. Players use the coins to purchase virtual items such as furniture, or "furni." Reportedly, the company generated over sixty million dollars in 2008.[13] The company has put a cap on kids' virtual spending, however, by prohibiting children from purchasing more than thirty-five dollars worth of coins each month via mobile phones.[14]

In addition to selling subscriptions and virtual stuff, another potential business strategy is facilitating, and taxing, user exchanges of virtual property. In this model, users can actually obtain cash benefits from selling the virtual things they have acquired or purchased. Making this model work is complicated business, but some companies pursue it, including Entropia Universe, an adult-targeted Swedish MMORPG. Entropia first sells virtual property to users by explaining that they should "invest" in their characters: "You may wish to purchase tools, weapons, real estate or a range of other items." However, it clarifies that such investments can pay off: "the virtual items inside the universe have a real value. . . . The unique and secure Real Cash Economy allows you to transfer your accumulated PED [Project Entropia Dollars] back into real world funds."[15]

In this sort of model, the company makes money not just from the initial sale of the virtual stuff to its users, but by facilitating its resale as well. Several MMORPGs recently bought into this concept by partnering with a company called Live Gamer. Live Gamer promises to enable "a complete marketplace solution for the player-to-player trading of virtual items."[16] Players in game worlds that use this service will have the option of "cashing out" their items by selling them to other players in exchange for real money. The MMORPG owners can then, like eBay, collect a listing fee or even a percentage cut from these player exchanges.

Second Life presents perhaps the most complex virtual world business model found today. It provides free access, sells premium subscriptions, sells virtual property, and taxes the ownership and sale of virtual objects. In 2008, a "basic account" in Second Life was free, but in order to own land, a user had to have a "premium account," which ran $9.95 a month. In 2008, fewer than one hundred thousand individuals had such accounts. Owners of a premium account had to pay a flat fee (to either Linden Lab or another user) for purchases of virtual land, but owning land also entailed paying Linden Lab a monthly "use" fee proportional to the size of the simulated land. So, for instance, in 2008, a sixteen-acre "private island" could be bought for $1,675 and would require the payment of a $295 monthly maintenance fee.

This is only a brief sketch of the technology and business models used by virtual worlds today, but it illustrates what a dynamic, innovative, and competitive market this is. There seems to be ample room for various business models, various levels of technological complexity, and various demographics. Those companies that manage to find the right blend have become very profitable very quickly. It is no wonder, then, that virtual worlds are currently an area that venture capital investors are eager to explore.

GENRES

In addition to the various business models and technologies found in virtual worlds today, they also vary by genres. Though one could slice the field in a variety of ways, three primary sorts of virtual worlds stand out.

First, there are the MMORPGs, the umbrella term (unfortunately) for both light- and heavy-client virtual worlds structured as games. Second, there are unstructured virtual worlds, such as Second Life. These are usually just called virtual worlds, but some people use the term "social worlds" to describe them. Third, there are virtual worlds targeted at children, which are sometimes in the MMORPG genre and are also sometimes called virtual worlds. I will call them "kid worlds" here. While there are important differences between these genres, there are no bright-line distinctions. The primary differences are about how the worlds are marketed (that is, to children or to adults) and what sorts of individuals are drawn to them (that is, gamers or content creators).

Perhaps the easiest way to understand the genres is to use the categories offered in an essay written by Richard Bartle, of MUD fame, in 1996. Bartle had noticed that players of MUDs approached them in different ways. He divided players into four sorts: achievers, explorers, socializers, and killers. These four player "approaches" were linked to different types of behaviors:

- "achievers" try to accomplish game objectives;
- "explorers" test and explore the game system;
- "socializers" chat with others; and
- "killers" enjoy dominating other players.

To be clear, Bartle suggested that these were styles of engagement with the software, not the equivalent of astrological birth signs. People do not play MUDs exclusively as explorers or socializers. Instead, they combine approaches. Bartle pointed out, however, that virtual world designers could make design decisions that might support or frustrate users pursuing these approaches. For instance, virtual worlds with smaller simulated geographies and multiple avenues of avatar expression would favor social interaction. Immense virtual worlds with few communicative options would make socialization very difficult.[17] So socializers could be helped or frustrated by the choices of the virtual world designer.

It is certainly possible to imagine other ways of framing player approaches to virtual worlds, and many people have done so (including Bartle).[18] However, the four original Bartle types were important in providing the insight, now well understood by most virtual world developers, that being a competent virtual world creator requires some level of intentional social engineering, facilitating certain group and individual behaviors through design and discouraging others. While all four of Bartle's approaches are present in most virtual worlds, the genres differ in terms of the dominant design approach to virtual community.

MMORPGS

Bartle's "achiever" approach is best suited to the structure of MMORPGs, since MMORPGs prioritize game goals. Almost all MMORPGs follow a very fixed convention of avatar "levels" of achievement. An avatar enters the virtual world at "level 1," being a virtual alter ego that is weak, penniless, and powerless. A level 1 avatar can only exist safely within a small corner of the MMORPG world, where "non-player characters" (NPCs) provide the user with menial tasks for equivalent rewards. Performing well in this little corner is the first step on a long journey: the game goal in any MMORPG is to obtain the highest level available in the virtual world.

To do this, a player must "level up," as it is called. In fantasy-themed MMORPGs, a level 1 avatar might be required to kill ten rats in the fields near a farm. By doing so, the avatar gains "experience points," a convention borrowed from Dungeons and Dragons. When sufficient experience is collected, the player advances to level 2. In a rich MMORPG, leveling up is a minor celebration: triumphal music might play, visual fireworks might be displayed, and the user's avatar might glow, momentarily. The outward appearance of the player's avatar will reflect, to other players, the new level of experience. A high-level avatar visually signals power within the game environment. As one player has written about game play in MMORPGs,

> It's not the process that's fun, it's the end product and the potential for recognition. . . . Players of MMORPG games are ultimately driven by a desire to improve their characters. It's not about winning so much as it is about obtaining a massive, glowing, meat cleaver of a sword. A sword visible to everyone else playing the game.[19]

It should be noted that in MMORPGs, this type of achievement is almost inevitable with a sufficient investment of time. MMORPGs are not skill-based games, generally speaking. If a user continues to play and pay subscription fees, eventually the highest level will be achieved. However, getting to this point may take thousands of hours of play time and require substantial help from other users.

Though leveling up is central to MMORPGs, it would be a serious mistake to think that this is all that occurs in them. Bartle's essay was about traditional MUDs and, in part, it was an acknowledgment that many users preferred to do things in MUDs that were not, strictly speaking, playing the game. Players explored and tested the limits of Bartle's creation, they hung out with each other in the MUD and chatted, and they spent their time simply attacking each other. To use Bartle's types, they approached the MUD not just as achievers, but as explorers, socializers, and killers.

In my personal experience, I have enjoyed "exploring" virtual worlds, including MMORPGs, much more than accomplishing game goals. In World of Warcraft, I have (through my avatar) navigated the ghoul-infested catacombs of the Horde's Undercity, wandered the streets of the Horde city of Orgrimmar, and spent time flying over the faux–Native American plains of Mulgore. Part of the pleasure of "achieving" new levels in a MMORPG is that doing so unlocks the potential for new sorts of experiences. (Even in Farmville, one gains experience points in the hope of one day having the thrill of owning a virtual tractor and growing tomatoes.) Achievement is intertwined with exploration.

In addition to exploration, social interaction drives user behavior in MMORPGs. Some players have even nicknamed World of Warcraft "World of Warchat." In my own experience playing the game, engrossing conversations with other users have more than once led my neglected avatar to an untimely death. Skilled designers of MMORPGs realize that they are social software and should be structured in ways that support, and even require, social interaction during play. For instance, avatars in MMORPGs usually have specialized roles, like positions on a sports team. When these various types work together, game objectives are easier to accomplish.

Finally, many MMORPGs also feature a different sort of social interaction, known as player versus player, or PvP for short. This sort of play is contrasted with the standard form of social play in MMORPGs, which is player versus environment, or PvE for short. In Bartle's original MUD, PvP was a key part of the game. Users could attack and permanently destroy other avatars, taking their possessions as a reward. While consumers have generally rejected this sort of "permadeath," competitive play in MMORPGs still exists.

Today PvP is generally limited in most MMORPGs. In worlds where it is not, experienced players tend to attack and kill lower-level players. Many new players do not enjoy getting killed repeatedly by more powerful players, so unconstrained PvP is not generally good for business. There are, however, some virtual worlds where the strong can and do prey on the weak. For instance, EVE Online is a popular space-themed MMORPG where the most lucrative and active zones feature unconstrained PvP.

In addition to exploring the world, socializing, and attacking other players, some users of MMORPGs enjoy them in unusual and unanticipated ways. My favorite personal example of an unusual approach to World of Warcraft is the base-jumping community. One day, when I was wandering through Azeroth, I found myself crossing the top of a huge dam at a place known as Loch Modan. Curious about the view, I placed my avatar at the edge of the dam and stared down at the churning waters below. The water seemed so far below that I found myself wondering what would happen if my avatar jumped off the edge. So I found out. What happened, of course, was that my avatar died. Yet for a moment, I saw the view from his eyes as he floated down toward the water. The experience of jumping was oddly fun, so I later found myself, every once in a while, jumping from other high places to certain (avatar) death. When I wrote a short blog post about this, I subsequently discovered a whole community of other users who were doing the same thing. This community shared lists of favorite places to go jumping in Azeroth. Large groups did jumps together. Some jumped on horseback. Some users even made videos of their elaborate jumping exploits and posted them on YouTube.

This is just one of a great many unusual things that users have found to do in MMORPGs. There are acting troupes, for instance, in Ultima Online. There are line dancers in other virtual worlds. Given that MMORPGs have tens of millions of users, you might imagine there are a great variety of ways that people can and do play within them.

SOCIAL WORLDS

Because MMORPGs *are* social, a separate category of "social worlds" is perhaps a misnomer. The term is only useful insofar as it highlights what these virtual worlds lack: the game trappings of MMORPGs. Social worlds are places where users "hang out" virtually without game goals to guide them in the use of their time. Some social worlds have evolved from game worlds where designers have failed to provide sufficiently interesting or engaging games. Habitat and Second Life, for instance, were both originally designed to be games, but the emergent activities of the users proved to be more interesting than the games. As a result, the designers changed their approaches.

The failure of designers to develop interesting content might seem like shirking a difficult task, but it also creates an opportunity for users. When virtual castles are no longer held out as prizes, users are free to build their own castles and invent their own rewards. Virtual world developers can switch from developing content to investing in tools that allow users to create their own worlds and amuse each other. TinyMUD and LambdaMOO did this with text, while contemporary virtual worlds like Active Worlds and Second Life offer users similar sets of tools for building visual simulations.

Today, Second Life largely dominates the field of adult social worlds, much like World of Warcraft dominates the landscape of MMORPGs. Although the media attention Second Life has received gives it a reputation more outsized than perhaps any other virtual world, it should be stressed that fewer people are attracted to social worlds like Second Life than are attracted to MMORPGs like World of Warcraft. Though it is the leading complex social world, Second Life only attracts about a million monthly users. This is a significant number, but it is smaller than the number of users for many MMORPGs and kid worlds. The lower numbers may be due to the fact that, in Second Life, you have to work to create and/or find your own fun.

In Second Life, avatars, buildings, and objects are built out of "prims," which are somewhat like flexible virtual Lego bricks. Prims can be programmed to behave in a variety of ways, triggering animation and sounds. Anyone familiar with basic software tools can easily build basic objects in Second Life. However, as it is with any creative enterprise, some people are better makers than others. And because there are no "levels" in Second Life, skill in building is one key way to stand out in this virtual society. As Tom Boellstorff and Thomas Malaby have noted, skilled creators in Second Life enjoy an elevated social status.[20]

The amount of new content generation that regularly occurs in Second Life is staggering. Cory Ondrejka, the former CTO of Linden Lab, reported that "as of June 2007, residents were adding over 300 gigabytes of data to the world every day, one million distinct items had been bought or sold in the preceding month, and tens of millions of scripts were running at all times within the Second Life grid."[21] Creators can produce and sell objects in Second Life for real profit. So those content creators who invest in Second Life are something like Marc Bragg. They may expend labor and anticipate that their efforts will pay off with real profits.

As noted in chapter 1, thousands of Second Life users have made over a thousand dollars a month in Second Life, and some have even managed to make a real living off of doing business in the virtual world. However, many people who create in Second Life make very little money, and very few major companies actually do real business in Second Life. Companies may create a Second Life presence, but often these virtual storefronts are essentially static three-dimensional web pages. Many companies such as Coldwell Banker publicly "entered" Second Life, rode the marketing wave with press releases, and then moved on.

There are important exceptions. IBM, for instance, has been more serious about Second Life, using it as an in-house platform for staff training and long-distance collaboration. Other organizations have entered Second Life for the purpose of facilitating online presence and community. For instance, several major universities have some sort of Second Life presence. To take one example, instructors at Harvard University have used the platform to hold extension classes where students interact with the instructors and each other in a virtual space.

Communities use Second Life for a variety of purposes. Some have used the spaces to create their own games, including MMORPG-type games. Others communities have used Second Life as a setting to host their original artwork (including sculptures made of prims). Some have used spaces to stage political protests or to raise funds for charity organizations. One creator used Second Life to create a three-dimensional homage to Vincent van Gogh. None of these things could be done in a conventional MMORPG, where players possess only rudimentary creative tools.

Creative tools are a strength and a weakness of social worlds. When each landowner in Second Life has the freedom to follow her own muse, the results can be a bewildering cacophony with very few unifying principles. It often seems as if the bits and pieces of flea markets, exhibition halls, classrooms, and speaker's corners were mixed together and then scattered randomly across the landscape of Second Life. Given that the environment is so flexible and so radically decentralized in its planning, the only unifying theme in Second Life is the prim. One Second Life travel guide sorts attractions into categories such as "shopping," "education," "entertainment," and "adults only," but much of what one sees in the virtual landscape defies any easy categorization.[22]

When I have explored Second Life, what I have found most striking is how closely much of the user-generated content re-creates offline spaces. For instance, Second Life features an amazing number of dance clubs, shopping malls, and homes. Some of these places are curious, given that doing "normal" social things via an avatar is in fact very different from doing those things with one's real body. For instance, dancing is a popular pastime in Second Life. While dancing in real life can be a fun and exhilarating use of the body, watching one's avatar dance is, to say the least, a different experience. Another common feature of Second Life that puzzles me is the common structure of an avatar's virtual "home."

Second Life does not require its residents to build homes, yet they quite often seem to build (or purchase) lavish, rich virtual dwellings with simulated furniture and ocean views. Inevitably, such homes have many architectural features that have no real function within the virtual world. Touring Second Life, I have seen home after home featuring a set of doors, a roof, and interior stairways. Given that Second Life avatars can fly, an interior stairway is actually more of a hindrance than a help to movement. The roof and the door also are not required, given that there is no temperature in Second Life and rain and snow do not fall. The enclosure of a virtual home may offer privacy, but the privacy is limited, given that Second Life users can adjust their viewpoint to, in most cases, see through walls. In any event, the specific architecture of a luxurious virtual home cannot simply be explained by a desire for privacy.

What the "homes" in Second Life strongly suggest to me is that many users of Second Life are engaged in something very much like the fantasy role-play found in MMORPGs. While MMORPG players have their fantasies designed by professional content creators with a penchant for heroic sword and sorcery combat, the fantasies made possible by Second Life give the user wider creative leeway. Private Caribbean getaways, Alpine chateaus, and fashionable dance clubs might appeal to people who don't particularly enjoy elves or spaceships but who still want to live a second fantasy life. It seems that many people use Second Life to fulfill their fantasies of wealth, status, and an alternative social existence.

KID WORLDS

Unlike adults, children are often encouraged to engage in the sorts of fantasy play activities found in virtual worlds. Children use props like "dress-up" clothes, dolls, and cap guns to facilitate fantasy play. Given that avatars resemble digital dolls, it is fitting that one of the most well-known dolls, Barbie, now has her own virtual world. Mattel claims that over eighteen million girls have registered for BarbieGirls.com, which launched in 2007 and bills itself as "The Hottest Online Hangout for Girls."

In BarbieGirls.com, girls essentially *become* Barbie by adopting a customizable avatar that resembles a cute and well-accessorized Barbie doll. Their alter egos wander the virtual world, purchasing new fashions and chatting with other avatars using various pre-programmed phrases such as "I would totally wear that! No joke!" "I'm daydreaming about my crush!" and "My Barbie Girl™ has a charm on it!" Barbie's virtual world includes a large shopping mall, a zoo, and even a theme park with an iconic fairy-tale castle sprouting from its center.

However, access to the virtual castle is limited to subscribers, known in the parlance of BarbieGirls.com as V.I.P.s. The web site explains,

> V.I.P. members have special access to the hottest stuff on BarbieGirls .com. With a V.I.P. membership, you can play exclusive games, adopt an online pet, unlock special areas, and get members-only hairstyles, outfits, and other super-cool stuff for your character (like a tiara!).[23]

Within BarbieGirls.com, the pre-programmed chat software offers girls the chance to endorse V.I.P. status with some stock phrases. Rather than typing out their own words, girls can choose a phrase to say, such as "I can't wait to be a V.I.P.!" "Being V.I.P. unlocks such cool stuff!" and "Hiya! Are you a V.I.P.?" Of course, girls are free to choose not to select these phrases, but the software flags that it is possible and easy to talk about the many wonderful benefits of V.I.P. status.

Plenty of other virtual worlds targeted to children mix this same sort of advertising enthusiasm with the social life of children's avatars. For instance, the owners of Bratz dolls and Hello Kitty merchandise have popular virtual worlds where their products play a prominent part. Lego is developing a virtual world featuring its popular toys. Nicktropolis is a virtual world tied in to Nickelodeon's television offerings. Even the fast-food giant McDonald's offers McWorld, a virtual environment with a Happy Meal theme.[24]

These kid-targeted, product-centered, brand-driven virtual worlds are quite different from World of Warcraft or Second Life, both of which serve primarily as adult playgrounds. The emphasis in many kid worlds seems to be not on serving up original content or providing creative tools, but on managing to make child-targeted advertising more interesting and interactive.

Chat functions are often disabled in kid worlds. While this may seem like a form of censorship, it is generally billed as a safety feature that protects children from revealing their personal information, such as name and address. Online safety is certainly a major concern of parents, but it seems the easiest way to ensure this is to design kid worlds in ways that significantly restrict creativity and expression.

Given that children have limited commercial power, the arena of kid worlds occupies a slightly different field, both practically and legally. For instance, it would seem very difficult for a virtual world owner to bind a child to the terms of an online contract, since minors generally lack the capacity to enter into legal contracts.[25] This means that if a Bragg-type situation were to arise with respect to a child, the contract would be less likely to protect the owner of the virtual world. By the same token, if two children in a kid world have a dispute about virtual property, litigation seems much less likely, given that neither will probably be able to hire a lawyer.

Children also receive special legal protection in many other ways, for instance in laws that shield them from exposure to certain types of "adult" content.[26] The risk of violating these laws is one reason that many kid worlds limit the expressive freedom of their young users. While adult content is a fairly common sight in Second Life, it is taboo in kid worlds. If millions of children had the freedom to shape Mattel's BarbieGirls.com and Disney's Club Penguin in any way they desired, reports of the presence of a few off-color creations could prove very bad for both branding and businesses.

Even though I have split virtual worlds and their technologies and business models into several categories in this chapter, in the chapters following, I will often group these diverse fields together. However, my general observations in the coming chapters should be weighed against the differences I have pointed to here. The technology, the goals, and the communities of various virtual worlds are often substantially divergent. This diversity raises some significant questions about the potential for any uniform legal policy. While all virtual worlds share certain things in common, it is doubtful that a single set of rules or principles would be best for all varieties of virtual worlds.[27]

4

regulation

The great inventions that embodied the power of steam and electricity, the railroad and the steamship, the telegraph and the telephone, have built up new customs and new law.

—Justice Benjamin Cardozo

In the early part of the twentieth century, the airplane transformed society. Concurrently, "aviation law" was created.[1] Today aviation law is an established field of legal practice, with its own specialized legal journals and law firms.[2]

The formation of aviation law took some time. In the United States and around the world, local, state, and national governments needed to create a new set of legal rules for the airplane or adapt old laws to apply to the new technology. This process took many decades to mature and the regulation of airplanes has never ceased its evolution. The birth of aviation law was a creative and contested process. Aviation law's particular shape was influenced by a series of military investments, lobbying by private business interests, numerous courtroom disputes, and major legislative proceedings. A brief consideration of this history can reveal some important points about the adaptation of law to new technology generally.

Though a history of human flight might start with Daedalus, the invention of the modern airplane is popularly associated with the Wright brothers and their flight tests at Kitty Hawk, North Carolina. In some ways, the law might be credited with a small role in that inventive work. The Wright brothers were clearly motivated by the prospect of securing a lucrative patent, which is an intellectual property right granted by the federal government. By granting patent protections, governments around the world attempt to encourage technological innovation. The work of the Wright brothers is often used as an example of patent law operating as planned, creating market incentives for new and useful technologies. In 1906, the Wright brothers obtained a patent. In later years, they devoted a considerable amount of time to enforcing their exclusive rights through patent lawsuits.[3]

The government also played a role in the invention of the airplane by being a primary purchaser and user of the new technology. Indeed, Orville Wright was arguably responsible for the first U.S. military aviation casualty when, in a demonstration at Fort Myer during 1908, his plane crashed, killing Lieutenant Thomas E. Selfridge.[4] Yet although the technology was clearly dangerous at the time, it was also understood to be an effective military tool. Shortly thereafter, the Wrights sold their first plane to the government. The National Advisory Committee for Aeronautics was founded in 1915, primarily to promote military usage of aviation. It later evolved into today's NASA.

However, though the federal government was certainly involved in the early evolution of manned flight, the legal status of airplanes was up in the air—no specific laws spoke to the new technology. It was only when wider commercial air services developed that aviation law began to come into its own. State legislatures began passing regulations concerning the technology, and scattered cases came before courts. By 1921, Justice Cardozo could describe, with apparent amazement, a "body of legal literature that deals with the legal problems of the air."[5] However, comprehensive federal legislation had to wait until 1926, when the Air Commerce Act (ACA) established an Aeronautics Branch in the Department of Commerce, which was the early ancestor of today's Federal Aviation Administration.[6] The ACA marked the beginning of uniform federal rules for the technology of flight, which took over two decades to arrive.

Even with the passage of the ACA, however, many questions about aviation law remained unresolved. It was not until 1946, well into the commercial use of the technology, that the Supreme Court finally set aside an ancient Roman maxim of property law, *cujus est solum, ejus est usque ad coelum et ad inferos* ("Whosoever owns the land, owns to the sky and to the bottom of the earth"). If this maxim were true in the age of the airplane, flying several thousand miles above someone's home would constitute a legal trespass. The Supreme Court concluded that the airplane, and more importantly, the legislative responses to the airplane, had modified this ancient rule.[7]

As Lawrence Lessig has observed, the airplane provides a useful example of old laws being revised to adapt to new technology.[8] However, the exact way that law should adapt to technological change is rarely clear. Nothing about aviation law was inevitable or preordained.[9] Today, it may seem like common sense that we do not own the infinite space above our land and that one needs a license to pilot a plane. We may think it perfectly reasonable that the government should impose standards of safety on airplane manufacture and commercial airline services. But these developments, though they may seem reasonable and just, only became established law within the last century. In the world after September 11, 2001, the legal status of the airplane is continuing to evolve. Despite a century of experience, it seems society still has not come to terms with the legal questions raised by the airplane.

A premise of this book is that virtual worlds, like the airplane, will create what Justice Cardozo described as "new law" for a "great invention." Yet for virtual worlds, what will be the path from no law to new law?

REGULATING TECHNOLOGY

In some cases, governments invent new rules for technology by direct legislation. The Air Commerce Act of 1926 is an example of this. The United States considered and created specific regulations in response to the airplane. However, in the absence of direct regulation, "new law" can still be established. When existing law is applied to new technologies by those charged with enforcing legal rules, this is new law as well. In the case of the airplane, new law was created by the Supreme Court's statement that those who own land actually do *not* own the infinite space above their homes. An old rule that seems to apply to the new technology was discarded. Likewise, when Judge Robreno faced Marc Bragg's claims and police officers faced Qiu Chengwei's claims, they interpreted legal rules that were ambiguous as to virtual worlds. Both decisions, by resolving the existing ambiguity, created new law, albeit in a less direct manner.

In either direct or indirect forms, the process of creating new law for new technology inevitably takes time. Indeed, one may say the process never ends. The history of the airplane suggests that law can take several decades to grapple with the basic questions posed by new technologies, even while those technologies continue to transform society in substantial ways.

The reactive stance of law toward new technologies is inevitable. Governments are always challenged by a range of contemporary issues, making them seem, quite often, flat-footed in their response to new technologies. In the United States today, new technologies are often created and financed by private businesses, which develop the technologies in relative secrecy and disperse them in a competitive market in the pursuit of profit. In such a system, a priori considerations of technology policy tend to be rare and limited to forthcoming technologies that pose known dangers.

So, for instance, technologies that are understood as threats to state power or social stability (for example, firearms or drugs) receive faster and more comprehensive regulatory consideration by legislators. The licensing of pilots and the regulation of air safety certainly took time, but setting safety rules for air travel was clearly an important priority for governments. By comparison, technologies that are viewed as relatively harmless, like most forms of entertainment technology, are rarely the subject of careful legislative deliberation.

Given the many challenges facing legislatures at present, I doubt the direct regulation of virtual worlds will be a very high priority for most governments in the near future. Like Disney World, virtual worlds are seen as technologies that provide entertainment and escape. We might predict, therefore, that the law of virtual worlds will grow gradually and through a piecemeal process, perhaps even more slowly than aviation law.

This is not to say there will be no legislative efforts directed at virtual worlds. Some laws targeted specifically at virtual worlds are already in place or are being proposed. For instance, in the United States, the IRS recently suggested that special regulations may be needed to address the question of taxation for virtual property and currencies.[10] In China, the government has passed some regulations directed at controlling how much time users spend in virtual worlds as well as policing the spread of virtual currencies.[11] In the Republic of Korea, legislators have passed consumer protection laws that balance company and user interests in virtual assets.[12]

But these are scattered efforts across the globe. No governments, at this time, are taking a comprehensive approach to the regulation of virtual worlds. Despite their contemporary popularity, the technology is still too young and unfamiliar to most lawmakers. As a result, the first steps toward the emergence of virtual law are being taken in courtrooms.

People are bringing their individual disputes and claims to courts and other legal authorities, who are tasked with applying existing laws to virtual worlds.

To the extent that this interpretive approach dominates, the law of virtual worlds will be understood, at least at first, as a subcategory of the broader law of the Internet. Virtual worlds are significantly different from web pages and e-mail, but they are still Internet-based communication technologies, and therefore they fall within the scope of many laws (and judicial interpretations of legal doctrines) that regulate the Internet specifically.

The notion of a "law of the Internet" (or "cyberlaw" as it is sometimes called) is about as old as the technology of virtual worlds. While virtual worlds have grown over the last two decades, courts and legislators have been struggling to adapt pre-existing law to Internet technology. Internet and computing technology, like the airplane, have led legislators to enact new laws and courts to come to new understandings of existing law. While virtual worlds have been a fringe phenomenon, web pages, e-mail, and computer software have been part of the broader social landscape for over a decade. As a result, the law of the Internet has been more fully developed. Virtual worlds have never played a central role in cyberlaw, yet they have played some role in the academic debates over the law of the Internet.

In order to explain how the history of cyberlaw relates to the law of virtual worlds, I should start with a brief overview of the birth of the Internet and state efforts to regulate it.

THE INTERNET

Like aviation technology, the Internet was born from a combination of efforts made by inventive engineers, military funders, and private business interests.[13] Perhaps the first true electronic computer, the ENIAC (electronic numerical integrator and computer), was completed in 1945, funded by the government and located at the University of Pennsylvania. It was originally tasked with computing artillery tables.[14] Later, in the 1960s and 1970s, the descendants of the ENIAC, business computers and electronic databases, arrived on the scene. The 1960s saw significant advances made in the science and technology of networked computing, including the birth of the early Internet as a project funded by the military.[15]

The structure of the contemporary Internet is, in some ways, rather counterintuitive. If you were to design a computer network from scratch, you would probably think it should be something like the human body, with a machine "brain" at its center that supervises and coordinates the various activities throughout the network. This is, indeed, how many digital networks operate and how virtual worlds tend to work. In virtual worlds, the central server supervises and coordinates all end-user interactions. The Internet, however, has a different structure.

Like a medieval landscape dotted by private and independent castles, the Internet has a network design that seems oriented toward circumventing, rather than enabling, central authority. Indeed, much of what happens on the Internet works on a principle of blind faith in the goodwill of other parties. One might compare an e-mail message sent across the Internet to a folded note passed by surreptitious students through a school auditorium. New data is handed from machine to machine in a step-by-step fashion without any real central control (by a central authority) that presupposes the route needed to reach the destination. Simple trust in the good faith cooperation of all intermediaries is what ensures that the e-mail, or any other form of Internet communication, will eventually reach its destination.

This decentralized "architecture" has some important advantages. It makes the Internet resilient, for instance. Again, by analogy, if one student does not show up at the auditorium on a given day (or is removed by school authorities), notes can still be passed through the auditorium. If there really is no plan, then the plan can't fail. In the same way, if one computer that passes data through the Internet is taken down, another computer can take its place in the chain. In fact, given the concern that one student might have a tendency to be overwhelmed by notes, Internet messages are ripped into small "packets," so that different parts of any communication can follow different paths en route to the recipient. And if one computer refuses to play along and drops the packet into oblivion, the sender will be informed that the data has been dropped, and the data will be re-sent and re-routed to the next available system.

One of the most significant advantages of decentralized computing architecture is that new computers can be added to the ends of the network organically, just as new students might be added to an auditorium. The Internet has always grown without the need to consult a central authority for permission to link up one, or a million, new computer systems to the data stream. As a result, the Internet has grown quickly. At the start of the 1970s, only a handful of computers made up the early, military-funded Internet. During the 1970s and 1980s, multiple academic and private networks were merged to create what we call the Internet today. By the mid-1980s there were over one thousand host machines on this network. By the mid-1990s there were one million. Today, the number is rapidly approaching one billion.[16]

Few people anticipated how rapidly the network would grow or what great utility it could provide for accessing information. The Internet surprised technologists as well as lawyers. The radical changes it heralded to information sharing and communication practices clearly indicated that this was one of Cardozo's "great inventions" that would require new law. By the mid-1990s, as stories about "dot-coms" made headlines on a regular basis, it became obvious to everyone that a significant shift in the social fabric was under way. A consensus started to form among lawyers and legislators that the Internet required various sorts of direct and technology-specific legislation.

A quick glance at law books today confirms that, just as governments responded in certain ways to the airplane, so they have responded to the Internet during the last two decades. Some people today advertise their services as "Internet lawyers," and they have a great number of specific laws to study and master. For instance, there are new, Internet-specific laws today that

- criminalize computer hacking and identity theft online;[17]
- prohibit certain forms of commercial e-mail;[18]
- protect personal privacy online;[19]
- grant legal property rights in Internet domain names (for example, www.mcdonalds.com);[20]
- create new protections for intellectual property online;[21]
- immunize Internet service providers from liability in certain circumstances;[22] and
- establish standards of online contract formation.[23]

In the following chapters, I will be describing the general contours of some of these laws. It is important to note, however, that none of these laws existed, in their contemporary form, twenty years ago. Many are currently subject to proposals for revision. Many are controversial in one way or another, with critics claiming they should not exist or should exist in a different form. Yet, despite the passage of so many new laws, it is common to hear claims from practicing lawyers that the Internet is moving too fast for the law.

So cyberlaw, or Internet law generally, is an example of computing technology being subject to legal regulation. The Internet generally has changed the law and it will continue to be a topic of legal debate and legislative efforts for many years to come. The law of virtual worlds, the focus of this book, occupies one corner of cyberlaw, arguably the newest and the strangest corner, yet many questions in this area have some important commonality with cyberlaw issues.[24] In any event, even where virtual worlds lack commonalities with the Internet, the laws crafted for the Internet will be some of the most important laws applied to the technology of virtual worlds.

Among the first and most hotly contested legal issues raised by the Internet was the question of jurisdiction, or what body should provide the law governing a dispute. Generally, legal jurisdictions are tied to particular geographic places. Early legal scholars therefore debated whether the Internet should be understood, legally, as a place. This is, in many ways, the same question I raised in chapter 1 with respect to the law of Lord British. While I have serious doubt as to whether most Internet web sites should be understood as legal places, I believe the argument that virtual worlds are places is more compelling. Because concepts of legal jurisdiction are so central to both the law of the Internet and virtual worlds, I will use the early debates over cyberspace jurisdiction as a starting point for exploring the concept of law in virtual worlds.

5

jurisdiction

We will create a civilization of the Mind in Cyberspace. May it be more humane and fair than the world your governments have made before.

—John Perry Barlow

Most popular news stories about virtual worlds ask, at some point, whether "real" laws apply to the communities that use them. We should probably start instead by asking the question, if laws apply to virtual worlds: *which* laws apply to the communities that use them? The problem is that there are actually many real laws, and only a few of these apply to a particular person at any given moment. Much depends on where that person is standing. For instance, Korean and German laws are perfectly real, but if you happen to live in the United States, you will probably be able to ignore Korean and German laws as you go about your daily business.

Traditionally, law has been closely tied to spatial territory. While independent castle courts challenged the legal authority of central rulers, they did so by carving out their own separate legal places on the map, making them good examples of the territorial nature of law. Castle lords could enforce their laws up to the territorial limits of the castle's military reach. Much the same is true of the world's current legal order. The system of territorial legal sovereignty (sometimes called the Westphalian system) is still the dominant framework for law, though some have observed that national sovereignty is increasingly eroded by the growing power of international and subnational legal regimes.[1]

The obvious reason for the centrality of territory to law is that nations making laws possess, not coincidentally, a monopoly on technologies of violence. If laws cannot be enforced outside of a given territory, those outside the territory are free to ignore the mandates of the supposed sovereign. As it did in the Middle Ages, might makes (legal) right, creating a necessary link between territory and law.

Yet there are other, more appealing justifications for linking territory to law. For instance, Thomas Jefferson (relying on John Locke) explained in the Declaration of Independence that "governments are instituted among Men, deriving their just powers from the consent of the governed."[2] To the extent that the governed are a collective, they have usually lived together as a territorial populace. It follows that diverse groups of people living together may have different cultures and ideals than those outside their geographic territory, justifying the fact that individual territories may govern themselves with different laws. Therefore, it makes sense for each country to have its own unique rules of law.

While this might be a justification for separate regimes of national sovereignty, it can be mapped just as easily onto smaller civic units (towns and cities) as well as larger units (treaty-based international organizations). These institutions certainly do exist as lawmaking units, though they lack the prominence and primacy of the nation-state. They also raise problems, since overlapping sets of lawmaking units will inevitably come into conflict, and these tensions may result, in the worst cases, in civil and revolutionary wars. At a minimum, however, overlapping jurisdictions create a great deal of legal complexity. There are mazes of legal rules about the proper relations between legal rules, such as are presented by international trade disputes, state and federal conflicts, and the abundant complexities found in harmonizing the European Union's competing institutions of governance.

Putting these territorial fractures aside, legal jurisdiction can also be divided by subject matter. Even in the age of the castle court, individuals who were located in one territory were subject to governance by multiple competing sovereigns with jurisdiction over various sorts of substantive affairs. For instance, though castle courts operated to settle some disputes, church courts, merchant courts, and lay courts also ruled over a variety of substantive matters, and disputes sometimes arose over which court was empowered to judge a particular matter.[3]

In the United States, subject matter jurisdiction is scattered among administrative agencies claiming the right to make specific rules for their particular (metaphorical) "turf"—for example, aviation, food and drugs, immigration, occupational safety, investments and securities, social security, telecommunication, agriculture, the environment, and intellectual property. Having specialized quasi-sovereigns for airports, farms, and medicine makes some sense, given the potential expertise agencies can develop. However, administrative quasi-sovereigns often have political and economic incentives to serve the interests of the subsets they govern rather than the general public. As theorists put it, specialized agencies are often subject to regulatory "capture."[4]

As I hope the above discussion illustrates, asking whether "real" law applies to virtual worlds is too simple a question, since it suggests that real law is a monolithic entity. Real law is actually a complicated array of different, and sometimes conflicting, authorities and rules. There are many real laws that might be applied to virtual worlds and many organizations that might be interested in making real laws for them. However, in order to know which of these laws applies to virtual worlds, we first need to determine which territorial and subject matter jurisdictions are the proper sources of rules. In other words, we need to know *where* World of Warcraft and Second Life are and *what* they are.

If we look to the "consent of the governed" for the answer to this question, problems arise immediately. The theory may have some theoretical and practical issues when applied to territorial communities, but it is not generally incoherent or impractical when applied in real space. In a small town, if your neighbor down the street smashes your car window or steals your bicycle, the local police and courts actually can provide you with some sort of justice, even if your claim only amounts to a few hundred dollars. In virtual worlds, territorial logic falls apart. To understand the problem, recall Alice and Neo from chapter 3. Neo is located in Costa Rica and Alice is in Scotland. Both are communicating via a server located in the United States, and neither person is aware of the immense distance between them. So exactly where, legally, is the virtual courtyard in which they are communicating? This matters because if Neo were to do something wrong—for example, if he were to criminally defraud Alice of valuable virtual cash—we would need to know which law of fraud applies. Would the appropriate legal jurisdiction be Costa Rica, Scotland, or the United States?

Neither Neo nor Alice lives in the United States, where one might say the virtual world (the server) is "really" located. Neo knows little about the law of Scotland. Alice knows little about the law of Costa Rica. If the two bodies of law diverge on particular points (and they do), "consent of the governed" seems consistent with whatever territorial law is applied.

Looking to territorial jurisdiction seems to be the wrong way to find the legal rule to govern the relationship between Neo and Alice.[5]

This problem is not unique to virtual worlds. The Internet has created very similar jurisdictional problems. For example, in 2002, two newspapers in the state of Connecticut published articles on the Internet that were critical of a prison warden in the state of Virginia. The warden brought a federal lawsuit in Virginia, alleging that many people were reading the stories in Virginia and that the newspapers had damaged his reputation in Virginia by publishing false statements.[6] The newspapers responded by asserting that they were not legally present in the state of Virginia, since they confined their newspaper business to Connecticut. Therefore, they should not be subject to Virginia law.

So where were these two online newspapers, legally? According to the court's decision in *Young v. New Haven Advocate*, the papers were not legally present in Virginia. The United States Court of Appeals for the Fourth Circuit refused to allow the lawsuit to proceed, reasoning that requiring the newspapers to travel to Virginia to defend against the prison warden's claims would be inconsistent with traditional notions of territorial jurisdiction. The Connecticut newspapers, the court said, had never "targeted" Virginia. For this reason, the newspapers could not be required to submit to Virginia law.

Several other federal courts have now adopted the rule in the *Young* case, and it is probably a rule that makes people feel less worried about the consequences of their online speech. For instance, if you posted something on a blog that turned out to be a false statement about another person, would you really want to travel to Alaska (presuming you don't live there) in order to defend yourself against a lawsuit? Likewise, if someone from Alaska were to publish something false about you on a web site, would you really want to travel to Alaska to seek a legal remedy?

The practical upshot of the *Young* rule and many subsequent cases similar to it is that the law today exercises less practical control over Internet speech. Virtual worlds make the "targeting" rule from *Young* even more problematic. For instance, if a newspaper were published in Second Life, exactly what community would the publisher of that newspaper be targeting? As a collective group, the Second Life community is not strongly associated with the legal system of *any* particular territory.

The cost of seeking the protection of territorial laws is also compounded in virtual worlds. For instance, Alice in Scotland does not know that Neo lives in Costa Rica. Indeed, Alice probably does not know Neo's real name. Of course, Alice might ask the owners of the virtual world to supply this information, but the owner of the virtual world may, for business or legal reasons, feel the obligation to protect the personal privacy of Neo against that disclosure. If Alice wants to know Neo's real name, she will probably need to find a lawyer from the United States who can file papers seeking a court order (a subpoena) requiring the disclosure of the information by the virtual world company in Virginia. This will probably entail considerable effort and expense for Alice. If and when Alice gets the information, she will have to hope that Neo provided an accurate name and home address to the virtual world company. If he provided false information, she is out of luck.

Even if she does pinpoint Neo's true name and identity, where can she go next? Is it worth the bother of trying to assert jurisdiction over Neo in Scotland or the United States, given that he will likely remain in Costa Rica? Even if Alice wins her case in Scotland, in order to collect any monetary damages from Neo, Alice must eventually deal with the government of Costa Rica to enforce the judgment. So it seems as if Alice will need to speak with lawyers from three countries to figure out how to pursue her claim against Neo. Unless she lost in excess of ten or twenty thousand dollars from the fraud Neo committed, it is probably not worth her while to do anything about the crime, given the current shape of the international legal system. Neo, realizing this, may seize upon the winning strategy of defrauding individuals in the virtual world in increments of around a thousand dollars or so.

Of course, not all legal claims arising on the Internet or with respect to virtual worlds are problematic in this way. If Alice lives next door to Neo and knows he controlled the avatar who defrauded her, jurisdictional problems may be substantially reduced. This may explain why the Republic of Korea, with a geographically concentrated population, can actually maintain a "virtual crime" beat that polices small-scale fraudulent transactions in virtual worlds.[7] But while the Internet does not completely defeat territorial notions of law, it does erode the practical power of territorial law to govern society.

LAMBDA LAW

The jurisdictional problems posed by cyberspace were recognized early in the history of Internet law. One radical question was asked early on: if the Internet creates jurisdictional problems, why not use the Internet to solve those problems? The Internet could be its own jurisdiction, with its own laws and courts created by its own "consent of the governed." There would be no need for "outside" law (the law of territorial sovereigns) to intervene. The "law of cyberspace" could be a new law formed by the consent of those who "live" in cyberspace. The early reception of this idea is worth discussing, since it seems to be replaying itself in the contemporary debates over virtual worlds.

The idea of a separate "Internet jurisdiction" was an appealing idea to many of the "netizens" who constituted the early community of the Internet. During the 1990s, many of the programmers and engineers who had laid the foundations of the Internet were concerned about the growing prospect of state regulation.[8] They saw prospective laws as a threat to the freedoms they enjoyed with a technology governed only by rough consensus and running code. A quasi-anarchic political philosophy was more or less in tune with the distributed architecture of the network, where decentralization and the near-absolute freedom of endpoints was a core design principle. Techno-libertarians (as they were called) formed a politics that privileged a free and self-governing Internet. Oddly enough, one of the ways this political sensibility found a voice in the legal academy was through a "rape" that took place in the virtual world of LambdaMOO.

In 1993, journalist Julian Dibbell wrote an article for the Village Voice that painted a picture of the early free-wheeling MUD, LambdaMOO. He described it as a "complex database, maintained for experimental purposes inside a Xerox Corporation research computer in Palo Alto and open to public access via the Internet." More importantly, Dibbell depicted LambdaMOO as a virtual community, populated by a mix of erudite techno-libertarians, anarchists, parliamentarians, sadists, and postmodernists.[9] To a public at the early stages of virtual reality hype, the story of LambdaMOO was fascinating.

The heart of Dibbell's narrative concerned the actions of an avatar known only as "Mr. Bungle." No one knew (or knows today) Mr. Bungle's true name, but according to Dibbell the (textual) appearance of his avatar was as a "fat, oleaginous, Bisquick-faced clown." The "rape" in question occurred when Mr. Bungle used a programmed virtual object, a "voodoo doll," to "take control" of two female avatars and simulate acts of sexual self-mutilation. These textual descriptions were accompanied by additional descriptions of Mr. Bungle's "distant laughter," which "echoed evilly in the living room with every successive outrage."[10]

The initial mental hurdle presented to the reader, and pondered by Dibbell as the guide, was what sort of relation the textual depiction of "voodoo doll rape" had to actual rape. The legal answer to that question has always been clear. A textual description of a rape in a MUD is no more a legal rape than a stage production of Shakespeare's *Hamlet* is a series of legal murders. The community of LambdaMOO may have been odd, but it was not so delusional that its members failed to realize that no actual rape had taken place. Still, many people felt that Mr. Bungle's user was, at the bare minimum, a jerk who had violated the unwritten rules of the LambdaMOO community. Just like a drunken and disorderly intruder might be kicked out of a private party, so some people wanted to kick Mr. Bungle out of LambdaMOO.

The problem was that LambdaMOO was a jurisdiction where the ruler had no interest, at that time, in enforcing any particular rules. By contrast, it seems likely that a contemporary Mr. Bungle would be quickly booted from a contemporary virtual world such as World of Warcraft, Club Penguin, or Second Life. As I will explain later in this chapter, most commercial virtual worlds have rules about communication and virtual conduct, and they remove and ban users who harass others. This makes financial sense. The cost of losing the revenues provided by one Mr. Bungle is less of a problem than dealing with the complaints—and potential lost revenues—of an entire community.

However, LambdaMOO was different. It was based in the famous Palo Alto Research Center (PARC) and it was open to everyone with an Internet connection. The PARC researcher who hosted LambdaMOO, Pavel Curtis, had no real commercial interests that led him to serve LambdaMOO users. Curtis and the other "wizards" (the administrators of the MUD) were doing their work for free and it was, at times, a thankless job managing a virtual community. The wizards were beginning to tire of policing claims of rude behavior by particular users. Curtis was essentially a virtual sovereign, but he received no personal benefit from arbitrating these sorts of etiquette disputes. Indeed, shortly before the "rape" occurred, Curtis had decided that the wizards should more or less abdicate their judicial thrones. As he put it:

I believe that there is no longer a place here for wizard mothers, guarding the nest and trying to discipline the chicks for their own good. . . . So, as the last social decision we make for you, and whether or not you independent adults wish it, the wizards are pulling out of the discipline/manners/arbitration business; we're handing the burden and freedom of that role to the society at large.[11]

So the LambdaMOO community was thrown, unwillingly, into a cyberspace version of the anarchic state of nature and was required to come up with its own laws. Curtis was forcing them to make their own rules if they wanted to handle situations like the one posed by Mr. Bungle. As it turned out, they were not quite up to the task. According to Dibbell, a small segment of the LambdaMOO community spent a long evening debating exactly what should become of Bungle. Some said his account should be deleted. Some disagreed. There was no formal consensus. The hour got late, the avatars logged off, and that was the end.

But even if an agreement had been reached, there was, at that time, no formal mechanism for enforcing the results of collective decision making in LambdaMOO. What ultimately occurred in the Bungle case was that one of the wizards, fed up with Mr. Bungle, "acted alone," deleting Bungle's account from the database.[12] Though this might seem like a harsh punishment, it had a limited practical effect. Mr. Bungle returned to LambdaMOO shortly thereafter (or so it seemed) with a slightly modified avatar. The "virtual death penalty" applied to an avatar, but from that user's perspective, the punishment was probably trivial.

However, the event did lead to some significant changes in LambdaMOO. The Bungle incident apparently spurred Curtis to make a further tweak to LambdaMOO's system of virtual law. Realizing that some sort of formal government was needed, Curtis added a system of parliamentary democracy to the software of LambdaMOO. Users were allowed to propose measures and vote on their enactment by Curtis and the other wizards. The wizards would then implement the system of rules agreed upon by the formal procedure.

Jennifer Mnookin examined the resulting "virtual government" of LambdaMOO in a fascinating 1996 article. It was also examined at length in a later book written by Dibbell.[13] The overall impression one gets from reading these accounts is that LambdaMOO governance tended to be complicated, theatrical, contentious, and time-consuming. While some of those who engaged in LambdaMOO politics were sincere, erudite, and passionate, many of the users seemed inclined to enjoy political theater as a form of collaborative entertainment and to resist the intrusion of real law. Mnookin stated that

> in an effort to shrink LambdaLaw down to size, a number of petitions and ballots have been introduced which have an anti-formalist, anti-legalist bent. All of these ballots have intended to mock the

formalist turn in LambdaLaw and add some humor to the adjudicative process.

As an example, Mnookin describes a "Wiffle" petition to resolve disputes through the use of virtual plastic toys (Wiffle bats) used to whap those who violate rules: "Any character who received a certain number of whaps would have been automatically banished from Lambda-MOO for a period of twenty-four hours." Mnookin describes one argument made in support of the Wiffle amendment to dispute resolution:

> I protest the introduction of violence into LambdaMOO society through the use of lawyers, arbitration, and legal red tape. This is a MOO, not a court of law. Support wiffle!

Another proposal was made to resolve disputes via the game of Scrabble. Another required that anyone who attempted to introduce a new petition governing LambdaMOO would have to wear a virtual placard reading "Moo-politician. Beware!" Many of these sorts of proposals, when submitted for voting, were actually endorsed by majorities, though they did not gain the super-majority needed for enactment. Tellingly, a measure introduced to outlaw virtual rape also gained majority support but failed to gain the super-majority needed to pass. The ban on virtual rape mustered only slightly more support than the Wiffle and Scrabble proposals.[14]

The skepticism toward the institution of law in LambdaMOO may have stemmed from the perception that, regardless of what the community wanted, the wizards still held the power over the software environment. They could still, if they wished to, make themselves invisible, destroy the avatars of those who opposed them, bend the laws of nature, and even unplug LambdaMOO. Though Pavel Curtis had failed to assert political power, he had never really abdicated his technological control. He later admitted this:

> Deep in its very structure, LambdaMOO depends on the wizards and on the owner of its machine. These are not and cannot be purely technical considerations. Social policy permeates nearly every aspect of LambdaMOO's operations, and only the wizards can carry out those operations.
>
> As a result, the wizards have been at every turn forced to make social decisions. Every time we made one, it seemed, someone took offense, someone believed that we had done the wrong thing, someone

accused us of awful ulterior motives. It felt a bit like the laws of thermodynamics: you can't win, you can't even break even, and you can't get out of the game.[15]

Unless they ceded the code of LambdaMOO to the users, the wizards would remain central to the virtual government. Technological omnipotence was in tension with the goals of Curtis's experimental democracy. So, slightly less than four years after abdicating power in 1992, Curtis reintroduced "wizardly fiat" in 1996, stating that while the petition system would still remain in place, the wizards would retain the power to trump community decisions if and when they felt this was necessary.

CYBERSPACE AS JURISDICTION?

The above account is a simplified version of the LambdaMOO story. However, it might be simplified further. Many people read the story and took away a simple observation: online communities could make, and might even *need* to make, new laws to address new sorts of problems. At a time when "online community" was a novel idea, this notion of new rules and laws for online behaviors was a novel idea as well.

If we associate separate places and communities with separate laws, it is not surprising that we might associate separate communities and rules with new places. The 1990s was a time when the Internet was talked about by many commentators not as a communications tool but as a virtual place. For instance, in 1993 the technologist Howard Rheingold wrote a book titled *The Virtual Community* in which he discussed various sorts of groups that were "homesteading on the electronic frontier."[16] In 1995, William Mitchell, the dean of the School of Architecture at MIT, wrote a book titled *City of Bits* that described how people were relying on visits to the Internet as an alternative to visiting real locations.[17]

If online libraries, museums, bookstores, and banks were replacing physical buildings, and e-mail Listservs and web sites were the basis for new friendships and community groups, then it was a short step to the conclusion that the Internet was a new sort of place. The language of the Web reflected this with terms like "home" pages, web "sites," Internet "addresses," and "domain" names.[18] And, of course, at the far frontier, there were virtual worlds like LambdaMOO that offered rich online communities interacting in virtual places that were built to mirror reality. (Mitchell and Rheingold both introduced their readers to MUDs and Habitat.)[19]

As legal scholar Julie Cohen has noted, our notion of whether the Internet is or is not a place is largely a matter of social construction.[20] In the early years of cyberlaw, legal scholars and judges often seemed willing enough to participate in the effort to make a legal space out of cyberspace. Even though they understood that the Internet was not a place, courts seemed willing, in many cases, to apply metaphors based on places in their efforts to shape the new law. Indeed, many compared the Internet to a sort of frontier town that required new legal sheriffs to tame its anarchy.[21]

The techno-libertarians seemed to enjoy the resonance of the frontier analogy, since it placed their native environment slightly outside the legalized confines of civilized society. The most well-known pundit in this area was John Perry Barlow, a former Grateful Dead lyricist and cattle rancher who co-founded the Electronic Frontier Foundation (EFF) in 1990. The EFF is a legal advocacy organization that has had a lasting influence on the law of the Internet. Today, the EFF continues to play an important and high-profile role in controversies concerning civil liberties online.

John Perry Barlow developed a reputation for his writings and speeches espousing techno-libertarian ideals. Much of his writing contrasted freedom in cyberspace to the intrusion of law. For instance, in 1994 Barlow delivered a keynote address at a New York University legal symposium that was organized to discuss how law might adapt to cyberspace. Barlow began by stating that he had a "virulent hatred of lawyers" and that law was "doomed" in cyberspace. However, he added that while some might brand him a "raving anarchist," he was instead primarily a cattle rancher who had an inherent cultural distrust of legal rules. Barlow said he felt "fairly safe in the ability of a community to enforce its will, by whatever means, on its constituents without resorting to law in a codified form at all."[22]

Julian Dibbell sat on a panel with Barlow at that symposium, and Barlow drew some interesting connections between the role of the newly formed EFF and the society of LambdaMOO. Barlow noted that he had "co-founded an organization to protect freedom of expression in digital environments such as Dibbell's LambdaMOO." While Barlow seemed dismissive of the significance of Mr. Bungle's actions, he did note that the incident raised "serious problems of jurisdiction. We have no idea where this crime took place, really."

Unsurprisingly, Barlow seemed to think that the appropriate jurisdiction for LambdaMOO, and for the Internet generally, was the jurisdiction where he felt they existed as places: cyberspace. Barlow suggested that there are "jurisdictions that have some authority in cyberspace and they tend to be defined by those places where you enter a password."

Barlow continued writing and speaking on these topics and, in 1996, made perhaps the most strident and well-known statement about a separate Internet jurisdiction to date by penning (actually e-mailing) his "Declaration of the Independence of Cyberspace." Barlow's statement was written in reaction to legislative efforts in Congress that sought to regulate speech on the Internet. In opposition to the legislation, Barlow offered a short and lyrical riff on the "consent of the governed":

> Governments of the Industrial World, you weary giants of flesh and steel, I come from Cyberspace, the new home of Mind. On behalf of the future, I ask you of the past to leave us alone. You are not welcome among us. You have no sovereignty where we gather. . . .
>
> Governments derive their just powers from the consent of the governed. You have neither solicited nor received ours. We did not invite you. You do not know us, nor do you know our world. Cyberspace does not lie within your borders.[23]

For some techno-libertarians, that poetry struck a chord. Barlow's "Declaration" was passed around by e-mail and posted on web pages. And even if the rhetoric was bombastic, Barlow's concerns were ultimately justified by the Supreme Court. The Communications Decency Act, which sought to keep minors from accessing offensive content on the Internet, was found to violate the free speech guarantees of adults under the First Amendment.[24]

Barlow's "Declaration," however, was more than a complaint about a specific law. It was a demand for the recognition of a new and independent jurisdiction in cyberspace. But what, exactly, did Barlow envision? For instance, what institutions could replace "flesh and steel"? How would Barlow's "we" secede from the tyranny of the territorial state? Toward the end of the document, Barlow even seemed to lapse into a sort of metaphysical muddle, as he stated:

> We must declare our virtual selves immune to your sovereignty, even as we continue to consent to your rule over our bodies.

Exactly what did *that* mean? Barlow's "Declaration" evoked a mood of secession from government by an online community, but it denied straightforward interpretation.

Law professors, while considerably less skilled at crafting lyrical and memorable lines, were generally better at articulating jurisdictional concepts that connected in useful ways with existing law. For instance, by 1995, prior to the penning of the "Declaration," several legal commentators had started to consider the possibility of "secession of the cyberspace community from geopolitical governance," as William S. Byassee put it.[25] Scholars like Trotter Hardy, Anne Branscomb, David Post, David Johnson, Ethan Katsh, Michael Froomkin, Henry Perrit, Joel Reidenberg, and Jennifer Mnookin were all part of an emerging dialogue about ways in which the new realm of cyberspace, as a new sort of place hosting a new sort of community, might come to be recognized as a separate jurisdiction.

Indeed, some legal authors seemed fairly passionate about the need for cyberspace sovereignty. In 1996, the same year that Barlow wrote his "Declaration," professors David Johnson and David Post argued in the *Stanford Law Review* that the recognition of new jurisdictional authority in cyberspace was not only possible, but necessary and inevitable. They stated that the Internet called for a new sort of governance:

> Territorially-based law-making and law-enforcing authorities find this new environment deeply threatening. . . . Separated from doctrine tied to territorial jurisdictions, new rules will emerge, in a variety of online spaces, to govern a wide range of new phenomena that have no clear parallel in the nonvirtual world.[26]

Soon came a wave of scholarly counterattacks to these sorts of claims. The most prominent critic of virtual jurisdiction to date has been Jack Goldsmith, who likened Johnson and Post's ideas to the advocacy of anarchy online (coincidentally the name of an early MMORPG). Goldsmith stated that territorial governments would not need to make any significant exceptions to tackle cyberspace. Rather, they would apply traditional regulatory powers and jurisdictional concepts to the Internet and resolve new questions according to existing rules.[27]

In a responsive article, Post stated that although Goldsmith was correct in his assertion that traditional courts would make efforts to muddle through the law of the Internet, Goldsmith had failed to grasp the main problem. The trouble was that, with the rise of the Internet, more people were coming into relationships with other people in remote places. While the law of jurisdiction might look to territorial rules to address the new situation, the existing theories failed to make sense, practically or theoretically, in a situation where community and commerce were no longer tightly tied to territory. As Post explains in a recent book, making web sites subject to the laws of potentially every jurisdiction in which they are accessible turns legal liability into a game of ex post "Jurisdictional Whack-a-Mole," where each sovereign polices the online conduct of anyone who shows up within its territory.[28] The most important claim of cyberspace exceptionalists, in other words, is not that law *will* change, but that it really *should* change.

In my opinion, Post and Goldsmith were both right, but Post and the cyberspace exceptionalists made the more important argument. While "real" laws (of nations) certainly do apply to the Internet and virtual worlds, and while the territorial approach to jurisdiction still dominates, the practical effectiveness and legitimacy of law is slipping today in response to the growing importance of online environments. The Internet might not exactly be overthrowing law, but ignoring and denying the important challenges it poses to law is not a very constructive way to work toward a better framework.

Applied to virtual worlds, Post's arguments against the legitimacy and effectiveness of territorial jurisdiction are even more persuasive. As Viktor Mayer-Schönberger has suggested, virtual worlds seem to fulfill John Perry Barlow's vision of "the new home of Mind." They are places that simulate territories without having territorial borders. They are independent and self-governing in some ways.[29] Even those legal scholars who have been most skeptical of cyberspace autonomy have seemed less willing to challenge the jurisdictional independence of virtual worlds. For instance, Tim Wu, who co-authored a book with Jack Goldsmith about Internet governance, can certainly be counted among the skeptics of techno-libertarian claims; however, in a law review article published in the late 1990s, Wu distinguished general ideas about "Internet jurisdiction" from questions posed by virtual worlds. Wu opined that although it would be strange to have online ticket purchases "governed by some weird law of Cyberspace," the ideas of Johnson, Post, Branscomb, Katsh, and others might apply fairly well to virtual worlds:

> For a group of MUD users whose environment is entirely virtual and who perhaps see their physical lives as distinctly secondary, allowing this group of people to make their own rules does not seem outrageous.[30]

This concession seemed slightly dismissive, but Wu later made it clear that MUD communities should have a "serious normative claim" to jurisdictional independence. Yet even if Wu, Post, Johnson, and others are correct that virtual communities should have the presumptive right to make their own separate rules, there is still a problem of getting from political theory to political practice. It seems doubtful that existing territorial governments will spontaneously recognize virtual jurisdictions as zones of legal autonomy merely because such autonomy might be deemed legitimate as a matter of political philosophy by legal commentators.

And even if LambdaMOO were entitled to deference as a self-governing community, it is not clear that contemporary virtual worlds have much in common with LambdaMOO. Claims about the jurisdictional autonomy of online communities make sense if we presume that the residents of online communities, like the residents of real communities, have some voice in establishing the rules that govern their behavior. In the case of LambdaMOO, Pavel Curtis attempted to promote this by crafting and coding the petition system and the institution of LambdaLaw. Yet if those who control the technologies governing online community do not give those communities the tools for effective self-governance, the "consent of the governed" has to be understood different. The "law" imposed in Club Penguin and World of Warcraft is not, like LambdaLaw, the result of an experiment in online democracy. Contemporary virtual worlds are "jurisdictions" much closer, structurally, to the jurisdiction of Disney World.

Certainly people like Disney World, and Disney certainly has an interest in attracting visitors, so Disney tries its best to create an enjoyable and attractive environment. But at the same time, Disney has little interest in giving its customers any legal right to make the rules for its park. (And most visitors to Disney World would probably not enjoy spending their time engaged in legislative deliberations!) In a similar way, commercial developers of virtual worlds try to please their users, but the contemporary market for virtual worlds has not led to many virtual worlds that re-create the experiment of LambdaLaw. Consumers are not attracted to virtual legislatures and companies are not rushing to create them: providing tools for virtual governments is seen as a way to lose money by developing a costly form of "customer service." The invisible hand of the market has shaped virtual worlds into zones of private corporate authority.

Indeed, there are few law-like rules in virtual worlds at all. The central document in the average virtual world is not some written constitution or, as Raph Koster once drafted, a "Declaration of the Rights of Avatars."[31]

Rather, the controlling legal document in commercial virtual worlds today is something that is probably much less inspiring to the soul of the early cyberspace revolutionary: the "click-wrap" contract. These are those long lists of oddly-worded terms and conditions that software and Internet users agree to abide by without actually reading.

CONTRACTS AND JURISDICTION

The law of contract is an ancient body of law that can be traced back, in many countries, to Roman roots. It is also an unusual form of law in that the rules of contract are not rules made by all for all, but instead consist of the government enforcement of private agreements. Property law, criminal law, and many other areas of law establish general social rules that govern all members of society. Contract law gives contracting parties the freedom to bind each other to the idiosyncratic rules they desire, within certain limits.

Contract law is premised on the notion of a mutually beneficial agreement made between two parties. For example, Neo and Alice agree that Neo will pay Alice one hundred dollars if Alice will paint Neo's fence. This is a contract and a court will enforce it. If Alice paints the fence, and Neo does not pay, a court will demand that Neo *must* pay and abide by the terms of the contract. We might ask why governments get involved in these sorts of matters. No legislature decided that Alice needed to paint Neo's fence or that Alice deserved one hundred dollars for the work she did. So why should the government enforce a private agreement? The dominant view is that society benefits from the institution of private contracts.

When two parties enter into contract voluntarily, both parties probably do so in anticipation that they will be getting a good deal. Both Alice and Neo must have thought that the benefits they would get exceeded the cost of performance. If most agreements are like this, then enforcing contracts makes us all better off, since it generally helps people to get what they want.

It may appear that contract law offers a sort of private and practical solution to many of the legal questions that arise with respect to virtual world jurisdictions. While governments may be unlikely to treat virtual worlds as independent countries with the sovereign power to rule their virtual territories, they will be willing to enforce private contracts. So virtual world communities can use contract law to bind themselves to unique sets of rules that territorial governments will enforce pursuant to the law of contract. If all virtual world participants are required to agree to the "laws" of the virtual world (expressed in the online contract), then the problem created by divergent jurisdictional rules and by the unique nature of fantastic environments could be overcome by setting more optimal rules through contract.

Yet there are significant theoretical problems with allowing contracts to be the exclusive means of legal ordering in virtual worlds. First, the law of contracts works best, from the standpoint of contract theory, when the terms of the contract are freely negotiated. This way, parties understand and control the terms of the agreement. Something much different happens with what is known as a contract of adhesion. Many "form contracts" today are offered on a take-it-or-leave-it basis. Car leases, bank loans, and insurance contracts are often presented to consumers as long documents with small print written in impenetrable legalese that simply must be signed before the transaction can be completed.

Often, consumers simply presume that the terms are reasonable and focus on those variables that they consider most important to the transaction. If you are renting a car, for instance, you will probably focus on the price of the rental and the time the car must be returned. You probably expect (reasonably) that if all goes well, as it probably will, the language in small print on the form will not be used against you. Additionally, you might suspect that if you object to a tiny term in the printed legalese, the rental that you are seeking will not occur, forcing you to seek a rental elsewhere, from a company that will have another long, impenetrable, non-negotiable contract. This use of non-negotiable consumer form contracts is not consistent with the animating theory and justifications of contract law. In practice, one party, the consumer, does not understand the terms of the bargain and is potentially bound to obey unknown (though ostensibly disclosed) rules.

Despite the problems with how these sorts of contracts are made, many courts in the United States are willing to enforce them. As a result, businesses that have the opportunity to do so will tend to use form contracts to protect themselves in the event of a legal dispute. There are some limits, however, on how far lopsided contracts will be enforced. In the United States, in instances where form contracts are "unconscionable" (offered under unfair conditions or containing unanticipated terms), courts may allow parties to escape from the rules of the contract, as Marc Bragg did with respect to the arbitration provision in the Second Life contract. In jurisdictions with significant consumer protection laws, such as many European states, certain terms in form contracts may not be enforceable. Yet the general rule today is that form contracts are enforced.[32]

In the business of consumer software, form contracts are a standard tool for setting limitations on user rights. In a well-known 1996 case, *ProCD v. Zeidenberg*, a defendant challenged the enforcement of a written contract that was included *within* a retail software product and therefore could not be read until after the purchase of the software was made. In upholding the contract, Judge Frank Easterbrook explained that if a customer were to find a provision indicating that she owed an extra $10,000, the customer could just return the software and reject the contract as offered. However, since the purchaser used the software, a court could presume that the terms were read and that an enforceable contract had been created.[33]

Though many commentators disagreed with Judge Easterbrook, this ruling and others like it encouraged early Internet businesses to use the online equivalent of form contracts to minimize their risks. Today, online contracts are generally known as click-wrap agreements, since individuals are required to click on a button that indicates they have read and agree to the terms of service. A variant of the click-wrap contract is the "browse-wrap" contract, which is often used on web sites. Even if a visitor to a web site is not required to assent to contractual terms (e.g., by clicking an "I agree" button), most web sites include a "terms of use" page that purports to bind the user to contractual terms governing the use of the web site.

For instance, the CNN.com web site is generally accessible online, but a page on the site states that "by using CNN Interactive," the visitor "agrees to comply with all of the terms and conditions hereof." According to CNN, they may change these terms of service at any time simply by posting a new version of them on the web site. Among the provisions are indemnification agreements, limitations of liability, consent to monitoring of communication, and various provisions that protect the intellectual property rights of the web site owner.[34]

Almost every commercial web site and software application today includes similar terms of use, licenses, and other legal documents that purport to set the legal rules concerning the relationship between the user and the creator of the software or service. On rare occasions, these contracts may become matters of public debate. For instance, in 2009, Facebook changed its terms of service in a way that suggested it would claim greater rights to the information contributed by its users. When bloggers started to spread the word about the terms, many Facebook users were alarmed. Stories about the controversy soon appeared in major newspapers and on network television.[35] Though Facebook has modified its terms in response, the fact is that Facebook's terms, while they may have been oppressive toward the user, were really no more oppressive than the terms posted on many other popular web sites.

The terms of service for virtual worlds are not much different.[36] For instance, players of World of Warcraft are required to, on a regular basis, assent to about twenty pages of single-spaced text that makes up the End-User License Agreement and the Terms of Use. Users of Second Life agree to abide by terms that are just as lengthy. Even Club Penguin has a fifteen-page agreement that purports to legally bind the children that use the virtual world, even though most contractual terms are not legally enforceable against minors.

The terms in these documents are almost never very attractive to users and offer no room for negotiation. For instance, in the summer of 2009, Second Life's terms began with the following statement:

> By using Second Life, you agree to these Terms of Service. If you do not so agree, you should decline this agreement, in which case you are prohibited from accessing or using Second Life.

The next sentence indicated that Second Life could amend the terms at any time by posting revised terms on its web site. The terms went on to state, among other things, that:

- Linden Lab may have no control over the "quality, safety, morality, legality, truthfulness or accuracy" of aspects of Second Life;
- Linden dollars are only a "limited license right" that can be used "when, as, and if allowed by Linden Lab";
- Linden Lab can interrupt access to Second Life "with or without prior notice for any reason or no reason";
- Linden Lab can cancel the account of anyone misrepresenting their identity, but Linden Lab will not be liable when people misrepresent their identity to you;
- Linden Lab can change or delete your avatar's name "for any reason or no reason";
- you may not transfer your Second Life account to another person without written permission from Linden Lab;

- when you upload creative content to Second Life, you grant Second Life a "royalty-free, worldwide, fully paid-up, perpetual, irrevocable, non-exclusive right and license" to use that content to promote Second Life;
- Linden Lab can delete anything within the world at any time for any reason or no reason;
- the user indemnifies Linden Lab for any breach of the contract; and
- any litigation between the user and Linden Lab will be covered by California law and the lawsuit must be brought in San Francisco.

And, as mentioned in the introduction, the Second Life agreement also states that users lack any persistent legal interest in the value of their avatars and virtual property:

> Linden Lab has the right at any time for any reason or no reason to suspend or terminate your Account, terminate this Agreement, and/ or refuse any and all current or future use of the Service without notice or liability to you. In the event that Linden Lab suspends or terminates your Account or this Agreement, you understand and agree that you shall receive no refund or exchange for any unused time on a subscription, any license or subscription fees, any content or data associated with your Account, or for anything else.[37]

Again, it is important to note that these contractual terms are not so unusual. They simply mirror, in the virtual world context, common language used in the licensing provisions of software and Internet services. Essentially, they operate to limit the liability of the company in a variety of circumstances, to obligate the user to protect the owner from liability, and to shift costs of potential litigation away from the company and toward the user by, for example, requiring arbitration in the home forum of the business.

In essence, the contractual rules of the average virtual world are not designed as mechanisms of governance but as defensive measures to protect virtual world owners. Given that online contracts are rarely read by users and are generally skewed to benefit the companies that draft them, some courts seem inclined to invalidate them in cases where their enforcement is deemed unjust or, as the law puts it, "unconscionable." This is what happened in the *Bragg* case.

Marc Bragg challenged the contractual provision that required him to travel to California to arbitrate his claim against Linden Lab. In order to decide this question, the court engaged in a lengthy discussion of the applicable law, which the parties agreed was the law of the state of California. Under California law, a contract could be unconscionable both procedurally and substantively. In deciding that the requirement was "procedurally unconscionable," the court noted that it was a non-negotiable contract. But the fact that seemed most crucial to the court's decision was that (according to the court) there were no virtual worlds that offered a true market alternative to Second Life. It based this decision on its understanding that "Second Life was the first and only virtual world to specifically grant its participants property rights in virtual land." Of course, it is questionable whether Linden Lab would have agreed to this statement.

In deciding that the requirement was substantively unconscionable, the court found that the agreement was not mutually beneficial, focusing on many of the provisions mentioned above:

> The TOS provide Linden with a variety of one-sided remedies to resolve disputes, while forcing its customers to arbitrate any disputes with Linden. This is precisely what occurred here. When a dispute arose, Linden exercised its option to use self-help by freezing Bragg's account, retaining funds that Linden alone determined were subject to dispute, and then telling Bragg that he could resolve the dispute by initiating a costly arbitration process. The TOS expressly authorized Linden to engage in such unilateral conduct.

The court also noted that costs of arbitration were likely to be well over twenty thousand dollars and that the required travel to California for confidential arbitration would favor Linden Lab. It concluded that:

> the arbitration clause is not designed to provide Second Life participants an effective means of resolving disputes with Linden. Rather, it is a one-sided means which tilts unfairly, in almost all situations, in Linden's favor.

The *Bragg* decision demonstrates that some courts, in some circumstances, may refuse to enforce contractual provisions that seem overly prejudicial toward those who use virtual worlds. Yet it is only one court decision and it is based on the peculiar facts surrounding Marc Bragg's use of Second Life. Many legal commentators found the ruling in the *Bragg* case rather surprising and presume that other courts looking at the contracts of other virtual worlds will be more likely to find them enforceable.

From the perspective of using a contract as a means of virtual world governance, it seems desirable to place limits on the contract's ability to set governance rules, at least given the current shape of these agreements. If virtual world contracts are primarily concerned with immunizing the virtual world owner from various legal liabilities, this leaves the relationships between users, at least under contract law, in the same state they were prior to the formation of the online contract.

As Joshua Fairfield has explained, setting the rules of virtual worlds in terms of the absolute power of the virtual world owner essentially makes the relationships between users anarchic, which is not, in the eyes of most legal commentators, a very desirable state of affairs.[38] So while the contracts that are found in virtual worlds undoubtedly play an important part in shaping the law of virtual worlds, they have problems from both a practical and a theoretical standpoint. Additionally, the current contracts of virtual worlds fail, as a practical and policy matter, to establish virtual worlds as legitimate and legally separate jurisdictions.

COMMUNITY RULES

Just because virtual world communities do not read or benefit much from the formal contracts that purport to bind them does not mean that new social rules are not created in virtual worlds. The community rules of virtual worlds are not laws per se, but they are norms that are enforced, informally, by communities of virtual world users.[39]

In his book *Order without Law*, Robert Ellickson studied how the established legal rules governing the pasturing, fencing, and herding of cattle affected the actions of cattle ranchers in northern California.[40] What Ellickson found was that the legal rules were practically ignored by the ranchers. Instead, the ranchers looked to social norms rooted in the traditions and conventions of the close-knit community. The cattle ranchers were enforcing their own rules, which were often at odds with the rules provided by law. Their social norms were not legal rules, not private contractual rules, but they were the rules that governed in the majority of circumstances.

Important social norms are found in many places. Consider the unwritten rules that govern conduct at a place of work, in a religious organization, or at schools and businesses. The failure to abide by such unwritten rules, when they exist, may have serious consequences. The same is true in virtual worlds. I will be discussing some of the specific ways that virtual communities have created their own social norms in chapter 8. For the moment, though, I want to focus on how owners of virtual worlds make efforts to influence community norms through contract-like mechanisms.

The owners of privately controlled spaces often make efforts to establish codes of behavior. For instance, Disney's theme parks prohibit clothing with offensive messages, thereby influencing social norms about appropriate attire in Disney World. Likewise, Disney's Club Penguin demands that children using the software "respect other penguins" and avoid "inappropriate" behavior. Establishing such rules can be a cost-saving measure for virtual world owners, since they provide prospective notice about the limits of tolerated behavior. The Club Penguin version of Mr. Bungle should not be surprised if he is summarily banned from the icy cartoon world, and those who encounter him doing his worst will know that he is violating a community rule.

Club Penguin has a set of "4 simple rules." They are: (1) Respect other penguins (no "mean behavior"); (2) Never reveal your personal information (including name, address, or password); (3) No inappropriate talk (for example, regarding sex, drugs, or alcohol); (4) No cheating: "Any use of third party programs to cheat is not allowed. Players who use any third party programs while playing risk being permanently banned."[41]

While many rules govern the things avatars cannot say, there are also rules about what avatars cannot *do*. For instance, Second Life promotes six behaviors as "Community Standards." A violation of these standards may result in expulsion from Second Life. Forbidden behaviors include: (1) intolerance (for example, insulting another user based on race, ethnicity, gender, religion, or sexual orientation); (2) harassment (including but not limited to sexual harassment); (3) assault (for example, unauthorized shooting of other avatars); (4) violating privacy (eavesdropping, sharing chat logs, or disclosing confidential information of another avatar); (5) indecency (displaying sexual, violent, or offensive material outside of "mature" zones); and (6) disturbing the peace (annoying other players with spamming or noise).[42]

Some of the standards, such as the prohibition on indecent and intolerant communication, are restrictions on what we would call speech in other contexts. But assault is not something that one might expect to encounter in a chat room. Apparently, however, complaints about avatar assault are fairly common in Second Life and are frequently acted upon by Linden Lab.[43] The assault prohibition points again to the primacy of the embodied avatar in virtual environments.

World of Warcraft has a different set of rules in the "Code of Conduct" portion of its terms of use that forbid some similar behaviors—for example, harassment, certain sorts of language ("threatening, abusive, harassing, defamatory, vulgar, obscene, hateful, sexually explicit, or racially, ethnically or otherwise objectionable"), advertising, and posting "any user's personal information." Assault, notably, seems to be acceptable behavior in World of Warcraft. The most peculiar rules are gamelike rules, which include prohibitions on speaking with players of the opposite faction.[44] Given that two player factions are at war, consorting with the enemy is essentially a violation of the fiction of World of Warcraft. Additionally, there is a prohibition on scamming or defrauding other players to get "gold, weapons, armor, or any other items that user has earned through authorized game play." So while Blizzard Entertainment (the company the produces World of Warcraft) denies that users possess any interest in virtual property vis-à-vis Blizzard, the rules of behavior suggest that users should respect virtual property interests in their dealings with each other.

The rules that govern user behavior in virtual worlds are certainly important to users, yet they have an odd relationship to both the contractual rules and the actual social norms that are respected by the community. Since most virtual worlds, including Second Life, World of Warcraft, and Club Penguin, reserve the right to arbitrarily terminate user accounts at any time for any or no reason, abiding by the rules provides no legal guarantee of continued access. By the same token, the rules may be merely symbolic if the virtual world owner fails to enforce them.

Presumably, most virtual world owners want users to comply with these community rules. To do this, they can create incentives for those who understand and enforce the rules. Club Penguin actually drafts children by promoting a semi-secret society of "secret agent" penguins. Children are encouraged to become secret agents by taking a test on the Club Penguin rules and solving some puzzles. Once they achieve secret agent status, children are asked to provide help to other penguins and to report penguins that break the four rules.[45]

In the real world, enforcement agents like the police are charged with responding to complaints about lawbreaking and investigating unlawful activity. When users of virtual worlds have complaints, they tend to page customer service representatives or fill out online forms describing the problem they are experiencing. For instance, in Second Life, users are directed to submit "tickets" that are divided into several categories, such as billing issues, technical issues, land and regional issues, and general feedback.

Often such tickets are designed to fix problems with the technology. If an avatar gets stuck inside a wall, for instance, or an error causes a loss of virtual objects, a ticket can be filed to request help. Of course, since tickets are a form of customer service, users sometimes complain about slow responses. Comments such as the following are not unusual:

> If I have learned anything in the 3+ years I've played this game [it is that] . . . if you don't get the answer you want from a [game master], put in another ticket immediately and keep doing it until you do.[46]

The same general mechanism is used with relation to violations of community rules. In Second Life, users can submit "abuse reports," which are the designated channel for complaints about violations of the community standards. The Second Life Knowledge Base states:

> Abuse happens when anyone violates the Terms of Service (TOS) or the Community Standards (CS). Every Resident when they register an account for Second Life agrees to abide by these rules. . . .
>
> Whenever you see one of these rules being broken, and you believe it to be intentional or malicious, everyone present at the incident should file an abuse report. The abuse reporting system exists to make the Second Lives of Residents more pleasant and satisfying.

Just because these reports are invited does not mean virtual world owners always address them. In MapleStory, for instance, users are invited to file abuse reports for offenses of scamming, harassment, and advertising. The web site notes, however, that

> we will not always personally reply to your reports or show up in the game regarding your user abuse report. It's not because we don't care about you =) You can be sure that the GMs are policing the game with the aid of your reports.

This comment from MapleStory's makers reflects the fact that virtual world owners generally make no binding promises that they will actually enforce the community rules they create. For instance, according to the Second Life terms of service, Linden Lab has "the right but not the obligation to resolve disputes between users relating to the Service." Additionally, Linden Lab denies that its governance has any "real world" effect, stating that "resolution of such disputes will be final with respect to the virtual world of the Service but will have no bearing on any real-world legal disputes in which users of the Service may become involved."[47]

So abuse reports and the like can be analogized to a loose system of law enforcement, where the commercial descendants of LambdaMOO wizards (paid customer service employees) dispense technological justice to the best of their ability according to the rules set by their employers.[48] While the ticket system is hardly law, it is a means by which virtual world owners enforce a system of community rules. Again, however, while the rules are ostensibly designed for the benefit of the community, the community receives only the rules that the virtual world owners provide and are willing to enforce. It is possible, though hardly assured, that in response to market demands, virtual world owners will at some point step up the robustness of their mechanisms for in-world dispute resolution.[49] At the present moment, however, the ticket system of customer service dominates as the preferred approach.

When virtual world owners fail to enforce their rules, it is theoretically possible that users could seek help from the state to enforce the virtual world's rules. However, while contracts create obligations between both of the contracting parties, they generally do not create obligations to third parties. So, for instance, if Alice agrees to paint Neo's fence, Flynn, as a non-party to the contract, would not have any right to complain if Alice failed to perform. In some situations, however, contracts *can* create obligations to third parties. For instance, if Alice had been paid by Neo to paint Flynn's fence, Flynn *could* sue if she failed to perform. In that case, Flynn would be the "intended beneficiary" of the contract between Neo and Alice, with legal standing to complain about Neo's breach of the agreement.

We might ask, by analogy, whether contractual rules that establish "community standards" in virtual worlds can be likened to Flynn's case— agreements designed not for the benefit of virtual world owners, but for the communities of virtual worlds. If that is the case, individual users might rely on contract rules, like the community standards of World of Warcraft, Club Penguin, or Second Life to bring claims against users who fail to abide by those terms. Mr. Bungle, in this case, might be sued for breach of contract, if nothing else.

Legal commentators disagree about the viability of this sort of claim.[50] Michael Risch has argued that certain clauses in virtual world contracts, such as anti-cheating clauses and anti-harassment clauses, do create contractual rights that can be asserted by users against other users who breach those terms. However, other legal scholars, such as Joshua Fairfield, are skeptical. Fairfield observes that virtual world owners do not generally intend such terms to create obligations between parties. In addition, there are important policy questions about whether they should be allowed to structure contractual relationships between users in this way.

In 2007, Anthony Hernandez, a player of World of Warcraft, brought a class action claim in federal court in Florida, alleging that IGE, a company specializing in the sale of virtual gold, had acted in violation of the World of Warcraft Terms of Use. In particular, Hernandez complained about the violation of the contractual prohibition against gold farming, arguing that IGE's actions ruined the game for the class of plaintiffs. Hernandez's case was supported by Blizzard Entertainment, and it might have offered some guidance on the question of whether virtual world users can be the intended beneficiaries of the contracts they sign. However, the litigation was settled before the case went to trial, with IGE agreeing to cease its operations in World of Warcraft for five years.[51]

While it is interesting to ponder whether users of virtual worlds might be the contractual beneficiaries of community rules, it remains to be seen if courts would support such claims. Though it may provide some legal traction to users, it does seem odd that two disputing parties should be bound by rules that neither party had a hand in drafting. Allowing virtual world owners to unilaterally set community rules by contract seems tantamount, for better or for worse, to treating them as sovereigns within their virtual domains.

On the other hand, if virtual world owners *lack* the power to set rules governing permissible and impermissible user interactions, on what basis could virtual communities ever set themselves apart with separate standards? If most users of virtual worlds believe that their conduct is governed by certain separate rules, and if those rules cannot be derived from the language of contracts or established by separate virtual jurisdictions, then under what legal framework might courts recognize the common law of Lord British, treating virtual worlds as independent legal spheres? One answer, suggested in the next chapter, might be to treat virtual worlds as games.

6

games

Games only repeat and repeat our effort to go back, back to a freedom we cannot recall, save as a moment of play in some garden now lost.

—Bart Giamatti

Ray Chapman was a shortstop for the Cleveland Indians. In August 1920, he was at the plate facing the Yankee pitcher Carl Mays. Mays was known for his unpleasant temperament and his unique "submarine" pitching style. He also had a reputation for pitching inside and sometimes hitting batters. At the start of the fifth inning, Mays pitched an inside fastball to Chapman. Chapman either failed to duck or ducked too late, depending on what account you read. Batting helmets were not used in the early twentieth century, and the ball struck Chapman's head with a loud crack. It bounced back toward the mound and, according to some, Mays fielded it and threw it to first base, thinking that Chapman had actually made contact with his bat.

But Chapman had collapsed. He was helped off the field and rushed to a hospital. According to some reports, Chapman asked his teammates to tell Mays "not to worry." Other accounts state that Chapman was unable to speak after being struck with the ball and was unconscious. The ball had fractured both sides of Chapman's skull and shifted his brain. Despite surgical efforts, he died the next day.

Mays surrendered himself immediately to the New York district attorney, who declared the death an accident. Mays blamed the inside pitch on a scuffed ball that failed to curve properly. The *New York Times* gave another explanation: "Chapman's left foot may have caught in the ground in some manner which prevented him from stepping out of the ball's way."[1] Other accounts suggest that Chapman lost sight of the ball. However, the easiest explanation for the accident was that Mays actually threw a baseball at high speed toward, or in the vicinity of, Ray Chapman's head. "Brushing back" is certainly part of the tradition of baseball pitching.

In the wake of Chapman's death, several ball clubs and players suggested that Mays should be excluded from the professional league. Though this did not happen, Mays felt that Chapman's death kept him from being voted into the Baseball Hall of Fame. This may have been true. But in some ways, Mays was lucky. Despite having been the cause of Ray Chapman's death in front of thousands of witnesses, Carl Mays never went to jail. The rules of baseball effectively exonerated him from liability.

A SEPARATE SPHERE

In his book *Spheres of Justice*, Michael Walzer argues that law should recognize the existence and independence of various "spheres" of human culture (for example, commerce, politics, education, religion, and intimacy).[2] According to Walzer, these spheres should be autonomous in order to prevent injustice. Power in one sphere should not be translated into power in another sphere. So, for instance, commercial power should not translate into political power or intimate power. Walzer suggests that the need for separate spheres accords with various prohibitions in laws and social norms, such as anti-bribery prohibitions in politics (money should not buy political influence) and laws prohibiting prostitution (money should not be used to purchase intimacy).

Whatever one makes of the desirability of independent spheres of justice, Walzer is surely describing something that is recognizable in many areas of human culture. We do recognize various domains of society where particular sorts of power are appropriately or inappropriately wielded. As Walzer's categories suggest, not all of the domains he recognizes as spheres of justice are domains we would associate with formal law.

Several years ago, when I started thinking about law and virtual worlds, I gave presentations on the subject at several law schools. In most gatherings, at least one professor would ask, "Aren't these things just games?" The answer to this question is fairly simple: yes, some virtual worlds are structured as games, but not all. However, to the extent that the answer was yes, there seemed to be an unspoken presumption: the project of "law and virtual worlds" was not worth pursuing. There was something obviously erroneous about making games the subject of legal examination.

As should be obvious from the previous chapters, I tend to disagree with that presumption. Most law schools today have courses in sports and entertainment law, making it clear that games and law do have some points of intersection. And the companies that make virtual worlds hire lawyers to advise them, making it clear that there is a legal practice concerning these technologies. To the extent that virtual worlds are indeed games, I still consider it possible, and important, to look at how they interact with the legal system. Yet, for some reason, even those who use virtual worlds frequently and seek to promote their importance often seem eager to distance virtual worlds from things that are "just games."

In 2008, at the first congressional hearing in the United States about the policy implications of virtual worlds, the focus was almost exclusively on the virtual world of Second Life. Many of the participants at the hearing made references to games, though these remarks were largely designed to create a distance between Second Life and games. Philip Rosedale, the founder of Second Life, submitted prepared testimony noting that Second Life had moved away from "game-play" and that participants did not fit the "gamer" profile. Another witness, who helped coordinate educational efforts in Second Life, told the representatives that Second Life "is not a game." The speakers seemed to be implying that lawmakers could feel comfortable taking the phenomenon of Second Life seriously, because it is not a game.

There are some good reasons that law might distance itself from games. For instance, some games have low stakes. To the extent that social disputes over games like Monopoly do not concern substantial and persistent investments, it follows that law should probably not bother itself much with disputes that arise in the game of Monopoly. Such disputes are not likely to come before courts, since it seems unlikely that victims defrauded of Marvin Gardens will bring lawsuits to recover damages. Law recognizes this with an old Latin maxim: *de minimis non curat lex.* In English, this translates to "the law does not concern itself with trifles." However, not all games involve trifles. The death of Ray Chapman was certainly not a "de minimis" event.

While we often tell ourselves that games are trivial and unimportant, that assertion seems to belie the depth of our commitment to games as social institutions. In the United States, an annual series of reports suggests that an average of five to ten high school football players die each year as a result of injuries directly related to playing that game.[3] The Centers for Disease Control estimates that more than a million injuries occur in the United States each year during sports activities.[4] These physical injuries are certainly not "de minimis" and might be avoided if other forms of activity were used to obtain physical exercise. We might ask why, then, does the law allow dangerous games to be played by dangerous rules.

I would argue that the gulf between law and games is not due to the triviality of games, but due to the fact that games constitute a rival regime of social ordering. The rules of games are inherently in tension with the rules of law. If one person throws a rock at another person's head and kills the other person, this is exactly the kind of conduct that leads to a murder conviction. Baseball, however, has its own rules and operates in its own separate sphere of society. As a professional player, Ray Chapman knew there was some risk that an inside fastball might be pitched. That pitch was thrown and it led to his death. The rules of baseball were never broken.

As a society, we seem willing to allow arenas of sports and games to persist as special social settings where separate rules apply. As the literary scholar Jackson Benson once explained,

> The game creates a small, independent world, with its own sharply defined structure of physical consequences, its own laws, its own tribal customs and rituals, its own hierarchy of participants, its own set of conflicts and emotions, and its own set of rewards and punishments.[5]

If games do actually operate in this way, then claiming that virtual worlds are games may not be too distant from claiming that they are separate jurisdictions. I would call them jurisdictions of play.[6]

LAW AND GAMES

One of the first scholars to write extensively on human play and games was the Dutch historian Johan Huizinga. In his 1938 book *Homo Ludens* (Man the Player), Huizinga claims to have found a cross-cultural "play element" that forms the basis for all of human culture.[7] According to Huizinga, the impulse to play is not only fundamental to games but is also the element of culture that animates law, art, war, poetry, ritual, and philosophy.

Since law is my main focus in this book, I want to stop to consider Huizinga's claim that law is rooted in play, since this seems to contradict my claim that law and play are separate spheres. Huizinga based his argument in part on the family resemblances between legal and playing fields, and on adversarial litigation in particular. In both games and law, the formal contest takes place in a set-apart space dominated by ritual (for instance, in the United States, lawyers generally begin their arguments by saying the ceremonial phrase "May it please the court"). In both games and litigation, a judge or referee, dressed in a distinctive and neutral ceremonial costume, supervises the field and holds contestants to fixed rules. Quite often, judges and referees are spatially elevated above the field, detached and superior to the battle below.

A certain ethic of sportsmanship and ceremony frames the adversarial process as skilled opponents compete according to the rules. They maneuver around each other, seeking vulnerabilities and priding themselves on inventive strategies. No one knows in advance who the winner will be, and the skill of contestants can be determinative. It is no wonder that lawyers often speak of litigation as a game.[8] Even John G. Roberts, the current Chief Justice of the U.S. Supreme Court, has made this connection. At his confirmation hearings, he began his opening comments by comparing himself to the umpire of a baseball game:

> Judges and Justices are servants of the law, not the other way around. Judges are like umpires. Umpires don't make the rules; they apply them. The role of an umpire and a judge is critical. They make sure everybody plays by the rules. But it is a limited role. Nobody ever went to a ballgame to see the umpire.[9]

Actually, at certain times and places in history, judges and umpires have been almost indistinguishable. For instance, several millennia ago, at the Olympic Games, the Greek *Hellanodikai* (literally, "judges of the Greeks") were elected from leading families to administer and supervise the Olympic competitions. Ten months before the games began, these judges moved into a large residence at the Olympic site, where they were instructed in the duties they would need to perform as "guardians of the law." The Hellanodikai presided over the Greek games as adjudicators, ceremonial authorities, and even as a police force with the right to whip those who cheated. Monetary fines were also levied against cheaters. When Olympic athletes made their procession to the stadium, they were accompanied by the Hellanodikai and passed twelve bronze statues of Zeus, called Zanes. Fines imposed on cheating athletes financed the creation of the Zanes; they were monuments to the shame of those who had defied the game rules.[10] Within the context of the Olympic games, the Hellano-dikai were judges. They learned the applicable rules, ascertained the facts, applied the rules to those facts, and meted out punishment.

We can only draw a distinction between the game's referee and the judge, I think, by insisting that law is *not* a game, and that legal rules have a privileged status. We might say there is something special about legal rules that separates them from game rules. For instance, we may claim that legal rules are rules of reason, designed to promote social welfare, where game rules are merely arbitrary. Though this is certainly a noble aspiration and a special respect for legal rules is socially desirable, it is not always clear that game rules and legal rules are so fundamentally different in character.

Some legal rules, like the rules of hopscotch or four square, can be elaborate and somewhat arbitrary social constructions. Indeed, in its procedure and substance, the legal system can sometimes resemble a complex and somewhat bizarre game. For instance, in my experience teaching first-year students in law school, I often witness the shock of a student who suddenly spots legal forms, like fantastic and powerful apparitions, appearing in the fabric of the world. As the introduction explains, the law of property often involves legal forms with bizarre names that are centuries old, such as the fee simple determinable, the life estate, the possibility of reverter, and the tenancy at will.[11] If you have not studied property law, you may not have heard of these creatures, but in legal disputes over land, understanding their nature can be essential to navigating legal rights.

No one looking at an acre of land would logically deduce the need for a legal rule establishing the property concept of a possibility of reverter, a future interest in a grantor of real property that follows the conveyance of a fee simple defeasible estate. The possibility of reverter interest is not eminently rational or socially necessary. The only way to truly understand it, and property law in the United States generally, is to know its historical evolution, including the key role of the military network of stone castles created in England by William the Conqueror. If all legal rules today were attributable to similar twists and turns of history and chance, it might be justifiable to think of law as a peculiar and specialized game played by lawyers. Indeed, the nineteenth-century philosopher and social reformer Jeremy Bentham essentially had this impression. After exposure to the law of his time, Bentham branded it the "Demon of Chicane" and quit the law-yering class.

Bentham, however, did not direct his efforts at overthrowing law, but instead at making its system of rules more sensible and better attuned to serving the public welfare. The current understanding of law as an instrument of social utility, valuable only to the extent that it is instrumental in achieving desirable ends, owes much to Bentham's utilitarianism. The true difference between the rules of games and the rules of law, therefore, may not be in their nature but in their aspiration.

So what do the aspirations of law, and the sense that legal rules must stand apart from game rules, tell us about the nature of game rules? We desire laws to be rationally designed to efficiently promote the common good. Do we desire the same thing of game rules? According to Johan Huizinga and several other play theorists, the answer is an emphatic no.

PLAY THEORY

Huizinga's definition of play in *Homo Ludens* has several components, one of which I emphasized above: the centrality of formal rules. However, the other components are worth careful attention as well. Huizinga defines play as a

> free activity standing quite consciously outside "ordinary" life as being "not serious," but at the same time absorbing the player intensely and utterly. It is an activity connected with no material interest, and no profit can be gained by it. It proceeds within its own proper boundaries of time and space according to fixed rules and in an orderly manner.[12]

According to Huizinga, the difference between legal rules and game rules is not procedural, but substantive. Game rules are different because games are different, in at least three ways.

First, games are disassociated from ordinary life in a way that makes them less serious than ordinary life. Law, on the other hand, is understood as very serious, given the violent and coercive powers of the state. Second, play absorbs players "intensely and utterly." Again, this differs from law. While legal disputes can be intense, they are rarely *intrinsically* absorbing for most participants. Third, and perhaps most important, Huizinga emphasizes that games are not materially productive. The utilitarian theory of law, on the other hand, envisions law as a productive and instrumental institution that advances social welfare.

Huizinga's most direct intellectual successor was Roger Caillois, an early sociologist who accepted Huizinga's theories in almost all particulars. Caillois particularly stressed Huizinga's observation that play is "irrational" and produces "no profit." Indeed, Caillois claimed that play is "an occasion of pure waste."[13] The philosopher Bernard Suits, who also wrote extensively about games and play, came to a very similar conclusion. In his 1978 book *The Grasshopper*, Suits defines play and games as unproductive and inefficient. The game, according to Suits, is characterized by

> activity directed towards bringing about a specific state of affairs, using only means permitted by rules, where the rules prohibit more efficient in favor of less efficient means.[14]

As one example of this sort of inefficiency, Suits points out how contestants in a race may run around a circular track in order to cross the finish line. They refrain from crossing the field's center even though this is the most direct path to obtain their objective. Hence, the racing game is intentionally inefficient.

Yet in games as in law, obedience to rules is perhaps the paramount feature. For Suits, the rule-abiding attitude of the player is crucial to the definition of the game. In order to play a game, according to Suits, a player has to possess a "lusory attitude," an intention to be bound by rules that serve no practical purpose. For instance, if a person were running from a hungry tiger and by chance ended up participating in a fifty-yard dash, that person would actually not have participated in a race. Even though her objective behavior matched that of the other racers, she lacked the lusory attitude.

If we agree with Huizinga, Caillois, and Suits, it would seem that games are spheres of human activity in which individuals maintain an intense devotion to a different set of rules.[15] This raises an interesting question: What happens when rules of games clash with rules of law? In essence, this seems like a conflict between two competing social jurisdictions. One solution to the conflict might be to cede to the rulers of games a certain degree of jurisdictional independence from law, just as criminal prosecutors ceded the policing of Ray Chapman's death to the rules of baseball. In some cases, courts have made their deference to the jurisdictions of games explicit. For instance, a 1981 case filed in Georgia alleged that a high school football referee had misapplied a game rule, costing one side the victory and the chance to play in the state championships. This loss was certainly not trivial to the losing team. Conceivably, college scholarships may have been lost due to the error. Yet, when the case came before it, the Supreme Court of Georgia refused to intervene. It declared itself to be "without authority to review decisions of . . . referees because those decisions do not present judicial controversies."[16] Other states have tried to place a similar distance between the rules of games and the rules of law. At least sixteen states have now adopted legislation that protects sports officials from liability for the decisions they make during games. This legislation essentially provides game referees insulation from conventional legal duties to abstain from negligence, tacitly acknowledging games as jurisdictionally independent spheres.

However, jurisdictional conflicts still occur, given that courts cannot completely ignore disputes involving the rules of games. Given that game rules are, from the standpoint of efficiency and instrumental utility, suboptimal, law may have difficulty balancing the competing interests in play when law encounters game rules. As John Barnes has explained,

> Sports maintain internal rules and structures to regulate play and organize competition. In sports law, the wider legal system impinges on this traditionally private sphere and subjects the politics of the sports game to the politics of the law game. The result is a double drama as the deep human concern for play combines with the concern for social justice.[17]

Two examples of lawsuits, involving the rules of football and golf, can help illuminate this point and its implications for law and society.

THE RESTRAINTS OF CIVILIZATION

On September 16, 1973, the Denver Broncos played an NFL game against the Cincinnati Bengals at Mile High Stadium. Though no one knew it at the time, it was the start of the first winning season in Broncos history. However, for Broncos veteran Dale Hackbart, the game marked the last season of a long career and the beginning of a lawsuit.

The Broncos were leading twenty-one to three in the first half of the game, when the Bengals took possession and drove to within scoring range. Dale Hackbart was in the end zone blocking Charles "Booby" Clark, a Bengals rookie fullback who was a prospective pass receiver. The pass was thrown, but it was intercepted by the Broncos. Hackbart, who had fallen to the ground in the course of blocking Clark, knelt on the ground and turned to watch the play continue. Clark, angry about the interception, slammed Hackbart on the back of his head with a forearm.

Hackbart did not complain at the time and even continued to play on two subsequent Sundays. However, he later discovered that the blow from Clark had fractured his neck. When the Bengals released him due to his age, he brought a lawsuit against Clark and the Bengals, alleging that Clark had intentionally assaulted him. Even though they had been playing football, Hackbart alleged that Clark had no business fracturing his neck simply to vent his anger. He considered it an assault, much as it would be considered an assault to strike a stranger on the sidewalk.

Judge Richard Matsch presided over the trial. He concluded that Hackbart had no claim. According to Judge Matsch, Hackbart had consented to the risk of injury by participating in a professional football game, where the normal rules of society were held in abeyance. Judge Matsch stressed that the rules of football, which governed conduct on the playing field, were ambiguous and not enforced uniformly or consistently. He also stressed that football players were encouraged by their coaches to become enraged and violent. Based on his understanding of football, Judge Matsch stated,

> It is wholly incongruous to talk about a professional football player's duty of care for the safety of opposing players when he has been trained and motivated to be heedless of injury to himself. The character of NFL competition negates any notion that the playing conduct can be circumscribed by any standard of reasonableness.[18]

However, even after finding that Hackbart had no claim under the applicable law, Judge Matsch went on to discuss how the policy of tort law related to professional football. Judge Matsch saw football as an occupation "hazardous to the health and welfare of those who are employed," yet found it strange that, unlike other hazardous occupations, the government did not seem to take much interest in protecting the safety of players. He considered it possible that "young athletes have been exploited and subjected to risks which should be unacceptable in our social order." However, he also noted that "professional football has received the implicit approval of government because these contests take place in arenas owned by local governments."

Judge Matsch lamented that good sportsmanship was not the norm in professional football:

> There are no Athenian virtues in this form of athletics. The NFL has substituted the morality of the battlefield for that of the playing field, and the "restraints of civilization" have been left on the sidelines.[19]

Though Judge Matsch was clearly not a fan of the enterprise of football, he concluded that if civil claims like Hackbart's were allowed, courts would be entangled in a "dense thicket" of conflicting game rules, social practices, and factual circumstances, all based on principles that seemed to contradict what he understood as ordinary and reasonable forms of human conduct. Essentially, the intersection of football and law was too difficult a problem for courts to police.

Hackbart appealed this ruling, and a panel of three federal appellate judges reversed the decision. While the court agreed with Judge Matsch that "subjecting another to unreasonable risk of harm, the essence of negligence, is inherent in the game of football," it also stated that "it is highly questionable whether a professional football player consents or submits to injuries caused by conduct not within the rules."[20] The appellate court maintained that the written rules of football at that time prohibited intentional blows. The applicable rule stated,

> All players are prohibited from striking on the head, face or neck with the heel, back or side of the hand, wrist, forearm, elbow or clasped hands.[21]

The appellate court determined that this rule of football was "intended to establish reasonable boundaries" in order to protect the safety of players. Given that football rules prohibited Clark's actions, the appellate court found it in error to conclude, as Judge Matsch had, that when a person plays football, "all reason has been abandoned" and "the only possible remedy for the person who has been the victim of an unlawful blow is retaliation."[22]

Essentially, according to the appellate court, although football is not a field of violent anarchy outside the law, the physical safety of professional football players is a matter fixed not by the standard rules of negligence, but by the rules of the professional game. The rules of football set some limits on the use of violence. Violence within the scope of the football rules is legal, but violence in excess of the football rules is a legal wrong. So Dale Hackbart won his lawsuit against Charles Clark because the court found that Clark had not been playing by the rules of football when he injured Hackbart.

We might ask whether the law, if it wanted to change the rules of football, could do so. The answer to that question, I think, is clearly yes. In many states, the violent sport of boxing is illegal. Where boxing is not illegal, it is subject to substantial regulation. The *Hackbart* case, however, makes it clear that although games are, in theory, subject to state control, courts seem willing to limit the degree to which legal rules intrude upon the sphere of games. Courts have granted the violent game of football substantial leeway to set up its own system of rules, allowing the game to operate outside the boundaries of traditional social expectations.

ARBITRARY RULES

In 1997, professional golfer Casey Martin brought a lawsuit against the PGA Tour, the organization that hosts the most important professional golfing events in the United States. At that time, Martin was one of the best golfers in the world. However, he also had a disability. He was born with a disorder in his right leg that made it painful and dangerous for him to walk.

During much of his career, Martin had managed to accommodate this disability. On many golf courses, golf carts are provided so that players can ride, rather than walk, between holes. In competitive collegiate golf in the United States, however, standard rules require players to walk between holes. Martin had been exempted from this rule to accommodate for his disability. However, when Martin sought this exemption in order to play in the PGA Tour, the organization refused to waive its "walking rule."

Martin sued under the Americans with Disabilities Act (ADA). The ADA is a federal law that prohibits discrimination against the disabled and requires places offering "public accommodation" to make "reasonable modifications" to allow access to those with disabilities. (For instance, a frequently required ADA accommodation for a business might be a wheelchair ramp providing building access.) Martin argued that the ADA applied to the PGA Tour's game and insisted that he be allowed to use a golf cart as a "reasonable modification" of PGA Tour practices.

The PGA Tour had two main arguments against the application of the ADA to Martin's situation. First, it claimed that the ADA was designed to protect the rights of disabled *customers*, not provide access to play in professional golf tours where golfers provide the entertainment. Second, it pointed to a provision of the ADA stating that it was not required to make a "reasonable modification" if doing so would "fundamentally alter the nature" of the service it provided. The PGA Tour argued that allowing Martin to ride a golf cart between holes would "fundamentally alter" the game of golf.[23]

The litigation made its way, ultimately, to the U.S. Supreme Court.[24] Justice John Paul Stevens wrote the majority opinion. On the first issue, Justice Stevens reasoned that because anyone could pay an entry fee and seek to participate in the PGA Tour, the competition was a public accommodation. The second issue is where things got interesting. The Supreme Court was required to decide whether Congress would have intended to allow the PGA Tour's interest in its rules to take priority over allowing disabled individuals to participate in public life. Though the case involved a statute rather than the law of negligence, this was a very similar problem to the one confronted in *Hackbart*.

The majority sided with Martin. They decided that requiring the use of a golf cart would not alter the fundamental nature of the activity in question, namely the game of golf. Stevens stated that golf had traditionally been a game about "shot-making," not walking between holes. Walking had never been "an essential attribute of the game itself."[25] Accordingly, the PGA could be required to provide Martin with a golf cart, since this modification of the rules did not change the fundamental nature of the services provided.

Justice Antonin Scalia wrote a scathing dissent complaining about the majority's musings on "federal-Platonic golf," as he called it. Scalia argued, with an interesting juxtaposition of claims, that "out of humility or out of self-respect . . . the Court should decline to answer this incredibly difficult and incredibly silly question." According to Scalia, games could not have any essential nature because "it is the very nature of a game to have no object except amusement," and this feature "distinguishes games from productive activity." Scalia rhetorically asked,

> Why cannot the PGA TOUR, if it wishes, promote a new game, with distinctive rules . . . ? If members of the public do not like the new rules . . . they can withdraw their patronage. But the rules are the rules. They are (as in all games) entirely arbitrary.[26]

As he explained, there is no good reason why three strikes, rather than four strikes, make a baseball player "out," whereas legal rules reflect careful and instrumental thinking. Later in his dissent, Scalia argued that athletic competitions generally are incompatible with the legislative intent of the ADA. Despite the goals of the ADA, the law would never be able to grant the disabled equal standing in physical competitions, since such competitions are premised on "the measurement, by uniform rules, of unevenly distributed excellence." According to Scalia, making modifications to game rules to accommodate competitors with disabilities would "destroy the game."

Justice Scalia's claims here are arguably in tension. If game rules are arbitrary, unproductive, and silly, then what is the harm suffered by the PGA Tour if the Supreme Court modifies its rules and requires it to provide golf carts? If the rules of games truly serve no purpose, then why should the law defer to them at all? It is interesting that while Justice Stevens and Justice Scalia were divided over the proper outcome of Martin's case, both claimed that federal law should be applied in a way that preserved the essential rules of golf. Scalia was actually the more ardent defender of the PGA Tour's rules, although he seemed simultaneously more dismissive of their character.

HETEROTOPIA

Scalia's observations about the unproductive nature of play accord with the observations of Johan Huizinga, Roger Caillois, and Bernard Suits. Rules of "ordinary life" (including legal rules) are understood as instrumental to obtaining desirable ends, often those related to material needs (for example, procuring food and shelter). Action and effort, by this account, should ideally be minimized. When seeking to achieve goals, we prefer the quickest and easiest way to attain them.

At a fundamental level, games invert this logic, because they are not instrumental activities. Instead, they allow players to escape to a more ideal realm of social action. Bernard Suits describes the game as a utopian practice—an activity suited for an ideal existence in which all material needs have been met. In such a setting, says Suits, play is no longer irrational, but the only rational activity. Johan Huizinga had a similar sort of respect for the activities he defined as unproductive and irrational. He claimed that play is a sacred activity, a means of satisfying "an imperishable need" to "live in beauty." He stressed that play "may rise to heights of beauty and sublimity that leave seriousness far beneath."[27]

These statements suggest that play is a hedonic activity, oriented toward a *process*, not a goal. The prioritization of utopian order and process, I think, can be seen in both game courts and the rules that organize play within those spaces. Bart Giamatti describes the American baseball stadium rhapsodically as "a green expanse, complete and coherent, shimmering carefully tended, a garden."[28] In many sports, game fields are arranged to maximize the pleasure and freedom of bodily movement.

Rules of play also prioritize the enjoyment of process. Actions are not generally explicable by desired goals, but rather goals are explicable by desired actions. The rules of games, at least those of good games, are designed to enable players to enjoy an optimal experience of free, purposeful, and enjoyable action. The ideal state is similar to what Mihaly Csikszentmihalyi has described as "flow."[29] According to Csikszentmihalyi, a flow state exists when an actor is optimally engaged, not overwhelmed by the task at hand or bored. Rules and goals of game play are arbitrary because this flexibility allows for the deliberate engineering of participant flow states that harmonize thought and action.[30]

The way that game rules support a hedonistic policy is perhaps best observed when game rules fail. If there were truly no guiding logic to the rules of games, if they were arbitrary in the absolute sense, they could not fail. Yet game rules do fail. Thomas Malaby, for instance, has pointed out that the shot clock rule in basketball was established to address a failure of the prior set of basketball rules.[31] Prior to the invention of the shot clock rule, the most effective strategy toward the end of a basketball game was for the leading team to obtain the ball and "dribble out" the remaining time. This led to a dull game ending for both competitors and spectators, since the dribbling out strategy did not promote spirited and competitive play. The shot clock rule fixed this failure in the rules of basketball to make them more optimally hedonic.

While the utopian and hedonic order of games may be rational in the sense that it is oriented toward process rather than result, it can conflict with those cultural values that value prudence and productivity over pleasure. John Stuart Mill once complained that the Puritans "endeavored, with considerable success, to put down all public, and nearly all private, amusements: especially music, dancing, public games, or other assemblages for purposes of diversion, and the theatre."[32] On the other hand, the Puritans valorized laborious industry as its own reward. The Puritanical agenda accords with the ancient criticism of pure hedonism, as exemplified in Aesop's fable of the ants and the grasshopper. When there is limited time and material, production is essential to sustaining life, and the path of productive labor is wiser than the pursuit of pleasure. However, as Thoreau once said, "It is not enough to be industrious; so are the ants. What are you industrious about?"[33] In the grasshopper's defense, Bernard Suits suggests that the ants are to be pitied because they have forgotten how to live, making their existence a life of toil for toil's sake—an odd sort of hedonic pursuit in itself.[34]

The valorization of productive labor seems particularly incongruous in post-industrial societies. Where material needs are largely met, achievement in the sphere of "ordinary life" may not be so far from achievement in the hedonic sphere of the game. As Thorstein Veblen cynically observed, the winners of the capitalist game often seem to "waste" the products of their labor in an effort to augment their own social status.[35] McKenzie Wark goes so far as to suggest that modern society is nothing more than a very big game:

> The whole of life appears as a vast accumulation of commodities and spectacles, of things wrapped in images and images sold as things. Images appear as prizes, and call us to play the game in which they are all that is at stake . . .
>
> The real world appears as a fun park divided into many and varied games. Work is a rat race. Politics is a horse race. The economy is a casino. Even the utopian justice to come in the afterlife is foreclosed: He who dies with the most toys wins. Games are no longer a past time, outside or alongside of life. They are now the very form of life, and death, and time, itself.[36]

I would hope that Wark is adopting a rhetorical pose here, inviting us to doubt the equations he is drawing. It is certainly valid to say that free market competition and materialism can give rise to a game-like social structure, that is, one that is ultimately more concerned with the intrinsic pleasures of the process than its instrumental utility. However, willfully equating labor and the game is, if nothing else, morally dangerous. There is nothing wrong with recognizing and obeying, at certain times, rules designed to maximize the intrinsic pleasures of process. But game rules, unlike the rules of law, do not even aspire to achieve social justice, much less prioritize those strategies that are efficient in doing so. A boundary can and should be identified between games and "ordinary life." Such a boundary is not only observable, but essential to the institution of government.

Games must occupy a separate sphere. They operate within delineated spaces and times, carving out what some, following Huizinga, have called a magic circle within which utopian and hedonic rules can function.[37] The notion here is not that game spaces are not interrelated with ordinary life, that there is no blurring between the game and everything else, but that games are, in an important way, oppositional to the logic of ordinary life. Michel Foucault coined the term "heterotopia" to describe such places, using it first in regard to "children's imaginative games," but broadening it to include a wide range of environments where existing social power can be challenged and reconfigured.[38] Importantly, the notion of heterotopic zones is premised on their opposition to some external rules. For play theorists, the game offers an escape from everyday life, conventional rules, and traditional value systems. Games are therefore one example of heterotopia. Game players move in a social environment governed by an alternative rule structure.[39]

As Julie Cohen has noted, virtual worlds also fit the definition of heterotopia fairly well.[40] They offer alternative spheres for social relations—spheres in which expectations of normal behavior may be vastly different. Games and virtual worlds clearly have much in common. Virtual worlds have their roots in computer games, marketed as games, perceived socially as games, and structured by separate rules in the same manner as games.

Yet, despite these clear connections, virtual worlds are not games. Instead, as Richard Bartle has explained, virtual worlds are online places where games are usually played. For example, not every interaction that transpires between two avatars in World of Warcraft will be governed by the rules of a game. It is certainly possible to hold the board meeting of a corporation using World of Warcraft as the platform for that event. A board meeting, even if it occurs through the use of troll and orc avatars in Orgrimmar, is certainly not a game. By the same token, just because many board meetings have been held using the Second Life platform, this does not prevent other residents from using Second Life as a play space. The conflict between games and law in virtual worlds therefore cannot be resolved by simply labeling virtual worlds as games, either dismissively or otherwise. Before law can defer to game rules—if it is to defer to game rules at all—we must have some sense of when and how game rules are present in virtual worlds.

The facts here will vary with each virtual world. The alternative rules a virtual world provides are usually peculiar to that virtual world, the genre it inhabits, and can even vary greatly among individual users. Mr. Bungle may have misunderstood the rules of LambdaMOO, but what are those rules, exactly? Even the system of LambdaLaw left much in doubt about the rules that were truly applicable in the online community. To the extent that virtual worlds are games, the lack of clear rules make it harder to square those games with the standard background expectations of law. In the *Martin* case, the Supreme Court could point to the centuries-old tradition and custom of golf, but there is no analogous tradition or custom in Second Life.

As an example of the difficulties this might pose for law, consider the phenomenon of disputes over virtual world property scams. As Orin Kerr explains, where game rules are clear and implicitly contractual, they can serve as a useful tool to resolve disputes over property:

A string of century-old card game cases from Texas illustrate the point. In these cases, individuals lost money in card games and tried to keep the money they had lost, either because they thought the game was rigged or because they claimed to have been cheated. When charged with robbery or theft, they argued that the money belonged to them and therefore they had committed no crime. . . . Courts always deferred to the announced rules of the game to determine who owned what.[41]

In other words, much like the courts in the *Hackbart* and *Martin* cases, the Texas courts focused on the application of fixed game rules to guide the proper interpretation of legal rules. But in virtual worlds, how can we be sure when virtual property is "fairly" stolen? In the case of Qiu Chengwei, our intuition might tell us that when Zhu took the Dragon Saber and failed to return it, he defrauded Qiu of the value of the property in violation of the game rules. However, based on my understanding of Legend of Mir, defrauding other players in this way is not part of the game. (Recall that this sort of behavior is expressly prohibited in the terms of service of World of Warcraft.) But what if the rules of the game made defrauding another player, like the act of bluffing in poker, an acceptable strategy?

EVE Online is a popular MMORPG operated by CCP, a company based in Reykjavik, Iceland, and it regularly raises this sort of question.[42] EVE owes its fantastic world to conventions of science fiction—it is set in a distant galaxy where competing empires and mega-corporations battle for control of scarce resources. Two features set EVE apart from other MMORPGs.

First, the virtual world is not "sharded," that is, split up into mirror copies of the game environment. Instead, all players (about three hundred thousand as of 2009)[43] share a single galactic playing field. This means that the player guilds in EVE Online (called alliances and corporations) can operate at a larger scale, actually dominating and controlling particular sectors of the virtual galaxy.

Second, EVE Online is a game where ruthless behavior is part of the game's culture. Players regularly infiltrate rival alliances and corporations with their agents, seeking to obtain valuable information or property or to otherwise exploit a rival's vulnerabilities. Likewise, in "null security" space, generally the richest zones for mining virtual property, player groups and pirates dominate particular areas and set their own rules. They often delight in destroying non-allied players to harvest the salvage from their spaceships.

In this environment in early 2006, a player who went by the name of Cally opened the EVE Interstellar Bank, or EIB.[44] The currency in EVE is interstellar credits, or ISK. Players who "invested" their ISK with Cally were promised high rates of return, which Cally regularly delivered. Cally's rates, in fact, beat standard investment rates in real currency, reportedly enticing some players to convert their real money to ISK (notably, in violation of the EVE terms of service) in order to make real returns off the virtual bank. True to the nature of EVE, however, it turned out that the Cally's EIB was a virtual Ponzi scheme. Cally disappeared with the virtual currency and posted a video bragging about his piratical performance, whereby he had made off with several hundred billion ISK. If this virtual currency had been sold on the open market, Cally would have made over one hundred thousand dollars from his Ponzi scheme—not bad for a virtual crime.

Despite the player outcry, however, CCP, EVE's owner, declined to take any action against Cally, simply stating that they would be watching carefully to ensure that Cally did not turn a real profit from his virtual Ponzi scheme. According to one blogger who attended a "virtual press conference" with CCP officers, CCP stated that it "is against scams and scam artists of this nature in general, but so long as people abide by the [terms of service], funds or assets acquired through what one would term fraud and/or embezzlement in real life are within the context of the game at-large, and thus not actionable by CCP."[45]

The statement is odd because, as Yee Fen Lim points out, EVE Online's terms of service actually do make reference to pyramid schemes.[46] While deception, treachery, and virtual violence are endemic in EVE Online, nowhere is it explicitly spelled out that running Ponzi schemes to defraud other players of investments is a fair manner of play. Rather, clause 9 of the EVE Online terms of service states:

> You may not advertise, employ, market, or promote any form of solicitation—including *pyramid schemes* and chain letters—in the Eve Online game world or on the website.[47]

This language, however, is arguably ambiguous. Presumably, players are free to advertise their private corporations and market their personal services as miners and bounty hunters—the game of EVE Online depends on this sort of thing. So perhaps this language means that Cally was privileged to market his *virtual* pyramid scheme and was only prohibited from marketing a *real* pyramid scheme? In any event, in the same document, CCP makes it abundantly clear that they, like essentially all virtual world owners, assume no affirmative duty to protect players against the loss of in-game assets due to the deception of other players.

But the failure of CCP, a private company, to address the harm done by a virtual pyramid scheme, would not bar a prosecutor from charging Cally with criminal fraud. Would the game rules of EVE Online prevent that prosecution? Tellingly, one commenter on a blog stated, "It's part of the game. It would be like suing someone you lost to at poker. Stealing from people is obviously part of the game."[48]

The analogy to poker brings us back to Orin Kerr's Texas card game cases, Casey Martin, and the relationship between terms of service and legal rules. It seems clear now, even if it was not previously, that the rules of the EVE Online "game" allow players, via their avatars, to engage in what would ordinarily be lawless behavior (that is, fraud). However, the exact scope of permitted lawlessness is not made clear by any formal mechanism (that is, contract), making it possible for various parties to have different understandings of what is and is not allowed within the game. Additionally, it seems possible that at least some "real world" investments (that is, cash) can be converted to the virtual currency of the virtual jurisdiction of EVE Online jurisdiction and vice versa.

At this point, we may wonder if EVE Online is properly understood as a game governed by rules at all. EVE is starting to resemble Judge Matsch's characterization of the NFL, a place where the "restraints of civilization have been left on the sidelines." When we defer to the "rules" of EVE Online under the aegis that it is "only a game," we permit the establishment of a very real and anarchic online frontier.

7

property

There is nothing which so generally strikes the imagination, and engages the affections of mankind, as the right of property.

—William Blackstone

I ended the last chapter with the story of Cally, the scam artist who made off with the equivalent of a hundred thousand dollars in EVE Online currency. In increasing numbers, the Callys of virtual worlds are being prosecuted. In November 2007, various news sources reported that a seventeen-year-old in the Netherlands had been arrested and charged with the theft of virtual furniture in Habbo Hotel.[1] The victims were other Dutch teenagers who logged in to Habbo Hotel and found their rooms stripped bare of their virtual possessions. In Habbo, unlike EVE Online, theft and fraud are not considered customary and acceptable. While CCP, the owners of EVE Online, defended the freedom of Cally to defraud his fellow players, the owners of Habbo, the Finnish company Sulake, actually aided Dutch police in their investigation of the Habbo crime.

The Habbo thief's modus operandi was one that is seen increasingly outside the context of virtual worlds. He stole the virtual furniture via a "phishing" strategy, directing users to false Habbo login screens where they unknowingly revealed their account passwords. The thief then logged in to their accounts and transferred their furniture to other accounts. The value of the furniture stolen in this way was placed at roughly five thousand dollars (presumably because this is the amount the victims had paid Habbo for it).

If the thief had stolen credit card account numbers rather than Habbo passwords and associated furniture, the crime would have been seen as just another case of online identity theft. Yet because the theft involved virtual property in a virtual world, and because Dutch police actually made an arrest, the Habbo case grabbed headlines. The teenager was subsequently convicted under Dutch law. At about the same time, two other teens in the Netherlands were also convicted of theft under Dutch law for stealing virtual items in another virtual world from another teen. The two boys had physically threatened a thirteen-year-old into handing over a virtual amulet and a mask in the MMORPG Runescape.[2] As in Qiu Chengwei's case, the physical violence was very real, but the property was virtual.

These were hardly the first cases, however, where criminal prosecutions were brought related to misappropriations of virtual property. According to *Harper's* magazine, by 2008, courts in the Republic of Korea had heard over seven hundred cases involving criminal allegations of the fraudulent acquisition of virtual property.[3] As early as 1999, Judge Ung-gi Yoon, an expert on virtual property law in the Republic of Korea, witnessed an arrest in one such case at a police station in Seoul:

> The two lads, now taken into custody by law enforcement officers, were sitting on their knees with their arms held up above the head, in a posture of atonement ostensibly ordered by the latter. The charge brought against them was fraud. The two youngsters, I was told, took money from a Lineage gamer for a number of in-game items that they promised, but never intended to deliver.
>
> The officer responsible for investigating this case was himself a Lineage player. He apparently collects evidence leading up to a case through his own in-game character.[4]

In the cases of the Habbo thief, the Runescape thieves, and the Lineage scam artists police arrested and prosecuted individuals for virtual property crimes, unlike the police in the cases of Geoff Luurs and Qiu Chengwei. However, all three cases involve different sorts of conduct. In the Habbo case, the thief used a form of deception to obtain unauthorized access to passwords granting access to virtual property. In the Runescape case, the boys used real violence to obtain an in-game transfer of virtual property. In the Lineage case, the boys took real money in exchange for a (false) promise to transfer virtual property. While all three arrests involved defendants doing something inappropriate with virtual property, the way that virtual property fits into each crime, from a legal doctrinal perspective, is actually quite important.

In the common law system of property, civil and criminal law both protect against the "conversion" of property. Though the exact rules about conversion vary between jurisdictions, conversion generally constitutes substantial interference with the property rights of another. For instance, if another person were to pound on your car with a baseball bat, that person would probably be subject to criminal prosecution, because a car is a form of legal property protected from this kind of interference. Whether traditional conversion law applies to virtual property generally hinges on whether virtual property is recognized as legal property. Notably, among the claims Marc Bragg brought against Linden Lab was the claim that Linden had converted his legal property, his virtual land.[5]

One interesting aspect of virtual property questions is that, in some cases, such as the Lineage case, the legal characterization of the virtual property at issue may not be of much concern. As Judge Yoon has explained, in the Republic of Korea, those who steal virtual property cannot be charged with the Korean equivalent of conversion prohibitions, given that virtual property is not "moveable" property; instead, virtual property is considered an intangible resource.[6] The Lineage thieves, however, could be prosecuted for fraud. They had misled their victim to obtain "pecuniary advantage," a category of criminal activity that is not limited to property per se.

So, as the Korean example illustrates, while property law plays an important part in determining the scope of remedies for wrongs involving virtual property, whether virtual property is recognized as property per se does not absolutely determine whether or not wrongdoing involving virtual property can give rise to legal liabilities. However, if we were to treat virtual property as legal property, the process of resolving disputes would be more straightforward, since property gives rise to all the standard legal interests that accompany property ownership.

In jurisdictions such as the Republic of Korea, the law at present does not permit virtual property to be regarded as legal property. The question I want to explore in this chapter is whether courts might embrace the idea of legal virtual property in common-law jurisdictions, and in the United States in particular.

PROPERTY DOCTRINE

William Blackstone, who is quoted at the beginning of this chapter, was one of the most influential authorities on the common law during the eighteenth century. In his *Commentaries on the Laws of England* (1765–1769), Blackstone explained both the substance and the logic of the English law of his time. His writings about property were particularly thoughtful and influential. Blackstone felt that property had a peculiar grip on the psyche. He even drew a link between human and animal property instincts, noting that animals possess

> a kind of permanent property in their dwellings, especially for the protection of their young; that the birds of the air had nests, and the beasts of the field had caverns, the invasion of which they esteemed a very flagrant injustice, and would sacrifice their lives to preserve them.[7]

Blackstone attributed a similar sort of irrational passion to the human attachment to property, which he famously described as a "sole and despotic dominion . . . in total exclusion of the right of any other individual in the universe."[8]

It seems clear that users enjoy, and virtual world owners seek to provide, compelling experiences that inspire the sort of passions that Blackstone described. In Britannia and many other virtual worlds, people obtain virtual property to get ahead, make friends, show off their success, and keep up with the virtual Joneses. Virtual worlds, as I noted in chapter 2, are largely about simulating the pleasures of going places and getting things. Since they want to please their users, the companies that provide virtual worlds have strong incentives to do their best to simulate the experience of possessing attractive and valuable forms of virtual property. And because property is more meaningful and valuable to its owners when it can be gifted, sold, and traded, virtual worlds owners have incentives to create virtual economies to please users, allowing them to use property to create and sustain social bonds.

Traditionally, the common law has recognized two forms of property: real property and personal property. The first of these, real property, concerns land, which was the predominant generator and form of wealth historically. All other varieties of legal property fall in the second category, described as personal or chattel property. The law of chattel property today primarily grants rights in tangible and movable things, such as cars and computers, though it also extends to some intangible things, such as statutory forms of intellectual property. Chattel rights in tangible things play a key role in virtual worlds. Servers are chattels, and it is the property interest in the server that allows virtual world owners to exclude others, technologically, from access to their platforms.[9]

The fact that computers are a form of legal property, however, does not necessarily preclude another form of legal property from being present on them. Just as computers are a form of property situated on some body of land, so other forms of legal property can, in theory, be situated on a network of computers. The key question, therefore, is whether virtual property, a form of property that is not tangible and not created by positive statute, can be recognized as an independent chattel property interest.

In the civil law system, the intangible nature of virtual property would bar its legal recognition. The common law is more flexible and has historically protected some forms of intangible rights as property interests. Blackstone himself discussed the law of "incorporeal hereditaments," a recognized form of chattel property that included such exotic property rights as offices, corodies, and advowsons.[10] (The last of these is a property right to nominate the rector of a specific church.) Blackstone realized that incorporeal hereditaments were rather odd forms of common law property, given that they were "invisible" and possessed only a "mental existence." Yet they were recognized as property nonetheless.

So, at least in common law systems, nothing precludes the recognition of property rights in intangible things. Indeed, in real property, the law recognizes future rights of ownership, including speculative future interests, as legal "things." So, for instance, say Alice is given a document that grants her ten acres in Pennsylvania if she one day becomes the president of the United States. Though Alice has no current right to take possession of the land, and indeed may never have that right, the law recognizes a legal property interest (an executory interest) that is in her possession. By law, she can sell her property interest to another or use it as collateral for a loan.[11]

Similarly, many other forms of personal wealth today are not directly bound in physical and tangible objects. Joint bank accounts, 401(k) plans, and investment securities are not discrete piles of cash that are in a drawer somewhere. Rather, they exist primarily in databases that delineate certain obligations on the part of some fiduciary toward an account holder. Much of our economy today is symbolic and virtual, represented and located in secure e-commerce systems that are just as intangible as virtual worlds.

It is also important to note as well that these forms of intangible property sometimes place encumbrances on the use of other forms of property. For instance, one of Blackstone's "incorporeal hereditaments" that is still very important today is the easement on real property. In their most common form, easements consist of a "right of way" across another owner's land. Though they are a form of property that grants rights in land, they are technically a form of chattel property (since they are not estates in land), and a very odd form of chattel property at that. Easements can only exist when someone other than the holder of the easement owns the land subject to the easement. If the owner of the easement comes into ownership of the land, the easement is "merged" into the land and destroyed as a matter of legal doctrine.[12]

If the law of easements sounds odd and needlessly arcane (which it is), the social value of legally recognizing easements is perfectly clear. Sidewalks, for instance, are easements allowing the community to walk on land that is privately owned. They generally increase the value and utility of land in a community. Other easements, such as access roads, sewer lines, or power lines, are also ways of structuring land use for common benefit rather than private exclusion. So, from the standpoint of policy, it is often the case that the "sole and despotic dominion" of property is not ideal. A web of overlapping and complex legal interests in things is preferable to an atomized regime of single owners with absolute private rights.

This insight is crucial to the enterprise of virtual property. To the extent that law recognizes virtual property, it must recognize something very much like an easement. Users, purchasers, and sellers of virtual property are all interested in a thing that depends on the operation of software, computing equipment and, most importantly, computer servers. To the extent that virtual property rights exist, virtual world owners will be constrained in the free use of their own computing equipment. The existence of easements demonstrates that it is fairly conventional to constrain private rights in tangible property in order to enforce someone else's lesser interests in that property. In the case of easements, placing burdens and limitations on rights of private ownership actually promotes public welfare. The open question is whether the same can be said for virtual property.

PROPERTY THEORY

Because intangible property interests are protected by various laws, when formal definitions of property are set forth in the statutes of many jurisdictions, they tend to be broad in their scope. For instance, the Model Penal Code, which exerts a strong influence on the criminal laws of the United States, defines property subject to theft as including "anything of value."[13] *Black's Law Dictionary*, commonly referenced by courts in the United States as a reliable source of traditional legal definitions, has a similarly open-ended definition of property. According to *Black's Law*, the term "property" can

> denote everything which is the subject of ownership, corporeal or incorporeal, tangible or intangible, visible or invisible, real or personal; everything that has an exchangeable value or which goes to make up wealth or estate.[14]

In other words, the formal definition of property suggests that essentially anything can be considered property, as long as the law is willing to recognize that thing as property.

Some cases push these sorts of definitions to their conceptual limits. For instance, in 1990, police arrested a man for selling AT&T long-distance codes at the Port Authority in New York City. Essentially, the defendant was selling fourteen-digit access numbers that could be used to make phone calls. The numbers, however, were "stolen" in that they were associated with accounts that the defendant had no right to use. Among other charges, the prosecuting district attorney claimed that the defendant, Johnson, had violated a statute prohibiting the possession of "stolen property."

Johnson's defense lawyer argued that this was nonsense. The fourteen digits, he said, were *numbers*, not legal property. Johnson certainly owned the tangible slip of paper on which he had written the three calling codes. If Johnson owned the paper, and if the court agreed that it was ridiculous to say that numbers were legal property, then Johnson could not be guilty of possession of stolen property. It seemed like a good argument.

Indeed, in a prior New York case involving almost identical facts, another judge had concluded that a string of numbers could not be considered property. According to that court, "the mere isolated knowledge of those numbers . . . has not yet been defined by the Legislature as a crime."[15] Yet the judge in Johnson's case disagreed. He explained that even if numbers were intangible ideas, they were a "thing of value" and therefore could fall within the criminal statute's definition of property. According to the court, the "number itself is what is crucial, and not who has the superior possessory interest in the paper."[16] The judge in the *Johnson* case clearly took a very broad view of legal property.

Not all courts, of course, have reasoned this way. For instance, although a person's happiness is certainly a thing of value, and an unkind criticism may deprive a person of that happiness, this is not an instance of legal conversion. By the same token, people are valuable, but thankfully, most legal systems no longer allow people to be treated as forms of property. In 1990, the Supreme Court of California additionally decided that a person's excised cells were not legal property, given the importance of allowing medical researchers the freedom to experiment with excised human blood and tissue without the risk of property-based claims from their former owners.[17] On the other hand, courts entertaining divorce suits have struggled over the question of whether a spouse's educational or professional degrees should be considered a property asset subject to division upon the dissolution of the marriage.[18]

We might hope that legal philosophy would provide clear guidance to courts puzzling over the borders of property. There have certainly been many attempts to make property law a more rational and coherent enterprise. Legal philosophers' efforts to provide a formal theory of property fill many heavy volumes. However, it should be admitted that attempts to theorize property law are inevitably post hoc efforts. As Blackstone noted, we seem to inherit the legal institution of property rights from much older and more primal arrangements and instincts. Although property rights can be *modified* by the state, attempts to formulate property regimes from first principles have been rare, and are even more rarely successful in practice. But if property rights *were* justified and rationalized on first principles, what would those principles be?

In the United States, perhaps the most influential theory of property rights, at least in the early years of the country, was that of English philosopher John Locke. Locke believed that property rights were natural rights, existing independently and prior to their recognition by government. This notion informed and partially explained Locke's commitment to the limited role of government in society. According to Locke, property interests could be acquired by the productive expenditure of one's labor. Individual labor comingled with raw materials created a natural right to property.[19]

Though Locke offered his theory as a universal truth, it is perhaps better understood as a statement of his ideology. That ideology still harmonizes comfortably with many modern liberal sentiments about the appropriate congruence between productive effort and property rewards. Many people intuit that they have a right to reap where they have sown. By the same token, they believe they have the right to prohibit others, including government, from depriving them of the fruits of their labor. So even if Locke's notion of property is founded on an ideology, that ideology still holds powerful sway in the contemporary world.

Though it may seem counterintuitive, Lockean ideals play a significant part in the shape of virtual property claims as well. Part of what virtual world owners offer is virtual property that is *difficult* to acquire. Most virtual world users have little regard for property that is superabundant and free, instead preferring to "earn" what they acquire, as Locke suggested they needed to do in order to acquire ownership. The labor of obtaining virtual property plays a significant role in the value it holds. Knowing that months or years of effort are required to obtain a virtual castle in Britannia is exactly what makes that virtual castle a marker of social status and achievement.

However, while Lockean theory may explain how many people think about property rights, as a formal legal matter, Locke's theories are often unhelpful. Locke's theory regarding property maps fairly well onto a society composed of self-sufficient yeoman farmers, reaping what they sow and demanding independence from oppressive external interference. It stumbles severely, however, when it is applied to industrial and postindustrial society, where vast and interrelated networks of individuals collaborate in chains of production. When people mix their labor with collective enterprises, Locke's theory offers minimal guidance.

To the extent that any coherent theory of property dominates today, the utilitarian view associated with Jeremy Bentham in chapter 6 probably comes closest to being dominant. Property law is a means to a civic end. It structures interpersonal relations concerning things in ways designed to further social welfare. When property rights create social benefits, they are justified. When they create more harm than good, they should be abandoned. Most legal scholars, philosophers, and judges in the common-law system seem to approach property rights in this way. They do not justify proposed property rules upon an abstract notion of what property *must* be, but instead upon the way proposed property rules might promote or frustrate valuable social goals. The benefit of this approach is that law becomes a flexible instrument in the service of the social good. The problem is that we must ascertain the social good in order to gauge the soundness of the law.

So, for instance, consider the issue of whether property law in a state should be modified in a way that would create incentives for certain tracts of land to continue to be used for agriculture purposes as opposed to residential development. Turning farmland into housing may meet market demands for affordable housing. However, the loss of local agriculture may lead to poorer health for the local population. Also, if those in urban areas relocate to rural areas, this may lead to the decay of urban centers, increasing automobile traffic and furthering environmental degradation. A utilitarian approach to property rights offers no clear guidance, only flexibility in response to political process.

Over the past thirty years or so, the utilitarian approach to property law has often been accompanied, in both scholarship and judicial practice, by an approach based in "law and economics." Law and economics adherents, such as Richard Posner and Frank Easterbrook, are utilitarian thinkers.[20] They tend to see legal rules as flexible instruments. While law and economics adherents generally profess to be indifferent to individuals' substantive goals, they privilege neoclassical economics as a tool for helping society *efficiently* achieve those goals. They also tend to support strategies based on the creation of private markets and free competition. This approach generally accords with what is known as "Chicago School" economic theory, which is in turn associated with the economic and political approach described as neoliberalism. Neoliberals and Chicago School thinkers are enthusiastic proponents of free market competition, economic deregulation, and strong rights of private ownership.

As a general matter, legal theorists who adopt a law and economics perspective are enthusiastic when it comes to the creation of new forms of private property rights in response to technological change. Private property is viewed as instrumental in avoiding a "tragedy of the commons," a systemic failure that occurs in the absence of private ownership rights.[21] When resources are owned collectively, individuals have little motivation to invest in the upkeep or development of those resources. Would you, for instance, voluntarily spend time planting a garden in a public park if you knew that everyone else could come and harvest the vegetables? Probably not. It might be altruistic to provide the world with vegetables this way, but your general altruistic impulses are probably crowded out by your interest in helping yourself and those close to you.

Additionally, your Lockean instincts probably tell you that if you plant vegetables somewhere voluntarily, you *ought* to have the exclusive right to reap the vegetables you sow. Though this may be a self-interested approach to property rights, Chicago School adherents argue self-interested behaviors are ultimately helpful to society. For instance, when you sell your home or the vegetables you grow, you obtain the benefit of your labor while your productivity affords the buyer something valuable. Law and economics theorists have a tendency to use these sorts of examples to promote a general program of furthering private ownership as opposed to common or state ownership. They explain that, aggregated across populations, private property and free markets lead to greater social productivity and more efficient development of resources. So, the story goes, new forms of private property rights can be desirable—even necessary—to make new social landscapes function optimally.

There are many reasons to be skeptical of this account, but my goal here is not to fully describe or criticize this approach to property rights. Instead, I just want to emphasize that many lawyers, jurists, and legal scholars in the United States endorse, or at least seriously entertain, this sort of approach to property law. The law and economics approach also explains and endorses the recent legal recognition in the United States of something very close to a virtual property right: the property right in an Internet domain name.

DOMAIN NAMES

At about the same time he decided in *ProCD v. Zeidenberg* that undisclosed software contracts could be legally binding (discussed in chapter 5), Judge Frank Easterbrook claimed that the law should recognize a new form of property.[22] The property he had in mind was the Internet domain name.

As a technical matter, a domain name is, like the property in the *Johnson* case, a string of numbers with importance to a computer network. Each computer connected to the Internet is identified with a number called an IP address (such as 185.23.53.102). While these long strings of numbers can be difficult to commit to memory, the mnemonic problem can be avoided by using instead a system of names, such as Rutgers .edu or Disney.com, that are keyed to a system of correspondence with particular numbers. Domain names are this system, linking names with numbers and, ultimately, with specific computers. The owner of a domain name is essentially a person who owns the right to associate a particular word, or string of letters, with a particular computer on the Internet.

The legal problem this presents is determining who should decide which words are associated with which computers. Domain names such as mcdonalds.com, sex.com, and madonna.com could point to any computer—or they could all point to one computer. To which computer *should* they point? In the 1990s, the engineers of the Internet decided that ownership of domain names should be handled on a first-come, first-serve basis. If you asked for a domain name, and that name was not taken, you'd generally get the name (unless the engineers thought you were up to something improper). In 1994, under these rather permissive rules, Joshua Quittner, a journalist for *Wired* magazine, applied for and received the domain name www.mcdonalds.com. Amazed, he published an article in *Wired* titled "Billions Registered: Right Now There Are No Rules to Keep You from Owning a Bitchin' Corporate Name as Your Own Internet Address."[23]

At the time, it was not clear that Quittner had done anything legally wrong. A domain name was not, after all, a tangible piece of property, and the domain name system was just a mnemonic shortcut that had been developed by well-intentioned computer scientists. It was not clear why a hamburger company, rather than Joshua Quittner, should "own" the Internet address mcdonalds.com. At the same time, the public value of mcdonalds.com was the reason Quittner was interested in owning it. The particular string of characters brought to mind, for better or for worse, a particular hamburger company. And that hamburger company, when it realized what was going on with the new technology, felt justifiably concerned that Quittner had appropriated the word that was associated with its business. So, when other companies with famous marks went to create their first web pages and found them already taken, they turned to the law. They brought trademark-based lawsuits claiming that they owned the exclusive right to link computers to the domain names associated with their brands. Around 1996, some judges started ruling in favor of the brand owners, often employing creative theories that distorted the rules of existing trademark law (which was ambiguous, at best, with respect to rights in domain names).

Three years later, Congress responded to this situation by passing the Anti-Cybersquatting Consumer Protection Act (ACPA), a law that explicitly recognized legal rights to domain names for companies that held corresponding trademark rights. Though the statute is complex, it is squarely targeted at those who seek to benefit from registering domain names in order to profit from their association with the owners of commercial brands. The law even allows companies to initiate "in rem" legal proceedings, or suits against the domain names themselves. Previously this sort of legal proceeding had been limited to cases involving tangible property. In in rem proceedings under the ACPA, courts can order that the ownership of the domain name be transferred to the successful plaintiff.

Congress apparently intended, by creating these in rem proceedings, for courts to consider domain names a form of legal property. Unsurprisingly, some courts began to treat domain names as property, and in particular as property interests subject to conversion. Traditionally, claims of conversion, like the laws of criminal theft, arose from interferences with tangible property. One well-known case, *Kremen v. Cohen*, involved the domain name sex.com. The sex.com domain name clearly had value—evidence submitted in the case claimed it produced over ten million dollars a year in advertising revenues. An enterprising con artist, Stephen Cohen, decided to grab that value from its registered owner, Gary Kremen, by filing a fraudulent transfer document with the agency that supervised the early domain name system. When he found out that he no longer controlled the computer linked to "sex.com," Kremen brought a lawsuit against both Cohen and the agency, alleging, among other things, that Cohen was liable for the conversion of the domain name.

The trial court refused to entertain the claim, because it felt that domain names could not be a form of property subject to conversion. It did not question that domain names were some sort of property, but it stated that, according to past decisions, they should be treated as "a form of intangible property which can not serve as a basis for a conversion claim."[24] When the case was appealed, however, a panel of three federal judges, with Judge Alex Kozinski writing the opinion, concluded that domain names *could* be subject to conversion.[25]

Judge Kozinski, having reviewed prior opinions indicating that tangible material must exist as the foundation for a conversion claim, concluded that such opinions were out of pace with the modern era. He stated that domain names were legal property because they were "a well-defined interest" that could be, and should be, subject to exclusive possession. He also noted that domain names were being traded on the market. He stated,

"Like other forms of property, domain names are valued, bought and sold, often for millions of dollars."

Not all courts will agree with the analysis in the *Kremen* case. Yet if the logic of *Kremen* proves persuasive, it may have important implications for virtual property. A domain name is really no more than the intersection of a particular number in a computer database with the social value it generates when exchanged. If, according to the law of the United States, a domain name can be a "well-defined interest" that is bought and sold and subject to the law of conversion, it follows that a virtual castle in Britannia can be such an interest as well.

VIRTUAL PROPERTY

Today there is a considerable amount of legal literature debating whether and how the law might recognize rights in virtual property.[26] Joshua Fairfield is a prominent commentator in this area and he has argued that the theoretical justifications for legal property rights in domain names and in virtual property are essentially identical. According to Fairfield, both domain names and virtual property use computer code to mimic real world properties. Specifically, what Fairfield means is that software rules create persistent and social artifacts with the key economic characteristic of being "rivalrous." One person's use of virtual property precludes or interferes with another person's use simply because this is how the simulation is coded.

Fairfield argues that because both domain names and virtual property have similar characteristics and are structured to function as rivalrous assets, they should be subject to the same rules of private ownership and market alienation that guide the tangible assets they are coded to emulate. According to Fairfield, who adopts a traditional law and economics approach, a free market in domain names and virtual property, like a free market in any other rivalrous asset, will encourage investment in the production of socially desirable resources and the distribution of those resources to the parties that value them most. It might be noted that this position is not inconsistent with cyber-libertarian approaches to the Internet, which tend to emphasize the importance of property rights, decentralized governance, market-based solutions, and individual autonomy.[27]

The strongest objection to Fairfield's argument, I think, is that virtual property is *artificially* scarce. The only reason a privately owned virtual castle can be offered for sale on Dagger Isle in Britannia is that the owners of the virtual world chose to create software rules to make virtual castles scarce, to make their acquisition difficult, to link private control of virtual castles to one account, and to provide a programmed mechanism for the owner to transfer the castle to the account of another. If those software rules were rewritten, perhaps everyone could have a virtual castle, or all virtual castles in Britannia could be held in common. Rules that apply to physical objects do not *need* to apply to simulated objects that are coded to behave like physical objects, primarily because the simulation does not *need* to behave like the reality it mimics.

However, such an argument might call into question the rights in domain names. The engineers who established the domain name system might have allowed mcdonalds.com to point to multiple computers, allowing anyone who wanted to "own" that name to include their machine on a list of locations corresponding to the name. After all, there are multiple people with the name Alice, so why not allow them all to claim ownership of the domain name alice.com? Some regime of shared ownership would be technically possible. For instance, someone looking for alice.com might be directed randomly to a computer owned by any one of the group of owners. But if domain names were coded to be non-rivalrous in this way, they would become nonfunctional. Domain names are socially valuable precisely *because* they point to a single computer and not to any number of random computers. If domain names were shared, or if anyone could own mcdonalds.com, the domain name system would lose its utility.

Virtual property could be largely non-rivalrous as well: everyone in Habbo Hotel could have huge rooms with tons of virtual furniture. Theft in that sort of world would be pointless, since superabundance would be the norm. Some virtual worlds, such as early MOOs, offered environments that were more or less like this, without very much resource scarcity. Even in virtual worlds like this, where superabundance is desired, certain physical and practical limits *do* apply to virtual property. For instance, too many virtual objects might tax the processing power of servers. However, these sorts of practical limits fail to explain why many forms of virtual property, like castles in Brittania, become valuable. The fact is that commercial virtual worlds seem to prosper more when certain things, like castles, igloos, blue hair, or ghostly virtual cats and dogs, are made artificially scarce. Even Second Life, a world that seeks to emphasize user freedom, codes artificial scarcity into its platform. If the market for virtual worlds is a guide to human psychology, it seems people are incapable of enjoying, individually or socially, simulations where they (and everyone else) can have everything and do anything. Such superabundance may seem utopian, but as chapter 6 explained, there are hedonic and social reasons for people to prefer at least some scarcity.

This harks back to the strange, inefficient, and economically counterintuitive logic of the game. The artificial scarcity of most virtual worlds, I believe, should be understood as similar to the "hedonic" sort of scarcity found in game environments. It is at least curious, therefore, to base arguments for virtual property's recognition on neoliberal theories about the ideal efficiency of markets, incentivizing production, and optimally allocating scarce resources. The very scarcity and inefficiency that is ordinarily understood as the "bug" in the system is actually revealed to be a key design feature.

One potential legal reaction to hedonic scarcity might reflect the law's reaction to games. Courts might identify a gulf between the privately regulated artificial scarcity of Habbo furniture and Britannian castles and the standard animating logic of property law, and use this difference to deny that virtual property should be recognized as a legal matter. Courts using this strategy might either focus on the intangibility of the interest or perhaps deny that the user's interest is a thing of value, given the contractual language that does its best, in most cases, to deny the existence of any virtual property rights.

Yet it should be noted that many commodities, such as baseball cards, diamonds, and haute couture clothing, are produced in intentionally limited quantities with the understanding that limiting supply increases demand. In some cases, a higher price signals the prestige value of a "luxury" or "limited edition" artifact. Goods whose high price drives demand are known as Veblen goods. Yet the legal system, when it fixes the value of good, does not discount the legal value of Veblen goods. When a diamond or luxury sedan is stolen, the law values that object at a market price that compensates owners for losses attributable to regimes of privately imposed scarcity.

While legal authorities could, in theory, turn a blind eye to the property interests at play in virtual worlds, by doing so they would risk of exacerbating social conflicts that flow from perceived injustices. The case of Qiu Chengwei is a perfect example. It certainly would have been beneficial to everyone involved in the case if the Chinese police had investigated the crime and attempted to provide some sort of remedy. To simply deny that anything has occurred when a person deprives another of an economically valuable virtual property interest is to cede the domain to anarchy. Private owners of virtual worlds will not necessarily be interested in stepping into the policing gap. As Cally's case in EVE Online demonstrates, it is not clear that virtual world owners always *want* to make their domains orderly.

My sense is that many jurisdictions will, like the Netherlands and South Korea, gradually come around to taking virtual property rights seriously. As virtual economies continue to grow in size, even in jurisdictions where virtual property rights are not recognized per se, states will feel increasingly obligated to pay attention to the structure of virtual property rights. The Republic of Korea is a prime example of a legal system where virtual property rights are *not* recognized as property per se, but the state is actively involved in regulating the impact of evolving technological practices on both businesses and consumers. By policing virtual crimes and passing legislation targeted at resolving questions about the status of virtual property, South Korea is in the vanguard of virtual law.

To summarize, virtual property's true legal problem is not existence or non-existence. Although some legal authorities in some jurisdictions will not recognize virtual property interests for a variety of reasons, it seems highly unlikely that all jurisdictions will reject virtual property rights in all cases. On the contrary, there is abundant evidence at this point that most courts in the future will, to some extent, recognize legal interests in virtual property. The key problem going forward, I think, is in sorting out the nature of virtual property rights.

The most troubling complexity in virtual property is that the user and the owner of virtual property, like a feudal lord and vassal, are bound together with respect to the property interest in play. Legally, the key document controlling this relationship is the online contract, which, as the *Bragg* case demonstrates, often denies that the user has any significant virtual property interest.

CONFLICTS

The recognition of virtual property rights has implications that extend beyond claims of conversion by either other users or virtual world owners. Consider, for instance, the problem of property inheritance. When a person dies in the United States, valuable property interests are normally passed on to heirs, whether those heirs are designated by will or otherwise. If online contracts deny user rights to virtual property, this means that the owner of a virtual world, rather than the user, will generally have exclusive control of virtual assets after the death of the user. Does this seem like the best rule, from the standpoint of public policy?

On November 13, 2004, U.S. Marine Lance Corporal Justin Ellsworth was killed by a roadside bomb in Fallujah, Iraq.[28] Like many soldiers before him, Ellsworth had corresponded during his tour of duty with his friends and family at home. But unlike prior soldiers, Ellsworth did not keep tangible copies of the letters he received from his correspondents. As about a hundred million other people do today, Justin used a free Yahoo! e-mail account.

Ellsworth's parents wanted to see their son's correspondence because, among other reasons, Ellsworth had told his father that he planned on making a scrapbook of his letters. If the letters had been tangible, they would normally have been returned to his parents along with his other possessions (unless Ellsworth had directed otherwise). However, because the letters were e-mail messages and their son had not shared his password, Ellsworth's parents had no access to his correspondence. Ellsworth's father, John Ellsworth, contacted Yahoo! and requested access to the e-mails. However, Yahoo! pointed to their terms of service, which indicated that the account was to remain permanently private. No one (except Yahoo!) would get the correspondence. Eventually, John Ellsworth hired an attorney and a court ordered Yahoo! to provide the family with the correspondence.

For Ellsworth's family, obtaining copies of his correspondence was nowhere near as simple as it would have been in the age of pen and paper.[29] Indeed, if you use a free e-mail service, you might wonder about your own e-mail. If you were to die suddenly, would you expect that your family would have access to your e-mail correspondence?

Virtual worlds will make this sort of question more pressing. Justin Ellsworth's e-mails are just the tip of the iceberg with regard to the disposition of virtual assets. To the extent that virtual currency, creative works, and personal histories of individuals are increasingly stored in distant servers, there are likely to be many more disputes of this nature.

It is important to say that there are a range of ways that virtual property will be raised before courts. At least three structural frameworks are possible, two of which involve multiple parties. There are:

1.   user lawsuits against virtual world owners;
2.   user lawsuits against other users; and
3.   lawsuits brought by non-users and non-owners.

The first of these types of conflicts is exemplified by the *Bragg* lawsuit. In such cases, virtual world owners will almost invariably argue that virtual property interests do not exist and will rely on their online contracts and any available legal precedent to establish this state of affairs. This is because, in almost all situations, a virtual property regime grants a legal entitlement to the user that poses a litigation risk to the virtual world owner. Bragg, for instance, claimed that Linden had converted his virtual property by denying him access to his land. A virtual world owner rarely anticipates any benefit from the recognition of virtual coins and castles on his servers as the protectable property interests of users.

Indeed, for reasons that might benefit users, virtual world owners may wish to maintain creative control over the virtual environment. For instance, those who own the virtual world might arrange for virtual castles on Dagger Isle to be attacked by a dragon. This may destroy the value of the asset, but (pursuant to the odd logic of games) players may find the challenge of confronting a marauding dragon exciting and desirable. Yet any move by the owner of a virtual world is going to have effects on the value of virtual assets. At one point, Linden Lab decided to do away with teleportation via "telehubs" (essentially fixed avatar teleportation stations) in Second Life and replace them with point-to-point avatar teleportation.[30] However, given that telehubs were high-traffic areas, the land around the telehubs at the time was highly valued. By rewriting the phenomenon of virtual transportation in Second Life, Linden Lab probably improved the user experience for many, but it also significantly devalued the interests of some virtual investors.

Yet, just as a real government needs the flexibility to build public transportation by condemning private land, it would seem appropriate for Linden Lab to have the power to adjust the rules of virtual transportation in a way that could adversely affect the interests of a certain portion of its users. While the *Bragg* case raised the difficult question of the appropriate limits of this control, the ideal policy for virtual worlds would certainly not leave owners hamstrung by attempts to improve the user experience.

Efforts by virtual world owners to prevent the downside risk of virtual property are also relevant to a second sort of dispute, the lawsuit between virtual world users. These are the sorts of claims that would be brought by the next Qiu Chengwei against the next Zhu Caoyuan or by the next EVE Online investor against the next Cally. While user conflicts over virtual property are common[31]—indeed, they are part of the design of many virtual worlds—lawsuits are relatively rare. The primary inhibitor is expense. As discussed in chapter 5, Alice will likely not sue Neo for fraud because the legal expenses will be much more prohibitive than those accompanying a claim of offline fraud. Absent a class-action mechanism, users with property losses will be unlikely to turn to the law for relief.

To the extent that virtual world owners have a say in such matters, they are generally opposed to allowing lawsuits to proceed between users. This is because when users *do* sue each other, virtual world owners are inevitably caught in the middle. The virtual world will probably have kept records that can provide information about the incident, will have information about the parties, will have written the contracts that set forth the explicit rules of the environment, etc. Producing all of this information will be a burden on the company, dragging it into disputes between users. This means that, at least in theory, the virtual world owner will have economic incentives to prevent disputes between users and perhaps even resolve such disputes economically via its power over the code. For instance, if two users are seriously intent on litigating the ownership of a Dragon Saber, perhaps the most cost-beneficial solution for a virtual world owner would be to provide both parties with a copy of the disputed virtual property, avoiding the costs of being drawn into litigation. From a legal policy perspective, it seems desirable for virtual world owners to satisfy opposing parties through a private alternative to the court system. The public would not be required to pay for the dispute resolution, and the virtual world owner would probably understand the nature of the dispute much better than a court. Private dispute resolution does not formally cede legal "jurisdiction" to the virtual world (since parties are free, in theory, to bring their claim to court), so it may be *less* problematic, theoretically, than the wholesale denial of virtual property rights. Yet it is unclear at present whether virtual world owners will be willing to invest in these sorts of robust models of alternative dispute resolution.

The third and final structural category of virtual property disputes involves conflicts between third parties and those who either use or own virtual worlds. Cases involving government officers, such as the Habbo theft, fall into this category. The hotly debated issue concerning the taxation of virtual property interests is another instance of the state keeping an eye on property transactions in virtual worlds. The case of virtual property heirs would be a third instance where outside parties might want to use legal process to make demands on either users or owners of virtual worlds. In such cases, users and owners of virtual worlds may find common ground. For instance, we can be fairly certain that while the IRS may have some interest in taxing transactions involving Linden dollars, neither those engaged in the Second Life transactions nor Linden Lab would be overly excited about taking on the burden of accounting for such transactions.

In summary, it seems that while virtual world owners have incentives to create the illusion of virtual property rights, they have few incentives to grant the users of virtual worlds legal interests in virtual property. It may not be so easy, however, for courts to deny that users have property rights in the context of conversion claims while denying that they have property rights with respect to virtual world owners. In the *Kremen v. Cohen* case, it should be noted that although Judge Kozinski had no doubt that a domain name could be considered property capable of conversion, it was not Cohen who was ordered to pay for the loss. Instead, Judge Kozinski strongly suggested that the domain name registrar (Network Solutions) could be held liable for Kremen's loss of millions of dollars. Kremen alleged that the registrar was the bailee (the party in authorized possession) of the domain name at the time of the theft. Kremen therefore alleged that Network Solutions was liable for his loss, just as a parking garage might be held liable for the loss of your car if they simply handed your car keys to a fraudulent thief. Judge Kozinski stated:

> There is nothing unfair about holding a company responsible for giving away someone else's property even if it was not at fault. . . . It would not be unfair to hold Network Solutions responsible and force it to try to recoup its losses by chasing down Cohen. This, at any rate, is the logic of the common law, and we do not lightly discard it.[32]

When I first read Judge Kozinski's opinion, I found his account of the "logic of the common law" surprising. Network Solutions was essentially no more than an administrative intermediary, duped by the fraudulent transfer form filed by Cohen. Judge Kozinski seemed to think Network Solutions was instead something like a bank, holding a set of expensive domain names like jewels in safe-deposit boxes. In response to the claim of Network Solutions that incurring this sort of liability would increase the costs associated with performing as a domain name registrar, Kozinski seemed unsympathetic: "A bank could lower its ATM fees if it didn't have to pay security guards, but we doubt most depositors would think that was a good idea."

Personally, I have doubts about the wisdom of recognizing an entirely new form of property right and then holding a company retroactively liable for the mistaken transfer of that right. But the point to take from the *Kremen* case is that, when real money is at stake in disputes over virtual assets, property law may well follow on its heels, drawing those who control virtual assets into the complex array of rights and duties that property law imposes. This alone is a good reason for virtual world owners to attempt to keep the full legal regime of property law at bay. It is not clear, however, how long they will be able to do so.

8

hackers

P.S. Sorry for ruining the economy and all that.

—"Methical"

As I mentioned in chapter 2, the most common protagonist in the fiction of virtual worlds is the hacker, a person skilled at manipulating computer interfaces and breaking the rules that constrain the coded capabilities of ordinary users. Neo in *The Matrix*, Mr. Slippery in *True Names*, Flynn in *Tron*, Case in *Neuromancer*, and Hiro in *Snow Crash* are all notable (and notably male) examples of the hero hacker. The hacker becomes a hero in these stories because the villains, who must be defeated, have seized power using oppressive technologies. *True Names*, *Tron*, and *The Matrix* all feature a rogue artificial intelligence that dominates a virtual world and seeks from its position of power to enslave or destroy all of humanity. The mysterious skills of the hacker are required to overcome it. Yet despite occupying the protagonist role, the hacker is usually portrayed as a morally ambiguous figure, quasi-criminal and quasi-anarchic, not quite comfortable in civilized society.

In virtual worlds, there are hackers. One frequently encounters clever users who have discovered ways to circumvent software rules. But it is rare to find the hackers trying to rescue others or to further the welfare of their fellow travelers in the virtual world. Their goals are generally much more conventional and follow logically from the discussion in the last chapter. Virtual property has real monetary value and is made artificially scarce by software constraints. Accordingly, those who can manage to overcome the coded restraints of artificial scarcity stand to gain power and wealth, both virtual and real. The easiest way to manipulate the code of a virtual world is to find an exploit, a gap in the overall logic of the simulation.

One of the earliest virtual worlds, Habitat, was also the site of one of the most well-known exploits of virtual world design. Like most contemporary virtual worlds, Habitat had its own virtual currency, called tokens. Tokens were granted as part of a regular allowance and could also be won as prizes. With tokens, users could purchase virtual objects, such as new avatar heads, from "Vendroids," which were simulated storefronts. Vendroids could also be used as pawn shops—they purchased virtual objects in exchange for tokens at slightly lower prices.

Unfortunately, there were two "bugs" in the Vendroid system. First, the simulation was shallow. Habitat did not simulate a limited pool of virtual currency, Vendroid inventories, or Vendroid balance sheets. It offered a Potemkin economy, so to speak. Second, to make prices *seem* as if they were affected by standard marketplace variations, the programmers created random price fluctuations between the Vendroids. For instance, a doll might cost 150 tokens at most Vendroids, but one Vendroid might (randomly) sell the same doll for 75 tokens. The potential exploit here is fairly simple to spot.

One weekend, some users discovered a Vendroid selling dolls for 75 tokens that a distant Vendroid would buy for 100 tokens. The users traversed from Vendroid to Vendroid, buying low and selling high, gaining tokens hand over fist. Soon they found and invested in a more expensive loophole, buying crystal balls at 18,000 tokens and selling them for 30,000 tokens. Since there was no deep economic simulation that undergirded the Vendroid system, the machines were essentially printing money. The net result was that the number of tokens in the Habitat economy quintupled as a result of the weekend of trading.[1]

Habitat's designers were caught flat-footed. Their logging system was not sophisticated enough to explain what had happened, so they chose to identify and directly confront the two wealthiest users:

Their reply was, "We got it fair and square! And we're not going to tell you how!" After much abject pleading on our part they eventually did tell us, and we fixed the erroneous pricing. Fortunately, the whole scam turned out well, as the nouveau riche Avatars used their bulging bankrolls to underwrite a series of treasure hunt games which they

Habitat *Copyright Lucasfilm Ltd.*

conducted on their own initiative, much to the enjoyment of many other players on the system.[2]

Despite the fact that the "scam turned out well," the designers still considered it a scam, suggesting that the Vendroid arbitrage strategy was not legitimate. In the offline world, of course, buying low and selling high is good business. The Vendroid "scam" is pretty much how businesses act in real markets. Yet buying low and selling high in this particular way in Habitat was deemed illicit, even though it broke no explicit rule and did not involve "hacking" the software code of the game.

The Vendroid scam tells a story about the nature of the technological power in virtual worlds. By virtue of creating a simulation and controlling the central servers, virtual world owners often seem to have a godlike power to destroy or reshape all objects and places within an environment. Yet their power is not unlimited. Users have the power to do whatever is made possible by the software. When users operate the code in a way that defies the expectations of the virtual world owner, as was the case with the Vendroid scam, disputes can arise. The makers of Habitat clearly felt that the users behind the Vendroid scam had done something illicit. The more interesting question from the standpoint of law is this: if they had sold the tokens for cash, would they have done something illegal?

CODE AS LAW

The Vendroid scam exemplifies the unpredicted consequences of creating an online community that has agency to interact and to influence a complex simulation. Users of virtual worlds demand at least a minimal level of agency within the virtual environment. For instance, most users expect the freedom to speak to other avatars, to move about the environment, and to have some effect on the environment. A virtual world without any form of user agency, with immobilized, paralyzed, and mute avatars, would not be popular with consumers. The ability to influence and shape the virtual environment is a desirable feature.

However, the results of user agency that is too powerful can be unpleasant for everyone. For instance, if all individual users had the power to delete the whole simulation (as the owners do), we might imagine that some disgruntled user would push that button, destroying the world for all the users. Keeping the authoritative server code secure and proprietary is therefore imperative for virtual world owners.

Balancing the demand for user agency with the requirement of control over key aspects of the simulation is a tricky business from the standpoint of technology and software. It is also a process with various legal and political implications. One of the first commentators to spot the interesting legal issues raised by the power of computer software was William Mitchell. In his book *City of Bits*, Mitchell points out that digital spaces have "architectures" that structure how people are able to use them. At one point, Mitchell cryptically suggests that these architectures are tantamount to legal rules:

> Out there on the electronic frontier, code is the law. The rules governing any computer-constructed microworld—of a video game, your personal computer desktop, a word processor window, an automated teller machine, or a chat room on the network—are precisely and rigorously defined in the text of the program that constructs it on your screen.[3]

This brief passage is loaded with interesting analogies. According to Mitchell, computer frontiers are actually governed by code that functions as law. For Mitchell, a key feature of this governance, from the user's standpoint, is the inflexibility of software rules. From the programmer's perspective, the opposite is true: software rules are *highly* flexible—they can be whatever the programmer wants them to be.[4]

Of course, calling software "law," while evocative, is a misnomer. The operations of a digital machine are private technological measures. They are like the high walls of a castle or the lock on a door rather than a law that prohibits trespass. People may use private technological force to bar access to domains, yet a private barrier is not always backed by legal endorsement. As the Edict of Pistres shows, the state is sometimes quite opposed to technologies that expand private power. To the extent that software exerts a new form of technological force, that force can uphold or oppose legal rules.[5]

Even though software architectures are not law, they can be more effective than law in some cases. As Mitchell states, you can't argue with the rules that an ATM imposes on a financial transaction:

> You cannot ask it to exercise discretion. You cannot plead with it, cajole it, or bribe it. The field of possible interactions is totally delimited by the formally stated rules.[6]

Human agents tend to be more flexible and less reliable in the process of rule enforcement. For instance, they may lack awareness of the scope of a specific rule, they may lack diligence in their duties, and they may be influenced by bribes or persuasion. Indeed, they may even realize that the policy justification for a given rule is not supported by its application to the case before them. The law has always entailed this sort of imperfect and contextual application. Mitchell's key point is not exactly that "code is law," but that the operation of software architecture follows set rules and, in some ways, is comparatively more powerful, consistent, and inflexible in the process of rule enforcement.

At about the same time that Mitchell published his book, many law professors were having the same realization about the growing importance of computers and the Internet. For instance, Joel Reidenberg noted that the technical structure of information systems could create rights and privileges that regulate information flows, serving as a potential substitute for legal regimes.[7] James Boyle explained how the technology of the Internet might, contrary to popular belief, not liberate, but constrain its users, as digital networks give government actors greater powers of surveillance over public information practices.[8] Ethan Katsh argued that the "software worlds" Mitchell described were enabling the formation of online communities with entirely different notions of time and space, changing the underlying facts that supported existing laws and social practices.[9]

Yet the most well-known legal commentator who explored the "code is law" analogy was Lawrence Lessig, who expanded on Mitchell's insight in a landmark book titled *Code and Other Laws of Cyberspace*. Lessig provided an extended treatment of the variety of puzzles that the Internet had raised for law, actually starting with a brief treatment of a dispute in a MUD. Lessig's book, unlike many legal tomes, reached readers far beyond the conventional confines of the legal academy.

Lessig is popularly associated with the claim that "code is law," yet as Lessig himself explains, the claim is not really an equation. Instead, "code controls behavior as law might control behavior: You can't easily rip the contents of my DVD because the code locks it tight."[10] A code structure, therefore, is not that different from a medieval castle. Building a castle wall excludes others from entering a place, protecting what is inside and preventing outsiders from interfering. Building a password wall has analogous effects. The private power to exclude outside influences ultimately may give rise to law. But the exercise of private power over architecture is hardly tantamount to the institution of law.

Indeed, Lessig's *Code* was written primarily in opposition to the notion that code is law-like. In debates over cyberspace self-governance, Lessig generally opposed techno-libertarians' calls for keeping cyberspace "free" from regulation. In his view, territorial governments needed to become more involved with the Internet because they were the social institutions best suited to preserve the values that had guided the Internet's development. According to Lessig, the choice was not between territorial law and cyberspace liberty, but between the institution of law and the technological sovereignty of companies like Microsoft, who were writing the code that would shape society online.

Lessig's predictions of an Internet without law have not come to pass. However, his notion that code is law is still particularly apt for characterizing the important regulatory role of software in virtual worlds. More than any other medium, virtual worlds, with their elaborate simulations, use software rules to shape online societies. Certainly, the rules of a DVD player or an ATM machine are important. If the ATM machine does not give you the option of withdrawing seventeen dollars, you are stuck with this rule. But in virtual worlds, the software rules have much more power. Code provides a framework for your identity, your community, your economic behavior, your creativity, and your communications. Code is the very substance of a virtual world. It may not be law per se, but the rules that software imposes on virtual world users may be more important to them than legal rules.

CODE AS WORLD

To get a sense of how deeply enmeshed software is in virtual society, we might start with the avatar. As I noted in chapter 2, the avatar is, in many ways, the body of the user within the virtual world.[11] Yet the avatar, although it may be seen as a second skin, is not a body that is legally "owned" by its user. It is an aspect of software code that is controlled, at least in part, by the creator of the virtual world.[12] The choices that individuals possess with respect to their virtual bodies are constrained by the options provided by the software. I mentioned in chapter 2 how the gendered and flexible appearance of user avatars can influence relationships among users. In other virtual worlds, the code can serve to disguise gender. For instance, children who use Disney's Club Penguin are not provided with a way to signal their gender to other users. Penguins are not categorized, by their virtual "nature," as males or females. Making a gender-blind world of colorful penguins may or may not have been a deliberate effort to engineer the child-centered society of Club Penguin, but it certainly influences how Club Penguin is used socially.

Virtual world software is also commonly designed, like the software of Facebook or MySpace, to allow users to create and manage customized social networks. In most all virtual worlds, from Second Life to MapleStory to Club Penguin, users can toggle a switch to establish a relationship coded as "friendship" by the software. Avatars are given additional information about their friends and are usually able to engage in chat despite virtual distance. In some virtual worlds, friendship relationships are made strategically important by the software. You may need friends, or at least find them helpful, when you attempt to accomplish the objectives of a game. For instance, City of Heroes allows pairs of heroes to form dynamic duos. Stronger avatars who pair up with lower-level "sidekicks" gain certain strategic benefits in play. The sidekicks also gain better powers, as well as the ability to explore more advanced environments.

Serious long-term relationships can also be made part of the software code. For instance, in the Korean MMORPG MapleStory, avatar weddings are common and software-facilitated. In order to marry, a male and female avatar must complete certain quests (the male avatar must obtain a ring for the proposal) and meet in a particular town, Amoria, where they formalize their union.[13] (Notably, same-sex avatar marriages are not permitted.) Strategic concerns can sometimes form the basis of these MapleStory marriages. As part of the MapleStory marriage ceremony, both players receive special items that are only available to married players. If players pay extra money for a "premium wedding," they may have a reception adventure in a nearby dungeon, where friends can be invited.

Marriage need not be forever, however. Divorce is possible. However, divorce costs money and imposes a temporary bar on remarriage. One day, a piano teacher in Japan who was a MapleStory user found herself unceremoniously "divorced" by her virtual husband. In retaliation, she logged on to the game, used the account code the "husband" had previously provided, and deleted the virtual husband's avatar. The virtual husband then called the Japanese police, who arrested his divorced "wife" for a violation of the laws prohibiting computer hacking. The arrest for "virtual murder" made news headlines because the only asset lost was apparently the virtual husband's avatar. According to news reports, the woman explained that she was motivated by a sense of betrayal: "I was suddenly divorced, without a word of warning. That made me so angry."[14] The strategic and socially prominent nature of marriage in MapleStory may explain her anger.

In addition to one-on-one bonds, most virtual worlds provide software tools that help groups and communities form collective associations. For instance, in World of Warcraft, players can form quest "parties," which are limited to five players. Within the quest party, players can share a party-only chat window and also have other party-specific software tools available to them. WoW players can also use another type of group interface to form "raids" of up to forty players, which are used to complete larger quests that have different specialized software tools.[15]

Finally, larger "guilds" and "groups" are also built into many MMOR-PGs. Players in guilds share a "guild chat" channel and have their guild's name displayed prominently above their avatar's head. Guild tools allow the designation of guild officers and guild leaders who have the power to appoint new members and remove members. Various forms of user-created social hierarchy and associated powers over the group are thus encoded via software.

In addition to mediating the virtual body and the virtual community, software tools also dictate how and when users of virtual worlds can create objects and shared spaces. This is why the ownership of "land" is important to users in Second Life. Land ownership entails control over content. The software allows owners of land to build what they please and affords them almost absolute dominion over who and what is allowed within the simulated metes and bounds of their virtual domain. MMORPGs can provide groups with similar sorts of customized virtual spaces. For instance, in the world of City of Heroes, groups of heroes and villains can create their own group "bases," complete with conference rooms, medical centers, and training facilities with access limited to those in the group and their recruits.

It is also important to note that though the software can be designed to support communities, it is also used to promote group antagonism, especially in those worlds that are structured as competitive games. In World of Warcraft, for instance, when a user of one faction attempts to communicate with the opposing faction (for example, when an orc tries to speak with a dwarf), the words are translated into meaningless gibberish. The software rule requires this inability to communicate in order to prevent players from "cheating" by siding with the opposing faction. Mutual unintelligibility helps arouse suspicions of the other side and promotes easier strategic cooperation with one's own side.

All of these software rules provide an architectural framework for virtual societies that structures and influences the community within them. The various forms of virtual currency (Linden dollars, WoW gold, EVE isk, and Habbo coins) should also be understood as part of this software structure, since forms of virtual property enable relationships based on trade and commercial cooperation. Given that avatars are designed to use, wear, and own various virtual objects, the particular form of those objects can also become markers of social status. In virtual worlds where users create and trade virtual objects with others, the code that enables these activities also influences the distribution of social power and status.

The software code in a virtual world is the physics and substance of the simulation and therefore becomes the medium through which the in-world community exists. It is not just a wall or a lock, like an offline technology, but the avatar body that encounters the wall, the reason that the avatar cannot pass through the wall, and, sometimes, the wellspring of the desire to move past it. It enables the request for help, determines who hears it and may even determine whether that request will be answered.

However, the code is generally understood to be a flexible structure. Just as people might complain about the options available on an ATM, users of virtual worlds tend to complain about various ways in which the software code shapes their experience. This is why, for instance, some users have circulated a petition seeking same-sex marriage in MapleStory while some Second Life users have asked Linden Lab to emulate MapleStory by coding forms of resident marriage into its software.[16]

While users of virtual worlds are certainly cognizant of the power that software has over their experience, they are not (generally) deluded into thinking that the owners of virtual worlds are legal sovereigns, or "gods," as they are sometimes called.[17] Instead, they accept the practical truth that virtual world owners have technological power over the software of the virtual world. In the absence of other alternatives, this power over code supersedes the power of law.

COMMUNITY AS CODE

Given that software rules are so important to virtual worlds, virtual societies can be divided into (at least) three classes of participants: wizards, users, and super-users. First, as the LambdaMOO incident suggests, virtual world owners (the "wizards" of LambdaMOO or Lord British in Britannia) are the class that has the greatest degree of power over the environment and controls the physical hardware. Second, there is a class of new users (called noobs) and conventional users that have some level of mastery over the software interface. And third, there are users who have, for whatever reason, a high level of technical mastery over the software's intricacies. Some of these "super-users" may know as much as the employees of the virtual world companies.

To the extent that law leaves virtual societies to their own devices, it effectively cedes power over virtual worlds to these groups. Among the groups, the "wizards" are clearly the party with the greatest technological power over the environment. Given this, and with an understanding that contract law is also slanted in their favor, James Grimmelmann has suggested that virtual societies are premised on owner-user relationships similar to those between lords and vassals in feudal societies. Virtual world users have limited rights, just as feudal tenants had limited autonomy with respect to their overlords. Others go further, suggesting that virtual world owners are not merely analogous to wizards or feudal lords, but are like deities within the environment.[18]

Yet as the example of the Vendroid scam indicates, the owners of virtual worlds are neither omniscient nor omnipotent. Perhaps the best-known example of the failure of a virtual monarch was when Lord British, controlled by Richard Garriott, appeared one day in Britannia to mete out virtual justice. By some oversight, Garriott had forgotten to make Lord

British's avatar impervious to harm. In a public forum, an audacious thief managed to assassinate the monarch, an event that has passed into Ultima Online legend.

Virtual worlds, like virtual monarchs, can be vulnerable to human errors. These include design flaws in their composition susceptibility to forms of external attack. In light of this, it is not uncommon for owners of virtual worlds to concede, usually with a tone of surprise, that they enjoy less authority over their creations than they had hoped would be the case. As the designers of Habitat stated in a retrospective account,

> It was clear that we were not in control. The more people we involved in something, the less in control we were. We could influence things, we could set up interesting situations, we could provide opportunities for things to happen, but we could not predict nor dictate the outcome. . . .
>
> Propelled by these experiences, we shifted into a style of operations in which we let the players themselves drive the direction of the design. This proved far more effective. Instead of trying to push the community in the direction we thought it should go, an exercise rather like herding mice, we tried to observe what people were doing and aid them in it. We became facilitators as much as designers and implementors.[19]

Part of the problem here is that, although the users of virtual worlds possess a limited agency within the virtual environment, they far outnumber the owners who control the code. As a result, like the members of any society, they tend to make their own rules and norms through the use of whatever technological powers they have been given. Though the wizards of virtual environments can put their rules into software code and exert their authority through technological means, they cannot afford to closely monitor even a fraction of the users of their environments. So, quite often, the users make rules for themselves.

In the MMORPG Everquest, there are many social norms that govern play. For instance, as T. L. Taylor explains, there was a norm in the early years of Everquest prohibiting "trains."[20] Trains were created when a player entered combat with one or more powerful monsters and realized that avatar death was imminent. In such a situation, it made abundant sense for the avatar to run away. But the monsters in Everquest were programmed to pursue relentlessly, which would lead to the formation of a train of monsters behind the player pulled by the fleeing avatar. If the train were pulled into a group of other players, the accumulated monsters would attack and kill them. Therefore, trains were formed due to one player's poor judgment but ultimately created a worse result for many other players. Failure to follow the anti-training norm led to a quick and sharply worded education. Repeat offenders were shunned, which was a significant punishment in a virtual world like Everquest, where teamwork was strategically important.

Another player norm in MMORPGs prohibits "ninja looting" and "kill stealing."[21] The problem here is that the software permits, just as reality does, one person to reap where another has sown. When a player has nearly defeated a monster, another player might come in at the last minute and finish the monster off, gaining (pursuant to the software) the valuable "experience points" for killing the monster. Likewise, when a monster is killed and drops valuable virtual property, a "ninja" might appear and make off with property that was not earned.

Though MMORPG norms against training, kill stealing, and ninja looting may seem bizarre and fantastic, they serve to prove the point about virtual governance that was raised with regard to LambdaMOO. Online communities, even when they are not granted tools designed to enable deliberative democracy, really do arrive at community norms of play that can be enforced. Not surprisingly, MMORPG norms express fairly standard "Golden Rule" reciprocal duties of care. The curious thing about these rules is that they formed in response to the physics of the code (the way combat and looting work) and the goals of the game (how virtual property and achievement are acquired), yet they evolved independently of the code and independently of any express mandate from the game designers. The community (not the developers) created and enforced these rules.

Dave Myers recently recounted a "sad and curious" tale of one avatar at play in the MMORPG City of Heroes.[22] The story provides an excellent example of community enforcement of social norms developed apart from fixed game rules. City of Heroes, like World of Warcraft, is a game where players must choose between two warring factions. Myers played a superhero named Twixt, who fought on the hero (as opposed to the villain) side and had risen to the highest level. At this level, players on opposing sides can do battle in a setting called Recluse's Victory, described as an "alternative dimension" where both sides are tasked with the game goal of occupying bunkers known as dimensional anchors.

In combating villains, Twixt adopted a tactic called droning, which involved using a teleportation power to send enemy villains into close proximity with deadly robots. Apparently, Myers was confident that the game rules permitted droning as a strategy. However, even if the owners of the virtual world did not forbid it, a portion of the community felt that droning was not a desirable strategy, and should be deemed a form of cheating. Nevertheless, Twixt intentionally and repeatedly engaged in droning. For this, he was vilified and ostracized by a significant number of other players. Notably, not only the villains complained, but his own cohorts condemned him as well. They used the powers at their disposal (for example, name-calling, threatening, shunning, and virtual attack) to try to force him to comply with the favored community rule that prohibited droning.

The lesson is simple: communities of users in virtual worlds can and do create and enforce codes of social conduct. This happens not just in social worlds, but also in virtual worlds styled as games. The rules they impose are responsive to the virtual terrain in many ways, but they are not absolutely determined by the rules imposed by law, code, or contract. Indeed, the community rules, the software rules, the contract rules, and the default legal rules can be in conflict.

HACKERS

Given that players can create and enforce their own rules within the code, it follows that players can take advantage of the code in ways unanticipated by designers, as they did in the case of the Vendroid scam. Among virtual world developers, the use of software in ways that lead to unintended and undesirable consequences is generally known as an "exploit" of a "bug" or "vulnerability." The code of virtual worlds is often so complex that it is practically impossible to make it bug-free prior to commercial distribution. Software vulnerabilities must be detected over time. Eric Raymond, a guru of the open source software movement, famously observed that "given enough eyeballs, all bugs are shallow."[23] In the open source software context, this means that large teams of collaborating programmers can find and fix bugs that avoid the detection of smaller professional teams. In the virtual world context, however, this leads to the conclusion that bugs will exist and will be discovered first by users.

Users will tend to notify virtual world owners when bugs are harmful to them. Virtual world owners ideally will respond by fixing the code. However, when users deem bugs beneficial to them—as was the case with the Vendroid scam—players will often not complain and simply exploit the bug for their own advantage. Those who exploit software are generally called hackers today. Among early programmers, however, "hacker" was often a term of respect, and among some communities it still has this meaning. In popular parlance today, the term "hacker" is usually associated with those who use computer technologies illegally.[24] Hackers are understood as individuals who "break" code for bragging rights or money.

In virtual worlds, there are certainly some super-users who are capable of exploiting software vulnerabilities in ways that grant them powers beyond those of other users. However, though sophisticated "exploits" may require skillful manipulation of computer code, many of those who "hack" virtual worlds are just lucky. The Vendroid scam was probably discovered by accident. It is not uncommon for ordinary users to stumble upon programming errors and take advantage of them, gaining competitive advantages and capabilities that the designers did not intend for them to have. For instance, in the early days of the MMORPG Asheron's Call, players found that when they "perched" in certain elevated locations, they could shoot arrows or cast magic spells on monsters that would not be able to reach them. In essence, perchers could shoot their opponents like fish in a barrel. Perhaps because the strategy seemed so simple and straightforward, it was unclear to some players whether it was really a bug in the software.

According to Tim Burke, when player perching become common, this changed Asheron's Call profoundly. Players started fighting for prime perching spots. They wrote "macro" programs that took control of their avatars and automated the mindless and unchallenging act of repeatedly shooting at helpless targets. With the macros working, they walked away from their computers. Like dribbling out the shot clock in basketball, perching was strategically smart, but it made game play uninteresting. As Burke recounts, this sort of behavior

> had rippling economic effects throughout the rest of the world, driving inflation, making macroing a more and more constant feature of gameplay, and so on. Developers were forced to spend time identifying and eliminating perching spots within the gameworld terrain and eventually banning macroing itself, though that came at a point where most of the players who objected to macroing had long since left the game.[25]

When activities like perching became linked to real world profits, user interest in identifying profitable exploits became even more pronounced. The emergence of gold farming and the associated real-money

Everquest II *Copyright Sony Online Entertainment, reproduced with permission*

trade (RMT) of virtual properties led to the commercialization of exploits. Those who discovered bugs in game software could gain not only virtual power and wealth, like the Vendroid scammers, but could also convert their virtual wealth into real money on eBay and other auction platforms. The Vendroid scammers wanted to keep their technique secret. Commercial exploiters have an even stronger motivation to guard the secrecy of their business methods. However, many stories of commercially lucrative exploits in virtual worlds are publicly known, even though the precise details are usually unclear.

One exploit with relatively clear—though contended—details occurred in 2004 in the MMORPG Everquest II. A story posted by "Methical," and later picked up by various news outlets, described how the Methical had become wealthy by duplicating virtual dogs called Halasian Maulers. According to one journalistic account, Methical was actually Noah Burns, a twenty-four-year-old from South Carolina who opened a storefront in Everquest II. Burns worked at a furniture store in real life, so he decided to make an attempt at being a proprietor of a virtual furniture store online.[26]

According to Burns, one of the items he was selling was a "Gnomish Thinking Chair." The client software normally listed items for sale in the user's inventory. In other words, other users shopping for the virtual furniture that Burns was selling could buy it from a separate sort of catalog screen. The furniture was not virtually present in the simulation. Burns, however, decided to remove the chair from the auction catalog screen and place it on the showroom floor of his virtual storefront. He was not sure what effect removing the furniture from the inventory screen would have on the pending sale. As he explained, "I figured it would either take it off the sale list, or it would poof off the floor if someone bought it."

Instead, due to a faulty line of software code, a copy of the chair remained on the showroom floor after the chair was purchased from the inventory screen. The purchaser had the chair, and Burns had retained a perfect copy. Burns quickly told his guild mates that he had discovered a "duping" (duplicating) bug. He thought about reporting it to the administrators of Everquest II, but then decided against it: "They would have just patted me on the back and said thanks." So, in his words, "I began to embrace the dark side."[27]

Much like the users of Habitat who executed the Vendroid scam, Burns and a friend increased their virtual capital pool and re-invested it in more expensive properties, moving up from chairs and finally arriving at the point of selling duplicated virtual dogs, which were extremely expensive. They soon amassed a huge fortune of Everquest platinum pieces. Like the Habitat users, Burns was now a virtual Rockefeller.

Burns's next step was to convert his virtual platinum into real cash by selling it on various online auctions. Though selling platinum pieces for real money was against the terms of service for Everquest II, Sony Online Entertainment could not effectively police the practice, since the game software permits the gifting of virtual items. (From the in-game perspective, selling a virtual item for real money looks like a gift, since the virtual world owner does not see the out-of-game transaction for money.) According to Burns, he eventually began dealing with IGE, the largest and most well-known company in the virtual property trade at the time.

The duping business that Burns had established was not without its problems. For instance, Burns reported that one of his clients failed to pay a five thousand dollar bill for virtual currency. The business was also short-lived. Burns stated that after three weeks, Sony Online discovered the duping and cancelled his account. However, Burns and his companions allegedly made about one hundred thousand dollars from their brief business, which Burns reportedly used to pay off student loans and take vacations in Hawaii and Paris. Burns, in explaining the events to a journalist, used the standard "cyberspace as legal frontier" analogy: "It's like the Wild West right now, and we're kind of like these outlaws."[28]

Perhaps the oddest thing about the Everquest Dog Duping was that the story was made public. For whatever reason, Noah Burns decided to share his story. Julian Dibbell provides a few other stories of lucrative exploits in his book *Play Money*, which focuses on Ultima Online.[29] But undoubtedly, the majority of commercial exploits are kept secret. Professional exploiting practice can involve significantly higher stakes. For instance, in 2003, Korean authorities arrested a twenty-two-year-old hacker and an accomplice. The pair had discovered a way to manipulate a game server and obtain payments worth 1.5 billion won, or roughly a million dollars—ten times what Burns made from his Halasian Maulers.[30]

THE LAW OF HACKING

In chapter 5, I discussed the questions of contract law raised in Marc Bragg's suit against Linden Lab. Yet there is another dimension to the *Bragg* case. During the court arguments, Linden Lab counterclaimed that Marc Bragg was liable to them. They claimed he had hacked the Second Life auction system through the use of an unauthorized software exploit. Linden Lab said that Bragg had violated state and federal laws by

> surreptitiously and without authorization accessing auction detail pages for parcels that Linden had not yet published on the main auction page of the Second Life site, and before Linden had set the minimum opening bid of U.S. $1,000.00. As these auction detail pages were unpublished, no user could access them by any method authorized by Linden. Therefore, the scheme required the use of an artifice or "exploit" to access the auction detail pages in advance of the legitimately conducted auction.[31]

Linden Lab's lawyers stated that because the auction had not been published, Bragg had purchased land for three hundred dollars that should have been priced no lower than one thousand dollars. From Linden Lab's perspective, this fully justified the decision to cancel Marc Bragg's account and confiscate his virtual landholdings. Bragg, in their view, was like a Vendroid scammer—he had improperly sought to exploit a loophole in the Second Life auctioning code. Linden Lab alleged that the exploit had cost the company real money.

If the allegations of Linden Lab were true, the technique in question was really not much more difficult or sophisticated than buying from Habitat Vendroids or duplicating dogs in Everquest. All land in Second Life has an identifying parcel number. By adding that number to the Second

Life auction URL, a user of Second Life could access an unlisted auction for land. Because the auction would not be advertised on the main page, the only bidding competitors would be those who were aware of the unpublished auction. So would this conduct alleged by Linden Lab really have amounted to a violation of federal computer hacking laws?

In the United States, the Computer Fraud and Abuse Act (CFAA) is the federal statute that criminalizes hacking. The language of the CFAA generally prohibits the act of obtaining "unauthorized access" to computer systems, though this takes a variety of more specific forms. For instance, one of the CFAA's provisions prohibits obtaining access to a computer "without authorization" in order to "obtain anything of value" and "with intent to defraud." Though the CFAA is a criminal law, the same conduct can form the basis of a civil claim if the victim can show "damage or loss" of five thousand dollars resulting from the conduct. The definition of "loss" under the CFAA is fairly broad. It includes the cost of "responding to an offense, conducting a damage assessment, and restoring the data, program, system, or information to its condition prior to the offense."[32] In other words, most all victim expenditures related to the unauthorized access can be counted as damage or loss.

In a fairly straightforward CFAA case, a defendant might discover and make unauthorized use of another user's password and intentionally cause damage to a computer system, for instance by deleting valuable files. This would be a straightforward violation of anti-hacking laws. However, in many cases, the application of the law can be more difficult. In particular, there are often difficulties presented by interpreting the meaning of the prohibition against "unauthorized access." This was certainly true in the case of Robert Morris, the first criminal defendant prosecuted and convicted under the CFAA.

Morris, who is now a professor at MIT, wrote a program that effectively crippled much of the early Internet, including many government systems. Most sources suggest that Morris had benign motives, indicating that he was testing security and counting the number of computers that comprised the Internet at the time.[33] His testing method entailed the distribution of a "worm" program that propagated itself throughout the network. However, the worm Morris designed proved too aggressive—it multiplied so fast that it rapidly clogged the network with a sort of electronic kudzu, overwhelming the systems and bringing normal network operations to a halt. It took substantial time and money to restore the network to its prior state.

The court found Morris guilty of hacking, but not exactly because he broke through some sort of electronic wall (though the worm actually did correctly guess some passwords, the analysis of the court did not hinge on that fact). Instead, the court focused on how Morris had failed to interact with the software tools "in any way related to their intended function."[34] According to the court's interpretation of the statute, unconventional and innovative uses of computer software, such as the exploitation of software bugs, could amount to criminal conduct if and when they caused damage to the computers of others.

Hackers using worms today have less benign motives. Compare the Morris worm to Taterf, a more recent worm that spreads through USB drives and that, as of November 2009, had been detected on more than four million computers.[35] Microsoft has warned that Taterf is one of the most prominent worms infecting systems today. Unlike the Morris worm, Taterf is not designed to reveal security flaws. According to a blogger for Microsoft, the intention behind Taterf is to automate the activities of Zhu Caoyuan or the Habbo thief:

> What do they do? Taterf, Frethog and their ilk are designed to steal your online game login details. The methods they use vary; from injecting into game clients and reading memory directly, to basic keylogging—but the end result is the same . . . u get pwned. Once they have your details, they are sent back to a remote location and are eventually sold to the highest bidder. After that, you may find your gold gone and toon naked upon your next login (zomg! My purplz!1!!).[36]

In other words, Taterf allows hackers to steal login details, rob accounts of their virtual property, and sell the ill-gotten gains on the market to the highest bidder. Under the ruling in the *Morris* case, the makers of the Taterf worm would clearly be liable for a criminal violation of the CFAA. However, it is unclear how the monetary damages to individual users would be calculated by a court.

In recent years, courts considering "unauthorized access" have sometimes taken a slightly different approach to claims of hacking. Rather than focus on how the defendant interacted with code, or upon the intended function of the code, courts considering "unauthorized access" have taken into account the contractual permissions granted to computer users by computer owners. In virtual worlds, these would usually be set forth in terms of service. If this sort of interpretation were to become the default rule, a mere violation of a virtual world's terms of service of could lead, in theory, to a felony conviction for hacking.

As an example of the breadth of this interpretation, consider the highly publicized case of Lori Drew.[37] Drew's actions were certainly reprehensible: she had pretended to be a sixteen-year-old boy on MySpace and used her fictitious persona to befriend and then torment a thirteen-year-old girlfriend of her daughter, saying, "The world would be a better place without you." The girl subsequently committed suicide. A federal prosecutor decided to charge Drew with violating the CFAA. As a legal matter, the crime allegedly was not against the girl, but against the MySpace web site. Drew had obtained access to MySpace in violation of its terms of service because, like most terms of service, they prohibited the submission of false and misleading information. These prohibitions were set forth in a "browsewrap" (rather than a click-wrap) agreement posted on the web site, meaning that users of MySpace did not need to be presented with the terms in order to be bound by them. On the basis of her violation of the terms of the browsewrap agreement, a jury found Drew guilty of violating the CFAA.

Subsequently, Judge George Wu overturned the jury verdict and acquitted Drew. In his written opinion, Judge Wu seemed concerned about the scope of private power over criminal law that could be created by a broad reading of the statute, stating that the prosecution's "approach makes the website owner—in essence—the party who ultimately defines the criminal conduct." The judge concluded that treating the violation of a web site's contract as a federal criminal offense would result in a law that would be unconstitutionally vague, transforming "otherwise innocent Internet users into misdemeanant criminals."[38]

Though I believe Judge Wu was correct to acquit Drew, the decision did not help to clarify the problem of unauthorized access. If access to a computer is not necessarily unauthorized under the CFAA when it is in violation of express contractual terms, then under what exact circumstances is access to a computer unauthorized? Who sets the line that separates unlawful hacking from a lawful but unanticipated use of a computer that causes some form of damage or loss? Other cases, some of which Wu cited in his opinion, *have* endorsed criminal convictions under the CFAA based on the violation of contractual prohibitions. This leaves the contemporary law of computer hacking in a state of confusion.

If the criminal law of unauthorized access ultimately makes it a crime to access any private computer in a way deemed undesirable by the computer owner, then the contractual provisions that govern virtual worlds might effectively be incorporated into the criminal code of the state. However, as Judge Wu recognized in the Drew case, this approach would seem to place unwarranted power in the hands of virtual world owners to make their own versions of substantive criminal law. It seems highly doubtful that Congress would have wanted to send users to jail for violating the terms of online agreements that most users do not read.

However, the approach taken by the *Morris* court, while more conservative, would also seem broad enough to make the unauthorized exploitation of software bugs in virtual worlds a violation of federal criminal law. For instance, the account of the Everquest II "dog duping" strongly suggests that Noah Burns recognized that he was taking advantage of a bug in the virtual world's software. Exploiting this sort of vulnerability while in contact with the computer could arguably be regarded as unauthorized access under the CFAA. To the extent that the owners of Everquest II spent time and effort to detect the duping bug, assess the damage it caused, patch the code, and restore the virtual world to its prior state, they suffered a quantifiable financial loss as a result of the exploit. At the very least, the case for a CFAA violation seems plausible.

Yet even though the CFAA would often seem to be on the side of virtual world owners, very few virtual world owners have actually used the CFAA aggressively in litigation. This is probably due to the fact that banning problematic users is less expensive and time-consuming than suing them. In many cases, however, banning those who intentionally exploit the code of virtual worlds will not prevent them from coming out ahead in the end. Noah Burns may have lost his Everquest II account, but he kept the real profits that he had obtained from his platinum sales. If account bans are the only tools used to address exploits, it seems likely that professional exploiters will keep up their work.

What is perhaps most confusing about the exploitation of bugs in virtual worlds is that it doesn't directly deprive anyone of anything. Noah Burns did not "steal" a single dog from any other user of the game. Actually, he was meeting a market need by providing something valuable to the Everquest II players who purchased dogs from him. The profits Burns made indicated a high level of pent-up consumer demand. If Burns made his dogs out of thin air and everyone was happy to have them, then who was really harmed?

The answer points back to discussion in chapter 7 about the odd characteristics of virtual property. Virtual world owners believe, with some justification, that unless virtual economies are premised on calibrated levels of artificial scarcity, they will prove unappealing to their users. At the same time, many self-interested users are willing to pay to speed up the process of virtual property acquisition by trading real money for virtual currency and property. Even if virtual world owners were to decide to sell virtual property directly to users, the business of exploits would not end. Instead, it would introduce greater market competition. Realistically, the cat-and-mouse game of virtual world exploits would only end if perfect software (lacking any vulnerabilities) were to be developed or if acquiring virtual property no longer brought advantages to users. Neither of those two options is a practical possibility, so the business of exploiting virtual worlds for commercial gain is likely to be a lasting enterprise.

The prominence of hackers in the early literature of virtual worlds was perhaps a tribute to the importance of code in technologically controlled spaces. If the communities of virtual worlds thought that their rulers were wholly illegitimate, virtual world hackers might be praised as heroes overthrowing tyrants. However, given that most virtual world users are not opposed to those who control their environments, the image of the hacker changes. The hackers operating in virtual worlds today look less like anti-heroes out to save the world and more like free mercenaries profiting from the uncertain legal status of virtual property.

9

copyright

Since when is it illegal to pretend to be your favorite superhero?

—Fred von Lohmann

At the time it was released, the City of Heroes MMORPG set a new standard for avatar customization. Cryptic Studios and NCsoft created what they labeled a "character creation engine," an immensely flexible program that let users choose the size, shape, and color of their avatar's body, hairstyle, facial expression, shoes, scars, gloves, utility belts, skin texture, chest symbols, sunglasses, etc. New players of City of Heroes would sometimes spend several hours working on their costumes before playing the actual game. Indeed, for some users, making costumes became the whole point of City of Heroes, as superhero fashion shows were organized in public areas of the game and player-judges awarded prizes to the most creatively designed costumes.

Unfortunately, all of this creative costume design was soon made the subject of a federal lawsuit. Marvel Comics owns the copyright interests in a variety of superheroes, such as the X-Men, Spider-Man, the Hulk, the Fantastic Four, Daredevil, and Iron Man. In 2004, Marvel sued the creators of City of Heroes.[1] Among other legal claims, Marvel alleged that NCsoft's avatar of the Statesman (essentially the equivalent of Lord British in the fictional universe of Paragon City, the virtual world of City of Heroes) looked too similar to Marvel's Captain America.

Lawsuits over infringing characters in film, television, or software are not that unusual. In the arena of video games, the makers of Pac-Man once

City of Heroes character generation engine *Copyright NCSoft, reproduced with Permission*

brought a successful lawsuit against a game featuring a Pac-Man look-alike.[2] What distinguished the City of Heroes case was that Marvel claimed that the players, in making their avatar costumes, were copyright infringers as well. In its legal pleadings, Marvel claimed that one could find "literally thousands of infringing Heroes roaming the streets of Paragon City." Marvel even attached some pictures of these "infringing Heroes" to its complaint, showing look-alike avatars of the Hulk, Spider-Man, and Iron Man in the virtual world. (It was later revealed that Marvel itself had generated some of the "infringing Heroes" it was complaining about.)[3]

Marvel requested that NCsoft delete the avatars of users who had infringed its copyrights, and NCsoft did so, scrambling the names and appearance of avatars to make them completely random. Yet Marvel claimed that these responses to specific requests were not sufficient. It also claimed that NCsoft's sale of the character creation engine was unlawful, given that NCsoft knew that users were infringing Marvel's copyrights and NCsoft was receiving financial benefits from these infringements. Essentially, Marvel sought to prohibit the distribution of the character generation engine itself unless the technology was licensed by Marvel.

Many people thought Marvel's claims were overbroad. Fred von Lohmann, a senior staff attorney at the Electronic Frontier Foundation, commented that Marvel might as well have sued Crayola, given how many children use crayons to draw infringing pictures of Spider-Man. However, when NCsoft made its copyright arguments to a federal court, the judge's reaction was considerably more cautious. The court refused a motion by NCsoft to dismiss the claims concerning the technology. Instead, it accepted that it was possible for players to infringe Marvel's intellectual property interests by creating and virtually donning the costumes of Marvel superheroes. The court also seemed to accept that, if a player did this, NCsoft could itself be liable for the distribution of a technology that enabled such "infringing" user behavior.[4]

As in the *Bragg* case, however, the early decision of the court did not lead to a final resolution of the case. Before the case could go to trial, Marvel and NCsoft settled the claims on undisclosed terms. So it is still not clear whether City of Heroes users, when they fashion avatars that resemble those of Marvel's superheroes, are guilty of copyright infringement. Future creators of virtual worlds will have to look at the court's decision and wonder about the potential illegality of tools they offer users to enable avatar customization. It seems quite possible that future virtual world owners offering more advanced creative tools will find themselves the targets of copyright infringement lawsuits.

INTELLECTUAL PROPERTY

In prior chapters, I explored how virtual worlds might pose interesting challenges to legal doctrines of jurisdiction, contract, property, and hacking. However, I intentionally ignored the laws of intellectual property. If I had explored this area of law in an earlier chapter, it could have easily eclipsed many other issues. In fact, it is not unusual for many people, including lawyers, to assume that because virtual worlds feature creative expression and forms of intangible value, they are entirely controlled through the laws of intellectual property.

That is not correct. While intellectual property law plays a key role in virtual worlds, it is a significant mistake to think that it occupies the entire field. For instance, virtual property rights are actually a very poor match for intellectual property law. Formally, virtual property resembles William Blackstone's "incorporeal heriditaments" more than it resembles any existing form of intellectual property. When Marc Bragg had his virtual land confiscated by Linden Lab and Geoff Luurs had his virtual inventory

cleaned out by an account thief, no one suffered a loss or gain of any traditional legal intellectual property right. A virtual castle in Britannia and
an account full of Linden dollars might be subject to exclusive possession
and market alienation, but the intellectual property rights in these virtual
objects (to the extent that they exist) are located in the hands of intellectual property owners rather than those users who might claim virtual
property rights.

To illustrate this point, let's say that Alice purchases a Harry Potter
novel. This book is now her chattel property. It is in Alice's possession. She
can sell it to someone else, burn it, pound nails with it, or swat flies with it.
She can even use it as a coaster for drinks. However, even though Alice is
the legal owner of the tangible book, the copyright in the book is not her
intellectual property. The property right does not belong to Alice, the intellectual property right belongs to J. K. Rowling. This means that Alice
can't make photocopies of the book to sell to her friends without the permission of Rowling. Perhaps she may be able to do this as a "fair use" in
U.S. law, but the exact scope of fair use is murky, and this particular use
seems like commercially motivated infringement. So, like a virtual property right, copyright law amounts to a limit on what people can do with
the physical (and presumably virtual) forms of legal property they own.
Yet, unlike virtual property, copyright protects no particular object
owned by a particular person; instead it grants a right to prevent the rep-
lication of a particular abstract information pattern (e.g., the sequence of
words in a book).

"Intellectual property" is a relatively new term, and some people claim
that it is actually a misnomer or at least has misleading connotations.[5]
Surveys of contemporary intellectual property laws usually identify three
"major" categories of intellectual property law: patents, trademarks, and
copyrights. Patent law grants to patent owners the right to exclude others
from making and using useful inventions. The Wright patent on airplane
technology is one example. Trademarks are rights in commercial brands
that are used to indicate the source of a company's goods and services.
McDonald's and Coca-Cola, for instance, are well-known trademarks.
Copyrights, which were at play in the City of Heroes case, are the rights
that artistic creators have in their creations, including things such as books,
music, artwork, animation, and computer software. In addition to these
three major forms of intellectual property rights, there are several other
forms of intellectual property interests that might be identified, such as
rights of publicity, trade secrets, and database protections.

Today, in the majority of jurisdictions, intellectual property laws are codified in statutes that spell out, with precision, the scope of the private rights established. In the United States, for instance, rights of trademark, patent, and copyright are set forth in lengthy sections of the United States legal code. However, other areas of intellectual property law, such as the right of privacy and the common law of trademarks, may have state common law and state statutory components. All these forms of intellectual property are relevant to virtual worlds. Virtual worlds employ technology (the subject of patent law) and are zones where commercial branding occurs (the subject of trademark law).[6] They are certainly zones where privacy law is implicated (they are, indeed, essentially panoptic environments)[7] and are even zones where celebrity identities are commercialized (making them subject to publicity rights). However, putting aside all other arenas of intellectual property, this chapter will focus on copyright law. Copyright is proving to be a primary wellspring of early legal conflict within virtual worlds over intellectual property.

COPYRIGHT AND CREATIVITY

In chapter 8, I described how the power of software code permeates virtual worlds. Given that copyright law applies to software code, this means that copyright law pervades virtual worlds as well. Copyright's influence, as the Marvel case shows, shapes the legality of what can be done in virtual worlds. In the tangible world, natural objects, like the earth, the sun, the moon, and the flora and fauna, are not products of human authorship. If you visit a national park with friends and take pictures of your companions and everything you see there, there is little chance that your pictures will raise copyright issues. You might have a copyright interest in your photograph, but chances are that nothing you photograph will be protected by copyright. Yet in a virtual world, all objects, even the bodies of your fellow avatars, are authorial fabrications protected by some form of copyright interest. If you happen to physically resemble a Marvel superhero, good for you. If your avatar happens to look like a Marvel superhero, you might have a copyright problem.

We might begin by asking why we have copyright law in the first place. As explained in chapter 7, the predominant justification for property law is utilitarian. Property law is justified because a world with property rights, all things considered, is believed to be a better world. The standard justification for copyright tells the same story: we are all better off with copyright law. However, while that may be the case, it is worth noting that the world got along pretty well without copyright for quite a long time.

Laws about tangible property and contracts existed in the earliest human civilizations. Copyright, on the other hand, is only about three centuries old, which makes it a comparative newcomer. It is also worth noting that copyright law, like the law of the airplane, was initially crafted to respond to a new technology. In the case of copyright, that technology was the printing press, and the state response was not one we would celebrate today. Copyright law originated with the formation of a commercial monopoly designed to censor popular speech.[8] Since this is not the most highly publicized version of copyright law, it deserves a brief explanation.

In the early fifteenth century, a commercial guild in England known as the Stationers' Company controlled the English trade in books. As the printing press expanded the production of books, the Crown granted the Stationers' Company a monopoly on the printing of books. Accompanying this legal right was the private power to shut down unlicensed printers and to seize and burn unlicensed heretical and seditious texts. So the early Stationers' Company can be understood as a state-sanctioned censorial cartel, one that functioned effectively and profitably for over one hundred years. Eventually, however, the social and political transformations of the Enlightenment took place, souring popular opinion about both censorship and monopoly, and therefore weakening the ties between the English government and the Stationers' Company. In 1694, Parliament refused to renew the Stationers' Company's monopoly over the book trade.

In 1710, however, the Stationers' Company finally succeeded in restoring a property right in the book trade. It did this through a political compromise with Parliament that marked the origin of contemporary copyright: the Statute of Anne. The Statute of Anne was, in a sense, a loss for the monopolistic Stationers. Under the Stationers' Company copyright, the members of the company, not the authors, enjoyed a proprietary monopoly in particular texts. However, copyright under the Statute of Anne was a legal right given to authors, not publishers.

The practical effect of the law, however, was to allow the Stationers' Company to retain many of its former powers through reliance on authors' copyrights. Authors who wanted to see their work in print generally had only one option: they had to sell their copyright to established publishers, who would then enjoy the exclusive legal privilege to print their work. So while the book publishers were no longer the direct beneficiaries of the new copyright law, they were still the primary commercial exploiters of the right. Today, publishers and commercial intermediaries are still the most vociferous parties when demands are made for extensions of copyright law. Most "professional" copyright creators today ultimately transfer their copyright to publishers or other intermediaries in the full-time business of producing, distributing, and profiting from the sales of works.

Given the history of copyright law, especially its recent history, I think it is fairly defensible to view the social operation of copyright law, both past and present, with a certain degree of skepticism. The law often seems written in order to channel economic benefits to publishers without much careful consideration of the public interest or even the interests of the authors that the law is, in theory, intended to benefit. Today, the prominent parties shaping copyright law in the United States are the motion picture industry, the music industry, the publishing industry, and the software industry. The major players in these industries have the funds to pursue legislative agendas and obtain the attention of Congress.

Yet, at least in theory, copyright is a law intended to benefit the public. It is designed to do so by promoting "the Progress of Science and useful Arts,"[9] or, as the Statute of Anne puts it, the "Encouragement of Learning."[10] The theory is that when creative authors and artists have an alienable property right in their creative work, they are encouraged to produce and sell more new authorial works. The public pays a certain "tax" by needing to respect copyright law, yet this tax is offset by the greater abundance and commercial availability of creative expression.

The chief right granted by copyright law is the exclusive right to reproduce a work—in other words, the right to make copies. But there are other rights as well, such as rights to control the distribution, performance, and display of a work, as well as the right to license translations, adaptations, and sequels of the work. These exclusive rights last for quite a long time today. While early copyrights lasted only a few decades, today most copyrights in most countries will last over a century. There is also no required registration for copyright protection and no required notice that must be given to the public of copyright ownership. So, as copyright law stands today in most countries, from the moment you draw a doodle in the margin of your notebook, take a picture with your cell phone, record a home video, compose a poem, or create a blog post online, you possess a copyright that will last for seventy years after your death. Another person who copies your doodle or poem or blog post may be liable for copyright infringement.

Applying the justifications for copyright law to the City of Heroes case, the theory of copyright seems to be that the artists who first depicted Spider-Man were incentivized in that creativity by copyright's prospect of a financial reward. They had the right to obtain this reward by selling their copyright interest to Marvel, a publishing company that specializes in monetizing and marketing works of creative authorship. Marvel now owns the exclusive right to reproduce Spider-Man, and that copyright will probably last roughly a century (unless it is extended by Congress). So, given that Marvel owns the exclusive right to reproduce images of Spider-Man, players should not be able to use the character creation engine to duplicate Spider-Man. This rule limits creative freedom in virtual worlds, but without this limit, the artist who might create the next Spider-Man may not have the incentive to do so.

This, at least, is how the story goes. In my opinion, the diversity of superhero costumes in City of Heroes actually tells a different story. It appears that hundreds of thousands of people are willing to create superhero costumes simply because they enjoy the creative process, not because they are seeking to make money from their creative artistry. However, if the tools that enable such creativity are outlawed by a copyright, this super-abundance of creativity will cease to exist. Therefore, if Marvel is successful in preventing users from utilizing the character generation engine to create Spider-Man clones, it also will prevent the majority of users—who do not want to make imitations of Marvel heroes—from having access to powerful creative tools.

In the United States, a potential defense to a claim of infringement is the doctrine of fair use, which exempts certain otherwise infringing uses from liability for copyright infringement. I strongly believe that the established doctrine of fair use should have protected City of Heroes players from liability for copyright infringement. To the extent that a player might make a clone of Spider-Man, that player would not profit commercially from the infringement, and may even do something creatively "transformative" with the Spider-Man character. However, the doctrine of fair use, contrary to popular belief, does not provide a categorical exception for noncommercial or "personal" copying. Instead, fair use in copyright law is determined on a case-by-case basis that makes it notoriously difficult to predict. It is very possible that the court in the City of Heroes case, if it had reached the matter, would have deemed player costumes infringing and outside the ambit of fair use doctrine. As in many cases of noncommercial personal copying, avatar infringement occupies a gray area of unsettled legality.

The City of Heroes lawsuit is just one example of many in which the laws of copyright are influencing the shape of virtual worlds. Copyright law speaks not only to the avatars in a world but to the world itself. There may be people, for instance, who want to spend time in a virtual world built specifically around Harry Potter or *The Chronicles of Narnia*. A group of artists and technologists might be more than willing to create such virtual worlds. But without the permission of J. K. Rowling or the C. S. Lewis Company, and some sort of deal regarding the distribution of profits, such virtual worlds are not legally permitted to exist. Virtual worlds based on *The Matrix, Star Wars, Star Trek, Conan,* and *The Lord of the Rings* have already been created, but deals were made with the relevant copyright owners first. As a result, creators of fictional worlds based on film and literature tend to own their potential paths of virtual world development.

Though fictional worlds can provide frameworks for popular virtual worlds, there can also be a mismatch between fictional and virtual worlds that can create problems. Fictional worlds are held together by central characters, while virtual worlds are online communities. So, for instance, the virtual worlds of Star Wars Galaxies and Lord of the Rings Online were licensed on terms that required the worlds to be developed consistently with the original fiction. Presumably, the owners of the copyrights in the fiction wanted to retain creative control over what the virtual worlds looked like. But requiring consistency can prove problematic. How can thousands of users collaborate in a shared virtual space that is consistent with a narrative featuring only a small group of heroes? The answer is that, in the virtual world, not everyone—in fact, probably no one—can play the part of the hero.

So, for instance, during the first few months Star Wars Galaxies was available, there was not a single Jedi. For the first couple of years, becoming a Jedi was nearly impossible for the average player. This kept the Star Wars Galaxies virtual world true to the fiction of the Star Wars universe, where Jedi were rare and legendary. But it clearly frustrated many players who anticipated a virtual life of wielding a light saber.

PUBLIC COPYRIGHT

Though intellectual property rights impact users of virtual worlds, users are rarely brought to court. In the City of Heroes case, although the legality of user behavior was directly at issue, Marvel sued NCsoft rather than the allegedly infringing users. Traditionally, copyright law has operated in this exact way, leaving the public out of the picture. Fifty years ago, this might have made some sense. Struggles over copyright law at that time generally pitted certain professional players in copyright industries (authors, artists, producers, broadcasters, publishers, and venues) against each other. These parties depended on copyright law's boundaries for their livelihood and therefore had personal stakes that made lobbying and litigation worthwhile. Because average people did not own broadcast networks or printing presses, the average person was rarely, if ever, seen as a threat to the copyright industries. And the average person therefore did not need to know or care about copyright. She could get through life being largely oblivious to copyright law, which functioned primarily as a law regulating a specialized trade.[11]

During the twentieth century, the law in the United States reflected this presumption. Congress tended to make new copyright laws by gathering representatives of various industries. As a result, our copyright statute often looks like a lengthy and complicated contractual agreement. There are incredibly complex rules about the duration of particular rights, limitations on varieties of performance, the retransmission of broadcasts by cable and satellite, and the variety of rights in digital and analog musical recordings. When I teach copyright, it takes several months to explain the basic details to students who are already well versed in standard legal principles. Copyright law today makes copyright lawyers necessary.

Yet technological change is increasingly bringing the average person into the world of copyright law. In the latter half of the twentieth century, the photocopy machine, recordable audio- and videocassettes, and the personal computer empowered users to make reproductions of works without depending on professional intermediaries to provide that service. These recording technologies made copying a part of everyone's life. This caused significant alarm in the copyright industries, which turned to legislators, courts, and public relations campaigns to preserve the status quo of copyright law and the business models that depended on it. In one famous case involving the Sony Betamax video recorder, the motion picture industry unsuccessfully attempted to put an end to Sony's technology, which enabled the widespread copying of television broadcasts.[12] In a 5–4 decision, the Supreme Court determined that although home taping of television broadcasts was not necessarily legal, the distribution of the recording technology could not be prohibited by law. The vote was extremely close, with Justices Sandra Day O'Connor and William Brennan initially favoring a verdict against Sony, but gradually coming to favor the legality of the technology.

The technology of the Internet has made the Supreme Court's Sony decision seem quaint by comparison. The Internet has put a tremendous strain on the logic of copyright. The Internet was built to make the popular creation and sharing of information dramatically easier and faster. The ensuing years have seen not only text but movies, music, images, and all other forms of information moving from degradable and tangible media (like vinyl, celluloid, and wood pulp) to the realm of electromagnetic digitization, where infinite personal copies can be made with perfect fidelity. It is hard to overstate the dismay the Internet has caused the entertainment industry. During the last decade or so, copyright professionals have made concentrated efforts with courts, legislatures, and the public to reverse the tide of free and ubiquitous copying of all manner of content. Based on the high economic stakes and the rhetorical intensity of public discourse, Jessica Litman has described the recent battles over digital copyright as the "copyright wars."[13]

The copyright industries have abundant reason to be concerned about the Internet. Cheap digital tools and Internet access now provide almost everyone with the ability to copy, upload, modify, and distribute content. Given this, a vast number of people are indeed making copies, not only of Marvel superheroes, but of many copyright-protected works that are economically valuable. A large part of the copyright problem is that copyright law has never concerned itself much with simple rules. Most people who use the Internet are not acquainted with the intricacies of copyright law, and to the extent that they are familiar with it, they have the intuition that their own personal activities are not going to be discovered by copyright owners. Most people don't think they will be sued for posting a Harry Potter picture on their web page, for making a mix CD and giving it to a friend, or for creating a Spider-Man look-alike in City of Heroes. Though the law may not always support this perception, most of the major companies in the copyright industries are understandably reluctant to sue members of the general public for personal and noncommercial infringements. Instead, the preferred strategy is to prevent the spread of technologies that enable public copying. Attempts to use copyright to discontinue Sony's Betamax and to shut down NCsoft's character creation engine are examples of this approach.

Copyright owners are also employing two more sophisticated legal tools to curb user copyright infringement. Both of these were made part of copyright law pursuant to the Digital Millennium Copyright Act (DMCA), a broad and multifaceted reform of copyright law passed in 1998 at the urging of the copyright industries.[14]

One provision of the DMCA grants copyright holders the power to notify online intermediaries when they spot infringements and demand that the infringing copies be deleted.[15] So, for instance, if an image of a Marvel superhero is posted to a web page, Marvel can contact the online service provider that hosts the web page and identify the infringing file. If the service provider quickly removes the infringing content, the DMCA provides a "safe harbor," meaning that the service provider will not be liable for facilitating copyright infringement. The law also requires the service provider to notify the user that the material has been removed and give the user a chance to contest the claim of infringement. If this "counter-notification" occurs, the material should then be restored, unless the copyright holder brings an actual lawsuit. These "notice and take-down" provisions are now part of the common practice of content owners dealing not only with web pages but with other content-hosting web sites such as YouTube and Flickr. The DMCA is used in virtual worlds as well. For instance, prior to and subsequent to the filing of its lawsuit against the makers of City of Heroes, Marvel used the DMCA notice provisions to demand that NCsoft delete particular allegedly infringing avatars within the virtual world.

Another provision of the DMCA created a more radical revision of copyright law. Searching for a way to limit user behavior, the copyright industries seized on the "code is law" ideas discussed in the last chapter and sought to make their code a substitute for the restrictions of copyright law. If new movies, for instance, could be technologically "locked" via digital encryption and proprietary technologies, then software prohibitions against copying could replace the need for copyright prohibitions. Indeed, technological protections are better than legal protections, given that legal prohibitions can be costly and difficult to police and enforce against users. If technological controls were effective, users would need to respect legal prohibitions against copying because the technology would provide no other choice. Even fair use rights could be technologically pre-empted. The FBI anti-piracy warning on DVDs can be used to illustrate the complicity between code and copyright. When this warning is displayed, the fast-forward function of the DVD player is suspended, leaving the viewer with no choice but to learn, yet again, that a conviction for criminal copyright infringement can subject a person to five years in prison or fines of up to $250,000. This sort of software control over the user experience of a work is known as digital rights management, or DRM.

The entertainment industry did not need a law to allow the use of DRM any more than the owners of virtual worlds needed a law to let them shape their code. The DMCA, however, made their technological control legally powerful by prohibiting users from "circumventing" the technological measures that limit access to a work. So, for example, most DVDs today are digitally encrypted to make it impossible to access them without licensed hardware. Although most people do not know how to decrypt DVDs, the DMCA makes it illegal to do so or to share DVD decryption tools with others. In an early DMCA case, a federal court of appeals determined that a web site that shared DVDs decryption tools—and that linked to other web sites with those tools—violated the DMCA.

From a conceptual standpoint, the DMCA's anti-circumvention provisions closely resemble the computer hacking laws described in the last chapter. Yet whereas the computer hacking laws prohibit individuals from obtaining unauthorized access to private computer systems, the DMCA prohibits individuals from obtaining unauthorized access to the objects they purchase. Consumers may purchase DVDs, but they have no legal right under the DMCA to freely tinker with the software on them.

By extending copyright owners' power to make their code into law with respect to the goods they sell, the DMCA has merged technological power with copyright power in novel and disturbing ways. Let's go back to the example of Alice, who could rip apart her old-fashioned printed book and use its cover as a coaster. The owner of a modern e-book generally loses that sort of autonomy. Consider what happened with Kindle, Amazon's e-book reading device, in the summer of 2009. Some customers had purchased a Kindle version of George Orwell's *1984* from the Kindle store. At a later date, Amazon realized that the company selling the text did not own the copyright. So, when Kindle reconnected to Amazon, as it regularly does, Amazon's software simply deleted the infringing copies of *1984* from purchasers' Kindles.[16] Though Amazon later apologized for its handling of the matter, the incident raises important questions about the future of the book as a legal artifact. Given market incentives, copyright industries will presumably continue to sell content in ways that enable ongoing control over what is experienced, how it is experienced, and what sorts of downstream uses can be made. Consumption patterns can be monitored and reported back to sellers. And, given the new rules created by the DMCA, tampering with the digital tethers that constrain the shape of the reader experience can be an illegal act in itself. In effect, the same sorts of coded controls discussed in prior chapters with respect to virtual worlds will increasingly exist in other media as well.

LAW AND HACKING REDUX

As discussed in previous chapters, virtual world owners possess significant control over users' experience. First, the law generally respects the exclusive right of virtual world owners to control the functioning of the key technology at play (the server). In addition, the law generally enforces the contractual agreements drafted by virtual world owners. Finally, property and contract are reinforced and extended by anti-hacking laws that prohibit unauthorized access to the machines hosting virtual worlds.

Copyright law allows virtual world owners to enjoy the additional benefit of copyright control over the code of their virtual worlds. Since the early 1980s in the United States, copyright law has regarded computer programs as "literary works." As a result, the code that is the basis of a virtual world is granted the same protections as the text of a poem. As many commentators and courts have noted, this is an odd rule, given that software is often primarily functional expression and not very much like poetry or other forms of creative writing. In addition, most consumers do not experience software code but instead have interactive experiences with the text, animation, music, and other content displayed when the program is operating. Protecting an authorial "work" that is largely invisible to users is not the typical way that copyright operates. Courts have therefore struggled with the application of copyright law to computer programs.

In addition to being out of synch with the other forms of media protected by copyright, copyright in software is problematic for another reason. When software operates normally, a reproduction of the software code is made in the memory of the computer running the program. For instance, when purchasers operate the World of Warcraft client software, a copy of the game program gets loaded into the random-access memory (RAM) of the computer. The creation of a RAM copy enables the software to run more quickly and with greater flexibility. Still, from the perspective of copyright law, a RAM copy is a copy and therefore needs to be authorized by the copyright owner before it is made. Though an exception in the copyright statute allows "owners" of software to make RAM copies, many courts have read that exception to be inapplicable to normal purchasers of software.[17] This is in part because the contracts that accompany software (generally click-wrap agreements) usually specify that purchasers are "licensees" (not "owners") of the program who must not make use of the software beyond the scope of the license. Therefore, just as a copyright infringement threat backs up technological control in the case of the DMCA, so it backs up contractual control in the case of software licenses. Failure to abide by the terms of the license can make RAM copies infringing copies, making those who violate the terms of software licenses liable for copyright infringement, even if they lawfully purchased the software.

To understand how both the DMCA and software licenses play out in practice, we can consider a recent lawsuit in Arizona involving Blizzard and an unauthorized "bot" program. In 2005, Michael Donnelly developed a program named WoWGlider (later renamed Glider) that is commonly described as a bot. Glider allows players to automate their avatars in World of Warcraft so that they can operate continuously when the user is not present. This essentially creates the same effect as the macroing and perching described in the last chapter with respect to Asheron's Call. However, given that Glider operates in an environment where World of Warcraft gold can be transmuted into real dollars, the software not only helped users who wished to advance quickly, it also may have presented an effective way for commercial gold farmers to turn a better profit. The numbers behind Glider attest to this. Donnelly began selling the Glider program in 2005. By late 2008, his company had sold over one hundred thousand copies and had made over three million dollars.[18]

Many users complained about Glider (as they had about perching in Asheron's call), and Blizzard attempted to use the powers at its disposal to stop Glider. It included a specific prohibition against bots in its contractual agreements and began to ban the accounts of Glider users. To determine who was using Glider, it employed a counter-cheating program that it added to the World of Warcraft client software. This program, called Warden, scanned the user's computer for Glider and other impermissible forms of software. Where such software was found, Warden would prevent the user from communicating with its servers. In response to Warden, Donnelly made further modifications to Glider so that it might avoid detection.

In late 2006, representatives of Blizzard confronted Donnelly in person at his home. According to the pleadings, Blizzard's agents demanded that Donnelly turn over his profits and stop selling the program. Donnelly instead contacted a lawyer, and MDY, Donnelly's company, filed a lawsuit the next day, seeking to enjoin Blizzard from interfering with its business. Blizzard responded to the suit by bringing multiple claims against MDY. Blizzard had three primary claims. First, Blizzard argued that Donnelly, by selling Glider, had unlawfully interfered with Blizzard's contracts with its customers. Second, it argued that Glider, like the character creation engine in City of Heroes, was a technology that played a key role in enabling copyright infringement. Finally, Blizzard argued that Glider violated the anti-circumvention provisions of the DMCA by providing access to the copyrighted content of World of Warcraft and circumventing the technological protection measure of the Warden program.

The contractual interference claim, according to Judge David Campbell, was fairly straightforward. Judge Campbell seemed quite confident that Glider was harming Blizzard's relationships with its customers. The copyright claims were more complex. First, just as Marvel had claimed that NCsoft distributed a technology that enabled infringement, so Blizzard claimed that Donnelly had distributed a technology that enabled users to infringe its copyright. MDY did not seriously contest that it was responsible for profited from users' operation of Glider. However, MDY argued that players who used the Glider bot did not infringe Blizzard's copyright.

Judge Campbell sided with Blizzard. He found that if WoW players violated the terms of the contract and used the Glider program, they were engaged in copyright infringement. This was due to the fact that the users made RAM copies of the WoW software each time they ran the program. If read broadly enough, such a rule might be somewhat similar to the jury verdict in the Lori Drew case, turning any violation of an online contract not into a computer hacking crime but into an infringement of copyright. Yet Judge Campbell was careful to emphasize that he interpreted the use of bots as a violation of a section of the terms of use relating to copyright interests rather than the violation of a "game rule," which would not implicate copyright.

With respect to its DMCA claim, Blizzard argued that Glider, like a software program that could be used to decrypt a DVD, allowed players to gain access to its copyright-protected software. Blizzard claimed that the Warden anti-botting software was a means of controlling access to World of Warcraft. By modifying Glider to evade Warden, MDY had created a tool that broke Blizzard's technology controlling access to the virtual world (that is, Warden's surveillance program). Notably, the copyrighted work that was accessed in this case was not the literal code of the game software but the dynamic and interactive environment of World of Warcraft that was created when the client interacted with the WoW server. This included

> the real-time experience of traveling through different worlds, hearing their sounds, viewing their structures, encountering their inhabitants and monsters, and encountering other players—[which] cannot be accessed on a user's hard drive. They can be accessed only when the user is connected to a Blizzard server.[19]

The court concluded that Glider did circumvent the Warden software and therefore violated the DMCA's prohibition against copyright hacking tools. Glider constituted an illegal technology under copyright law. The court therefore ruled in favor of Blizzard on all three claims. As of the writing of this book, MDY's appeal of the court's judgment is pending. Unless the case is settled, the copyright claims will certainly be re-argued and revisited by the appellate court.

The story of the Glider litigation is interesting because it reveals the gulf between the theoretical goals of copyright and contract law and how they play out in practice when applied to virtual worlds. Copyright law is supposed to provide monetary incentives for the production of works of creative authorship. Glider is itself a work of creative authorship that many people were willing to purchase. And Glider's botting software does not copy Blizzard's creative work or distribute it. Contract law, in theory, is supposed to promote mutually beneficial bargains, such as the sale of software products. Yet, in the Blizzard case, the non-negotiable contract Blizzard created was interpreted to put ordinary users of its software at risk of liability for copyright infringement if they breached the contract. Judge Campbell's opinion in the MDY case, while it is arguably correct as a matter of existing law, is fairly far from serving the traditional objectives of contract and copyright theory.

Yet, at the same time, allowing Blizzard to prohibit unauthorized software that harms the collective experience of users in its virtual worlds seems appropriate. My impression is that the majority of players of World of Warcraft would prefer a game with a more level and more social playing field, where avatars are actively controlled by other human beings rather than piloted by automated software. As Mia Consalvo has noted, the automated avatar bots tend to undermine both virtual economies and the social capital acquired through play.[20] They also undermine community: a virtual world of avatars set on autopilot is essentially a world of zombies. And while the prohibition on Glider may be counterintuitive from the standpoint of promoting market exchange, World of Warcraft is a game-like environment where market exchange is actually counterproductive at times. If this is all correct, it seems appropriate that Blizzard should have *some* legal tool to help it discourage companies such as MDY from facilitating "cheating" for profit.

We might analogize Blizzard's situation to that of Disney World. Occasionally, some visitors to the park may engage in antisocial behavior such as "cheating" by cutting lines or harassing other visitors. Disney, via its right of private property, has the power to exclude those who violate its rules. By having this level of legal control over its environment, Disney can create a more enjoyable experience. Similarly, users of World of Warcraft may benefit from Blizzard's ability to police the use of software that threatens its carefully calibrated game environment.

Even if such is the case, however, we should worry about the collateral effects of using copyright law as the cudgel of choice. Linking copyright power to contractual rules and technological control allows virtual world owners to acquire an even stronger set of controls over user behavior. Virtual world owners already have property, contract, technology, and traditional copyright on their side. Do they need RAM copies and the DMCA as well?

USER-GENERATED CONTENT

The virtual world and the video game are new forms of media that were not in existence at the time of copyright's creation. Indeed, when the last major revision to United States copyright law was made in 1976, video games were in their infancy. The traditional work of copyright is something like a book, a song, or a movie that is passively experienced by consumers.[21] People do not meet in books like they meet in virtual worlds. As Sal Humphreys has noted, the "legal discourse of intellectual property relies on a linear production process rather than a networked one."[22] Interactive media is remarkable in the scope of control the user has over the work. In many cases, the user verges on being an author herself. For instance, the City of Heroes character creation engine is primarily a tool that permits users to do the work of authors. The Glider program allows

Julian Dibbell's user-generated content in Farmville *Copyright Zynga, reproduced with permission*

users to interact with World of Warcraft in an unauthorized way. The fact that both cases involved claims of copyright infringement seems odd in that the infringers in both cases were more like authors and actors than unauthorized readers and viewers.

The notion that users of interactive software might be authorial actors was recognized some time ago in a case involving the classic video game Defender. In 1982, Williams Electronics, the makers of Defender, sued another company, Arctic International, which had created a look-alike version of the game. This was fairly early in the history of software copyright, and one argument made by the defendant was that the game play of Defender did not qualify for copyright protection. Unlike a book or a film, Defender required an interactive player at the controls and was therefore a different experience every time it was played. Arctic claimed that because "the player becomes a co-author of what appears on the screen," there was "no set or fixed performance."[23] Therefore, according to Arctic, there was no "work" definite enough to be protected by copyright, only a field of decisions offered to the player.

Judge Delores Sloviter rejected the claim:

> Although there is player interaction with the machine during the play mode which causes the audiovisual presentation to change in some respects from one game to the next . . . , there is always a repetitive sequence of a substantial portion of the sights and sounds of the game.[24]

In other words, even though players were authorial in some way, Williams could lay claim to copyright protection in the fixed and repeated elements that made up the various "props" of Defender. Williams could claim copyright in the fluid interactive environment it had set before the player. Whether Defender players were authors was not explored. From a practical standpoint, it did not seem to matter: Defender players had little stake in the fleeting authorship of the game performance. After all, they were not selling or distributing videos of their game play for profit.

In today's virtual world, however, users are invested in authorship. Numerous scholars in the humanities have argued that virtual worlds place a special emphasis on the user's authorship. Espen Aarseth, for instance, argued in his early exploration of computer games as literature that while most digital games can be understood as a form of navigable interactive literature (a "cybertext"), MUDs more closely resemble a form of improvisational theater. According to Aarseth, the most significant literary events that occurred in MUDs took place in users' conversational interactions.[25] Torill Mortensen largely agreed with Aarseth's analysis, noting how MUDs could place users in a position "dangerously close to being an author."[26]

Indeed, in LambdaMOO and many other more free-form MUDs, users created not just avatars but rooms and interactive objects as well.[27] Contemporary virtual worlds, even MMORPGs such as City of Heroes, tend to give a prominent place to user creativity as well. Looking at contemporary MMORPGs, Lisbeth Klastrup has explained that virtual worlds do not create narratives as much as they enable "tellable" experiences, offering players both the stage and the props to create a shared narrative experience.[28] Yochai Benkler, writing about early MMORPGs, says something very similar.

> In a game like Ultima Online or EverQuest, the role of the commercial provider is not to tell a finished, highly polished story to be consumed start to finish by passive consumers. Rather, the role of the

game provider is to build tools with which users collaborate to tell a story. . . .

The individual contributions of the users/coauthors of the story line are literally done for fun—they are playing a game. However, they are spending real economic goods—their attention and substantial subscription fees—on a form of entertainment that uses a platform for active coproduction of a story line to displace what was once passive reception of a finished, commercially and professionally manufactured good.[29]

The shift from professionally created content to interactive and "user-generated" content is not limited to virtual worlds. The World Wide Web has become a powerful tool for "amateur" authors.[30] In recent years, web sites such as Wikipedia, MySpace, YouTube, Flickr, and Facebook have provided online platforms on which users create and share forms of information that are, at least ostensibly, governed by the law of copyright. The size of amateur copyright content is staggering. There are now billions of freely accessible web pages that hold more information than can be found in all the volumes of the Library of Congress.

Virtual worlds have been a harbinger of the trend toward user-generated content, yet as they seek to partner with traditional media models, they must struggle to balance copyright law with a community of users empowered with creative tools.[31] Given that copyright law protects all varieties of creative works, handing creative tools to users can put virtual world owners in a position where they must seek copyright permission from users. Virtual world owners, after all, are intermediaries in the reproduction and distribution of the content authored by their users. Whether users regard themselves as authors or not, copyright makes their authorial work legally real and this implicates the virtual world owner. Just as players must make RAM copies to run their client software, so NCsoft *must* make electronic copies of user creations in order for participants in the virtual world to "see" what has been created by other users. The legal strategy used by NCsoft to deal with this problem should be familiar by now: the online contract.

The terms of service of most virtual worlds require that (1) all content provided by users does not infringe the rights of any third party (if it does, users are generally required to indemnify the virtual world owner from liability), and (2) all content created by users within the game becomes the property, or at least is subject to the licensed use, of the virtual world owner. For instance, the terms of service of Lord of the Rings Online require that users transfer (assign) their creative contributions to Turbine, the owner of the virtual world. If, for some reason, this term is not enforceable, the virtual world owner requires

> the sole and exclusive, irrevocable, sublicensable, transferable, worldwide, paid-up license to reproduce, fix, adapt, modify, translate, reformat, create derivative works from, manufacture, introduce into circulation, publish, distribute, sell, license, sublicense, transfer, rent, lease, transmit, publicly display, publicly perform, provide access to electronically, broadcast, communicate to the public by telecommunication, display, enter into computer memory, and use and practice the Content, all modified and derivative works thereof, all portions and copies thereof in any form, all inventions, designs, and marks embodied therein, and all patent, copyright, trade secret, trademark and other intellectual property rights thereto, and/or to incorporate the same in other works in any form, media, or technology now known or later developed. To the extent permitted by applicable laws, you hereby waive any moral rights or rights of publicity or privacy you may have in the Content.[32]

It is doubtful that most people who create original content within Lord of the Rings Online read or fully understand this language. Most users participate creatively in virtual worlds because they find it pleasurable to do so, not because they anticipate commercially exploiting their creative labor. They may not even be troubled if they realize that they are required by contract to transfer their copyright ownership to virtual world owners. And while terms like those set forth above seem extremely one-sided, it seems unlikely that, in the majority of cases, Lord of the Rings Online anticipates that the works created by its community of users will be valuable and monetized. A more sympathetic reading of this rather extreme language would be that the owners of the virtual world want the freedom to operate their virtual world without the risk of infringing the copyrights of users, something that is increasingly hard to do in online environments, where regular copying is unavoidable.

However, even if a virtual world owner is confident that it will not infringe the rights of its users, it may fear that its users will infringe the rights of third parties, just as Marvel alleged players had done in City of Heroes. While contractual agreements requiring indemnity and the DMCA "notice and takedown" provisions should protect virtual world owners in such cases, Marvel's lawsuit demonstrates that some copyright holders may be even more aggressive about attempting to enforce their rights. Virtual world developers have therefore adopted different approaches to providing creative tools for users. For example, NCsoft's highly flexible character creation engine might be contrasted with the rather rudimentary tools for avatar customization in World of Warcraft, where many avatars look similar to each other.

As an additional example, Lord of the Rings Online and Star Wars Galaxies took divergent approaches to providing tools for user-generated music. In the fictional universe of *Star Wars*, cantinas play an important role. In 1977, coinciding with the release of the first movie, the tune played by Mos Eisley's bug-eyed cantina musicians actually topped the Billboard charts.[33] Accordingly, cantina music was featured in the design of the Star Wars Galaxies game. Players were required to visit cantinas after adventures and be "healed" by the music and dancing of other players. Players could also choose to be cantina musicians, working to advance in their profession by earning tips for the quality of their services.

However, all music played in the cantina was from "canned" selections authored by the game designers. Players protested, arguing that they should have the freedom to write their own music for their slitherhorns, ommni boxes, and mandoviols. But the requests fell on deaf ears. According to one of the game's producers, the problem was copyright law: "If we allowed someone to play anything they want, they could play a song by Madonna and then we'd have licensing issues."[34] Additionally, there was the problem of making the cantina music scene consistent with the hit song from 1977 and the Lucasfilm notion of what cantinas in Star Wars should sound like. Madonna tunes would be inconsistent with the desired Star Wars theme. So, due to copyright concerns, the musical instruments in Star Wars Galaxies were coded to be non-creative.

Musical performance was also a key part of Tolkien's fictional world. Tolkien's hobbits would regularly burst into song, as would elves, Ents, and warriors of Gondor. Accordingly, Lord of the Rings Online also offered players the option of becoming virtual musicians, similarly playing songs to lift the spirits of other players. While the "functional" songs are, like those in Star Wars Galaxies, limited to canned music, Lord of the Rings offers minstrels the power to convert their computer keyboards into piano keys and write songs in a rudimentary form of musical notation. They can play their own original songs at public locations in Middle Earth. As might have been anticipated, not all original songs are so original. Elves and hob-bits in the virtual Shire will, on occasion, play well-known tunes by Metal-lica, Led Zeppelin, and Rick Astley. While giving creative musical powers to players undoubtedly makes Lord of the Rings Online a more pleasurable and expressive experience for users, it raises the multifaceted copyright problems that Star Wars Galaxies avoided by avoiding these tools.

To the extent that users have creative powers in virtual worlds, it is rare that their creativity is limited to the medium of the virtual environment. Many users of virtual worlds export their works to the Web in ways that blend their creativity with the authorship of the virtual world owner. For instance, a community of Lord of the Rings Online musicians currently exchanges song notations via several web sites. In addition, hundreds of musical performances within Lord of the Rings Online are documented in the form of videos on YouTube.

Many other YouTube videos feature creative scenes taken from other virtual worlds. Videos that rely on virtual worlds as stages are called ma-chinima. (The practice is just as common in video games.) Machinima techniques can be used for many purposes: there are comic news reports from World of Warcraft, tours of guild strongholds in Everquest II, mov-ies made in Second Life, music videos set to MapleStory combat, videos of kids trying their best to get banned from Club Penguin, and documenta-ries of various memorable "public" events in virtual worlds. Machinima is rapidly entering the mainstream. In recent years, machinima from World of Warcraft has been used to make an episode of *South Park* as well as a Toyota commercial. There is even an Academy of Machinima Arts and Sciences in New York that holds an annual awards festival.

Filming in a virtual world can pose some practical problems, how-ever. The *Washington Post* recently reported on the efforts of one group of filmmakers to make a video in World of Warcraft:

> There's no real way to rope off an area when they want to film a scene, so Taylor and his team have production assistants on patrol, logged on as powerful characters, whenever they're trying to film. If a mon-ster comes near, the PA's job is to kill it, if possible. If another War-craft player is about to stumble onto the set, that PA tries to steer him away, with bribes if necessary. The crew has paid out about 10,000 pieces of virtual gold in bribes so far. (Entrepreneurial Warcraft fans could sell that amount for around $500 in real-world currency.)[35]

The legal problem with machinima is that, like Spider-Man avatars and hobbits that play "Stairway to Heaven," it is legally suspect under copyright law. A video of a virtual world posted on YouTube is inevitably a reproduction and distribution of, at a minimum, the visual artwork and animation provided by the software of the virtual world. As the Defender case established, this is material protected by copyright law. Still, it may be legal to reproduce and distribute some forms of machinima because, for instance, noncommercial and creative transformation of virtual world content might be a fair use in the United States. However, depending on fair use is a case-by-case gamble, and if machinima is not fair use, it is likely copyright infringement.

Machinima is currently flourishing, however, primarily because the owners of the copyrights are not keen on suppressing it. Most virtual world owners see fan-created video as a way to build community around the virtual world. Subscribers who invest their creative effort in the game are more likely to continue subscribing and serve as viral advertisers of the game to a broader audience. Blizzard, for instance, currently states on its web page that it "strongly supports the efforts of its World of Warcraft community members who produce 'Machinima' movies . . . using video images, footage, music, sounds, speech, or other assets from its copyrighted products . . . subject to a few conditions."[36] The primary condition Blizzard places on machinima is that it must be noncommercial, but it also limits the use of its material for third-party promotional purposes and requires that machinima videos be consistent with World of Warcraft's "T" (teen appropriate) rating. Blizzard currently grants awards to quality machinima and hosts the videos on its own site, including one video titled "Associate Professor Evil Kills All Gold Farmers," in which the avatar of an undead mage attacks and destroys the gold farmers who are devastating the virtual economy and taking all the fantasy out of the game.

The growing acceptance of machinima videos proves that many forms of noncommercial user-generated material can effectively support, rather than challenge, the businesses of virtual world owners. The limitation of machinima to noncommercial uses, however, ensures that machinima creators will be primarily amateurs and hobbyists. By requiring that profit-seeking machinima artists negotiate for a copyright license, Blizzard effectively avoids situations like the MDY case, in which it must deal with legally savvy and commercially aggressive businesses that seek to profit from its virtual world.

SECOND LIFE AND COPYRIGHT

So far the story told about copyright is typical to most virtual worlds to-day.[37] Copyright law grants the owners of virtual worlds heightened power beyond the already substantial legal and technological power they enjoy. To the extent that users take on the role of author, virtual world owners can use contract, technology, and copyright to limit that power or to channel it in directions that are consistent with business objectives. But virtual world owners are free to pursue other strategies as well. The most unusual of these strategies is probably the model pursued by Second Life.[38]

Second Life faces many of the same problems as other worlds that feature user-generated content, though in the case of Second Life, such problems tend to be exacerbated, since the content within Second Life is almost exclusively generated by users. Players can upload such a tremendous variety of complex and dynamic content that, as explained in chapter 3, Second Life accurately describes itself as a virtual world "imagined and created entirely by its Residents."[39] While other virtual worlds allow users a certain level of creative input, Second Life originated as a nearly empty landscape that provided users with tools for sculpting and animating complex avatars, places, and objects.

Like other virtual worlds, Linden Lab requires that users grant it legal rights sufficient to use uploaded content in order to operate the Second Life platform as it desires. Linden Lab also requires, contractually, that users refrain from posting infringing content, and it complies with the DMCA "notice and takedown" requirements. However, Second Life's copyright situation differs from that of most other virtual worlds in an important way. As part of its effort to attract a community of creative users, Second Life allows users to economically exploit their creativity (including their copyrights) within Second Life. Perhaps just as important, it advertises to users that they retain their copyright and that they have the right and the ability to monetize their creativity.

Many Second Life users have obtained real money by creating and selling original objects, such as clothing, avatars, and buildings. However, only a select few can make a living by creating content in Second Life. One of the most successful entrepreneurs is the virtual sex mogul Kevin Alderman, known by the avatar name Stroker Serpentine. Alderman is the owner of Eros, LLC, a manufacturer of virtual objects that are designed to facilitate and improve the appearance of avatar sex. Among his creations is the Sex-Gen bed, in which Second Life avatars can assume a variety of carefully crafted positions. The virtual beds cost around twenty-five U.S. dollars (converted from Linden dollars). In various new reports, Alderman has stated that he is making "six figures" from his Second Life businesses.[40]

Alderman's business thrives on the fact that his beds in Second Life are simulated to be as hard to duplicate as real beds. Objects in Second Life can be programmed by their creators to behave in various ways, including a setting that prohibits duplication. For instance, a new object can be set to "no mod, no copy, no trans," a setting that generally prohibits basic users from modifying, copying, or transferring the virtual object. Just as Halasian Maulers in Everquest II are made valuable through artificial scarcity, so the user-controlled DRM of Second Life is designed to allow content creators to make their custom-crafted virtual objects artificially scarce and economically valuable.

However, just as Halasian Maulers can be duplicated by exploiting software flaws and just as the encryption of DVDs can be cracked by wily hackers, there are Second Life users who know how to circumvent the code that prohibits the copying of objects in Second Life. In 2007, Kevin Alderman found that someone had managed to duplicate his Sex-Gen beds and that exact copies of the beds were selling in various venues at a steep discount. So Alderman brought a lawsuit in federal court in Florida (his home state) alleging that unknown defendants were infringing his copyright in the Sex-Gen beds. With the aid of a subpoena sent to Linden Lab, Alderman tracked down and identified the infringer, and the lawsuit was quickly settled.[41]

Alderman's lawsuit demonstrates how users with real financial stakes in their copyrights may be inclined to turn to the law to protect their commercial interests. The problem for virtual world owners is that users who invest in lucrative content creation on their platforms will probably look to the virtual world owners for a remedy before they resort to the legal system. Platform owners who entice users with promises of virtual business but then fail to take an interest in the financial stakes of their community may find their users rebelling against them. This happened in Second Life in 2006, when a new piece of software shook the community of Second Life creators in much the same way that file-sharing software shook the music industry.[42] Copybot, a user-created program that interacted with Second Life, allowed users to disregard the DRM setting on objects like the Sex-Gen bed. Users of CopyBot could copy all objects in Second Life at will without the permission of creators. Second Life creators and entrepreneurs protested to Linden Lab about what they viewed as the failure of Second Life's DRM. Although Linden Lab eventually stated that the use of Copy-Bot constituted a violation of its terms of service, users complained that Linden Lab had a duty to actually prevent the use of CopyBot. Essentially, those protesting the harms created by CopyBot seemed to want Linden Lab to take the same aggressive stance toward CopyBot that Blizzard took with regard to the Glider program.

In September 2009, Kevin Alderman and a co-plaintiff refashioned these broad complaints about Second Life's failure to protect user-generated intellectual property as a class action lawsuit on behalf of Second Life creators.[43] Just as Marvel had accused NCsoft of designing a technology that led to contributory and vicarious infringement of its intellectual property rights, so Alderman accused Linden Lab of failing to adequately protect the rights of the creative community in Second Life. While the legal merits of Alderman's lawsuit are debatable, it demonstrates the risks inherent in the Second Life business model. First Marc Bragg sued Second Life based on its promotion of economic investments in the ownership of virtual land, and now Kevin Alderman has brought suit against Second Life based on its promotion of economic investments in the creation of original content.

There is an unfortunate lesson to be learned here, and it may not bode well for the future of richly imagined user-generated worlds. When virtual worlds empower users with a wide range of creative freedom and encourage them to take economic ownership in their productions, those worlds are more likely to attract lawsuits from all directions. Large scale financial stakes and uncertain rules are a dangerous mixture. It may be that the majority of successful virtual worlds will not follow the Second Life model, limiting the scope of creative contributions from users so as to avoid legal headaches.

Copyright in virtual worlds has two faces. With respect to the creativity of the virtual world owners, copyright law adds additional power to the already substantial control enjoyed via contract, property, and technology. Virtual worlds are often rich and complex artistic creations, so their protection under the aegis of copyright is certainly deserved. In the case of the user, however, copyright law is more often perceived as a source of risk that needs to be defused and harnessed in ways that serve the interests of those who are monetizing the platforms. Like peasants tilling fields around a medieval castle, users will lend their copyright labor and creativity in ways that build the value of the virtual world platform, often paying for the privilege to do so.[44]

conclusion

Our inventions are wont to be pretty toys, which distract our attention from serious things. They are but improved means to an unimproved end, an end which it was already but too easy to arrive at.

—Henry David Thoreau

The legal issues I have addressed in this book will not go away or be resolved conclusively anytime soon. In fact, chances are that they will become more vexing and complicated as virtual worlds become more popular. Legal struggles over property, crime, contract, and intellectual property will become increasingly frequent. Other legal issues mentioned only briefly in previous chapters, such as free speech, trademark, and privacy rights, will surely spur new lawsuits, new controversies, and new twists in legal doctrine.

As I suggested in the introduction, the most remarkable thing about the application of law to virtual worlds today is the incredible degree of control and autonomy that the law grants to virtual world owners. Virtual world owners are essentially the sovereign lords of their fantastic jurisdictions, with almost complete autonomy over the forms of value created through the use of their platforms. Admittedly, Disney must still entice consumers to its new virtual kingdoms, but there seem to be few problems presented on that front. Hordes of people, and especially younger people, seem to be flocking to this new electronic frontier.

What those visiting virtual worlds will find, legally, is something that resembles a new feudal order, with a separate and different set of rules governing their rights and duties. Virtual sovereigns are minting their own currencies, crafting and drawing wealth from their own societies, fine-tuning their own economies, and casting out those who dare to flaunt their decrees. All of this suggests that virtual worlds are becoming, in essence, separate jurisdictions governed by separate rules. As a matter of legal doctrine, these rules may not qualify as "laws," given that no territorial government has recognized the formal sovereignty of virtual worlds. But as a matter of effective legal practice, the doctrines of contract, property, hacking, and intellectual property all serve to greatly empower those who own and administer virtual worlds, effectively insulating their actions from legal review.

The ultimate question is: What should we make of this trend?

In the recent past, our world had a significantly greater diversity of social structures, rules, and rights. To the extent that virtual worlds today support freely created alternative societies, bound by separate rules, they may hold out the hope of restoring that sort of diversity of frontiers. There may be some attractions associated with a new and decentralized virtual order.[1] Many users of virtual worlds seem to be drawn to them because they offer escape into a fantastic and alternative existence. The creative tyranny of virtual world owners may be exactly what permits users to escape, if they wish to, into a sphere separate from ordinary life and ordinary law.

Courts and legislatures around the world will need to decide whether the law can tolerate such forms of escape.[2] If we do not change the law, virtual worlds will likely grow into increasingly profitable, entertaining, and social realms dominated and policed by powerful corporate wizards employing an array of legal and technological tools designed to attract and monetize social relations within virtual communities. Legal servitude to online overlords may seem counter to what the law would seek, yet the law today largely helps, rather than hinders, the construction and maintenance of the new domains being built within virtual castle walls.

Ideally, I think, the law might aspire to find more democratic and participatory structures arising on this new virtual frontier. Yet how far can democracy extend to technologically mediated sites of fantastic escape? Users of virtual worlds today seek primarily to be transported and entertained, not to elect representatives and listen to virtual campaign speeches. The hard work of democratic governance seems to be at odds with the nature of the experience these worlds provide.

Indeed, it may be that the slippage of virtual worlds from traditional legal expectations reflects something fundamental about their nature and their appeal. Perhaps the effort I have made here to clarify the popular stakes in virtual law is ultimately an effort to change the nature of virtual worlds. Perhaps what makes virtual worlds so appealing is the inherent ambiguity present in the virtual realm, where things can be and not be all at once. If we could clearly see and weigh the risks and rewards present in virtual worlds, clarifying the legal status of our interests in them, it might be that we would limit, for better or for worse, the sorts of pleasure they currently provide.[3]

NOTES

INTRODUCTION

1. Lise E. Hull, Britain's Medieval Castles 98 (Praeger 2006). I should note that my adoption of a feudal law analogy to begin this book was inspired by the work of others who have used the analogy to describe similar shifts in law. See Alfred C. Yen, Western Frontier or Feudal Society? Metaphors and Perceptions of Cyberspace, 17 Berkeley Tech. L.J. 1207 (2002); James Grimmelmann, Virtual World Feudalism, 118 Yale L.J. Pocket Part 126 (2009); Peter Drahos and John Braithwaite, Information Feudalism (The New Press 2002).
2. Robert Liddiard, Anglo-Norman Castles 40 (Boydell Press 2003); M. W. Thompson, The Rise of the Castle 33 (Cambridge 2008).
3. Thompson, Rise of the Castle 9.
4. Hunt Janin, Medieval Justice: Cases and Laws in France, England, and Germany: 500–1500, 46–48 (McFarland 2004); Robert Cowley & Geoffrey Parker, The Reader's Companion to Military History 71–73 (Houghton Mifflin Harcourt 2001).
5. Georges Duby & Cynthia Postan, The Chivalrous Society 42 (University of California Press 1981).
6. Thompson, Rise of the Castle 163.
7. Max Weber, The Vocation Lectures 38 (eds. David Owen & Tracy B. Strong, trans. Rodney Livingstone, Hackett 2004).
8. Susan Reynolds, Fiefs and Vassals: The Medieval Evidence Reinterpreted (Oxford 1994) (offering a critique of the concept of feudalism).
9. A. W. B. Simpson, A History of the Land Law 47–102 (Oxford 2d ed. 1986).
10. Id.
11. Id.
12. Oliver Wendell Holmes, The Path of the Law, in Pragmatism: A Reader 145, 154 (ed. Louis Menand, Vintage Press 1997); Jesse Dukeminier et al., Property 173 (Aspen 6th ed. 2006).
13. Richard E. Foglesong, Married to the Mouse: Walt Disney World and Orlando 6 (Yale University Press 2003).
14. Steve Rajtar, A Guide to Historic Orlando 85 (History Press 2006).
15. See Cinderella Castle, available at: http://disneyworld.disney.go.com/parks/magic-kingdom/attractions/cinderella-castle/ (last visited June 2009).
16. Foglesong, Married to the Mouse 75–77.
17. Id. at 89–93.
18. Id. at 70–71.
19. Id. at 103. Disney's planned community of Celebration, built within the Disney-controlled region and modeled on the original goals of Epcot, came later.
20. Id. at 3, 100–200.

21. For some visitors, entering Disney World may be even more significant: anthropologist Conrad Phillip Kottak has suggested that visits to the Magic Kingdom have some of the same structural features as pilgrimages to religious shrines. Conrad Phillip Kottak, Anthropological Analysis of Mass Enculturation, in Researching American Culture: A Guide for Student Anthropologists 55–65 (University of Michigan Press 4th ed. 1982).

22. See Ultima Online, available at: http://www.uo.com/ (last visited June 2009).

23. Julian Dibbell, Play Money (Basic Books 2006); Brad King & John Borland, Dungeons and Dreamers 148–169 (McGraw-Hill 2003).

CHAPTER 1: LAW

1. Victor Keegan, Virtual Worlds Take Over the Online World, The Guardian, July 10, 2008, Technology at 4; Gordon Pitts, Time to Embrace Your Avatar, The Globe and Mail, June 2, 2008, at B11; Edward Castronova, Exodus to the Virtual World: How Online Fun Is Changing Reality 18–19 (Palgrave Macmillan 2007).

2. See Richard Bartle, Designing Virtual Worlds 102–104 (New Riders Game 2003) (discussing "mobs").

3. Bruce Damer, Avatars: Exploring and Building Virtual Worlds on the Internet 400–406 (Peachpit Press 1997).

4. Amanda Lenhart, Sydney Jones, & Alexandra Macgill, Adults and Video Games, Pew Internet and American Life Project, December 7, 2008, available at: http://www.pewinternet.org/Reports/2008/Adults-and-Video-Games.aspx (last visited June 2009). The Pew report makes a distinction between game-like virtual worlds and nongame virtual worlds, suggesting that the latter are less popular.

5. See, e.g., more than ten thousand Harry Potter stories available at http://www .fanfiction.net/book/Harry_Potter/ (last visited June 2009).

6. As Ted Castronova has explained, this is the primary difference between virtual worlds and earlier notions about virtual reality. Edward Castronova, Synthetic Worlds: The Business and Culture of Online Games 287–294 (University of Chicago Press 2005).

7. Books include: Wagner J. Au, The Making of Second Life: Notes from the New World (Collins Business 2008); Bartle, Designing Virtual Worlds; Tom Boellstorff, Coming of Age in Second Life: An Anthropologist Explores the Virtually Human 94–95 (Princeton University Press 2008); Castronova, Exodus; Castronova, Synthetic Worlds; Lynn Cherny, Conversation and Community: Chat in a Virtual World (Center for the Study of Language and Information 1999); Damer, Avatars; Julian Dibbell, My Tiny Life: Crime and Passion in a Virtual World (Henry Holt 1998); Julian Dibbell, Play Money (Basic Books 2006); Benjamin Duranske, Virtual Law: Navigating the Legal Landscape of Virtual Worlds (American Bar Association 2008); Peter Ludlow & Mark Wallace, The Second Life Herald: The Virtual Tabloid That Witnessed the Dawn of the Metaverse (MIT Press 2007); Thomas M. Malaby, Making Virtual Worlds: Linden Lab and Second Life (Cornell University Press 2009); Howard Rheingold, The Virtual Community: Homesteading on the Electronic Frontier (MIT Press

2000); T. L. Taylor, Play Between Worlds: Exploring Online Game Culture 9–11 (MIT Press 2006).

Collected essays about virtual worlds can be found in: Hilde G. Corneliussen & Jill W. Rettberg, eds., Digital Culture, Play, and Identity: A *World of Warcraft* Reader (MIT Press 2008); Ralph Schroeder & Ann-Sofie Axelsson, eds., Avatars at Work and Play: Collaboration and Interaction in Shared Virtual Environments (Springer 2006); Ralph Schroeder, ed., The Social Life of Avatars (Springer 2002).

8. Sherry Turkle, Life on the Screen: Identity in the Age of the Internet 185–190 (Simon & Schuster 1997).

9. Daniel C. Miller, Note: Determining Ownership in Virtual Worlds: Copyright and License Agreements, 22 Rev. Litig. 435 (2003).

10. Many books today offer extended investigations of Second Life. See, e.g., Au, Making of Second Life; Boellstorff, Coming of Age; Ludlow & Wallace, Second Life Herald; Malaby, Making Virtual Worlds.

11. Taylor, Play Between Worlds 9–11.

12. For a description of the economy of Ultima Online, see Dibbell, Play Money. For broader accounts of virtual economies, see Castronova, Synthetic Worlds; Castronova, Exodus 137–158.

13. Tuukka Lehtiniemi, How Big Is the RMT Market Anyway? Virtual Economy Research Network, available at: http://www.virtual-economy.org/blog/how_big_is_the_rmt_market_anyw (last visited June 2009); Julian Dibbell, The Kingpin of Azeroth, Wired, December 2008, at 180; Richard Heeks, Current Analysis and Future Research Agenda on "Gold Farming": Real-World Production in Developing Countries for the Virtual Economies of Online Games, in Development Informatics working paper, no. 32 (Institute for Development Policy and Management, University of Manchester 2008), at 453–469.

14. The first legal books about the intersection of law and virtual worlds were Jack Balkin & Beth Noveck, eds., The State of Play: Law, Games and Virtual Worlds (New York University Press 2006) and Duranske, Virtual Law. More than two hundred law review articles and student notes have been written on the topic. An important early article was Jennifer L. Mnookin, Virtual(ly) Law: The Emergence of Law in LambdaMOO, reprinted in Crypto Anarchy, Cyberstates, and Pirate Utopias 245 (ed. Peter Ludlow, MIT Press 2001).

15. I do not explicitly address the virtual tax question here, but there is already abundant—and conflicting—literature on the topic. See Bryan Camp, The Play's the Thing: A Theory of Taxing Virtual Worlds, 59 Hastings L.J. 1 (2007); Leandra Lederman, Stranger Than Fiction: Taxing Virtual Worlds, 82 N.Y.U. L. Rev. 1620 (2007); Scott Wisniewski, Taxation of Virtual Assets, 2008 Duke L. & Tech. Rev. 5 (2008).

16. Brad King & John Borland, Dungeons and Dreamers 158–162 (McGraw-Hill 2003).

17. Id. at 161–162.

18. See Ultima Online Harrassment Policy, available at: http://support.uo.com/harass.html (last visited June 2009).

19. Eric Goldman, Speech Showdowns at the Virtual Corral, 21 Santa Clara Comp. & High Tech. L.J. 845 (2005). For additional investigations of free speech rights

in virtual worlds, see Peter S. Jenkins, The Virtual World as a Company Town—Freedom of Speech in Massively Multiple Online Role Playing Games, 8 J. Internet L. (2004); Jason S. Zack, The Ultimate Company Town: Wading in the Digital Marsh of Second Life, 10 U. Pa. J. Const. L. 225 (2007).

20. Farhad Manjoo, Raking Muck in "The Sims Online," Salon.com, available at: http://www.salon.com/tech/feature/2003/12/12/sims_online_newspaper/print .html (last visited June 2009).

21. Amy Harmon, A Real-Life Debate on Free Expression in a Cyberspace City, New York Times, January 15, 2004.

22. Id.

23. Ludlow's career as a virtual muckraker is described in Ludlow & Wallace, Second Life Herald.

24. Boellstorff, Coming of Age 94–95.

25. Au, Making of Second Life; Daniel Terdiman, The Entrepreneur's Guide to Second Life: Making Money in the Metaverse (Sybex 2007).

26. Terdiman, Entrepreneur's Guide; Au, Making of Second Life 141–181; Boellstorff, Coming of Age 205–236; Malaby, Making Virtual Worlds.

27. Terdiman, Entrepreneur's Guide 8–9.

28. Second Life, Economic Statistics, available at: http://secondlife.com/statistics/ economy-data.php (last visited June 2009).

29. Terdiman, Entrepreneur's Guide 106.

30. Press Release: Coldwell Banker° Entrance into Second Life° Makes Virtual Home-ownership Easier for Millions of Residents, available at: http://www.coldwell bankerpreviews.com/servlet/ResourceGuide?action=showArticle&article Id=53889 (last visited June 2009).

31. Greg Lastowka, Coldwell Banker Selling Homes in Second Life, Terra Nova, available at: http://terranova.blogs.com/terra_nova/2007/03/coldwellbanker_ .html (last visited June 2009).

32. Autumn Gray, First Life Second Life, Albuquerque Journal, August 26, 2007, at A1.

33. Sam Ali & Charlie Young, Guiding Coldwell Banker into Virtual Realty, Newark Star-Ledger, August 3, 2007.

34. Id.

35. *Bragg v. Linden Research*, 487 F. Supp. 2d 593 (E.D. Pa. 2007).

36. Marc Bragg, Virtual Land Dispute Spills Over into Real World, available at: http://www.chescolawyers.com/bragg.pdf (last visited June 2009).

37. Ejected Online Game Player Claims Virtual Real Estate Was Wrongly Confiscated, 11 BNA Electronic Commerce Report 22, May 31, 2006, available at: http:// ipcenter.bna.com/ (last visited June 2009).

38. The current Second Life terms of service are posted online at: http://secondlife .com/corporate/tos.php (last visited June 2009). They have been revised subsequent to the *Bragg* lawsuit.

39. Yannis Bakos, Florencia Marotta-Wurgler, & David R. Trossen, Does Anyone Read the Fine Print? Testing a Law and Economics Approach to Standard Form Contracts (October 6, 2009), available at: http://ssrn.com/abstract=1443256 (last visited November 2009).

40. *Bragg v. Linden Research*, 487 F. Supp. 2d 593 (E.D. Pa. 2007).

41. Robert Hassan, The Information Society 17 (Polity 2008); Ung-gi Yoon, A Quest for the Legal Identity of MMORPGs—From a Computer Game, Back to a Play Association, Journal of Game Industry & Culture (June 5, 2006), available at: http://ssrn.com/abstract=905748 (last visited June 2009).

42. Numerous papers carried brief accounts of the story. See Ansa English Media Service, China: Online Player Kills Opponent Over Cyber Sword, June 8, 2005; Sam Leith, A fantasy world might be man-made, but it's perfectly real to those who live in it, The Daily Telegraph (London), June 18, 2005.

43. John Brewer, When a Virtual Crook Struck This Gamer, He Called Real Cops, St. Paul Pioneer Press, January 31, 2008.

44. Susan W. Brenner, Fantasy Crime: The Role of Criminal Law in Virtual Worlds, 11 Vand. J. Ent. & Tech. L. 1, 58 (2008).

45. Michelle Levander, Where Does Fantasy End? Time.com, June 4, 2001, available at: http://www.time.com/time/interactive/entertainment/gangs_np.html (last visited June 2009).

46. Richard Heeks, Understanding "Gold Farming": Developing-Country Production for Virtual Gameworlds, 5 Information Technologies & International Development, no. 3 (2009), available at: http://itidjournal.org/itid/article/view/383/179 (last visited June 2009).

47. Julian Dibbell, The Life of a Chinese Gold Farmer, New York Times, June 17, 2007, at Sec. 6, p. 36.

48. David Barboza, Ogre to Slay? Outsource It to Chinese, New York Times, December 9, 2005, at A1; Dibbell, Chinese Gold Farmer; Jon Burstein, Video Game Fan Asks Court to Ban Real Sloth and Greed from World of Warcraft, South Florida Sun-Sentinel, Thursday, April 10, 2008; BBC News, Poor Earning Virtual Gaming Gold, August 22, 2008, available at: http://news.bbc.co.uk/go/pr/fr/-/2/hi/technology/7575902.stm (last visited June 2009); Dibbell, Kingpin; Heeks, Understanding "Gold Farming."

49. Barboza, Ogre to Slay.

50. Dibbell, Chinese Gold Farmer.

51. Dibbell, Kingpin.

52. Id.

53. Heeks, Current Analysis; Heeks, Understanding "Gold Farming."

54. Lehtiniemi, How Big; Dibbell, Kingpin.

55. BBC News, Poor Earning.

56. Dibbell, Chinese Gold Farmer.

57. Id.

58. Dmitri Williams, The Video Game Lightning Rod, 6 Information, Communication & Society, no. 4 (2003).

59. Dmitri Williams, Nick Yee, & Scott E. Caplan, Who Plays, How Much, and Why? Debunking the Stereotypical Gamer Profile, 13 Journal of Computer-Mediated Communication (September 2008); Amanda Lenhart et al., Teens, Video Games and Civics, Pew Internet & American Life Project, September 16, 2008, available at: http://www.pewinternet.org/Reports/2008/Teens-Video-Games-and-Civics.aspx (last visited June 2009); Amanda Lenhart, Sydney Jones, & Alexandra

Macgill, Adults and Video Games, Pew Internet and American Life Project, December 7, 2008, available at: http://www.pewinternet.org/Reports/2008/Adults-and-Video-Games.aspx (last visited June 2009).

60. Williams et al., Who Plays.

61. Mia Consalvo, Cheating: Gaining Advantage in Video Games 3 (MIT Press 2007).

62. Dmitri Williams, Groups and Goblins: The Social and Civic Impact of Online Gaming, 50 Journal of Broadcasting and Electronic Media 651–670 (2006).

CHAPTER 2: HISTORY

1. Sherry Turkle, Life on the Screen: Identity in the Age of the Internet 210–232 (Simon & Schuster 1997).

2. Julian Dibbell, My Tiny Life: Crime and Passion in a Virtual World 195–228 (Henry Holt 1998).

3. Simon de Bruxelles, Second Life Affair Leads to Real-Life Divorce for David Pollard, aka Dave Barmy, The Times, November 14, 2008, available at: http://women.timesonline.co.uk/tol/life_and_style/women/relationships/article 5151126.ece (last visited June 2009); Divorced from Reality, The Sunday Independent, November 23, 2008; Jill Insley, Cyber Affairs Cited in Breakdown of Real Marriages, Guardian Unlimited, May 27, 2009.

4. Matthew Acton, I Caught My Hubby Virtually At It with a Man, News of the World, February 8, 2009, available at: http://www.newsoftheworld.co.uk/news/168122/Lisa-Best-caught-husband-John-having-virtual-sex-with-a-man-while-in-bed-with-her.html (last visited June 2009).

5. Many virtual world histories exist. See, e.g., Richard Bartle, Designing Virtual Worlds 1–35 (New Riders Game 2003); Tom Boellstorff, Coming of Age in Second Life: An Anthropologist Explores the Virtually Human 32–59 (Princeton University Press 2008); Bruce Damer, Avatars: Exploring and Building Virtual Worlds on the Internet xiv–xxii (Peachpit Press 1997); Bruce Damer, Virtual Worlds Timeline, available at: http://www.vwtimeline.org/ (last visited June 2009); Dibbell, My Tiny Life 51–63; T. L. Taylor, Play Between Worlds: Exploring Online Game Culture 21–28 (MIT Press 2006).

6. See, e.g., Bartle, Designing Virtual Worlds 3–4; Edward Castronova, Synthetic Worlds: The Business and Culture of Online Games 4–5 (University of Chicago Press 2005); Mark Bell, Toward a Definition of "Virtual Worlds," 1 Journal of Virtual Worlds Research, no. 1 (2008), available at: http://journals.tdl.org/jvwr/article/view/283/237 (last visited June 2009) ("A synchronous, persistent network of people, represented as avatars, facilitated by networked computers").

7. Elizabeth Mansfield, Too Beautiful to Picture 26–27 (University of Minnesota Press 2007).

8. Plato, Republic, Book 7, 208–211 (trans. C. D. C. Reeve, Hackett 2004); Boellstorff, Coming of Age 33–34.

9. See, e.g., McKenzie Wark, Gamer Theory 001–025 (Harvard University Press 2007).

10. The short story is reprinted in Jorge Luis Borges, Labyrinths (New Directions 1964).

11. Boellstorff, Coming of Age 37.
12. Thomas M. Disch, The Dreams Our Stuff Is Made Of (Simon and Schuster 2000).
13. Ray Bradbury, The Illustrated Man (Bantam Books 1952).
14. See, e.g., Daniel F. Galouye, Simulacron 3 (Bantam 1964) (depicting a simulated society inside a computer).
15. Vernor Vinge, True Names (Baen 1987). Vinge describes the history of the publication in Vernor Vinge, True Names and the Opening of the Cyberspace Frontier (ed. James Frenkel, Tor 2001).
16. William Gibson, Neuromancer (Ace Books 1984).
17. Neal Stephenson, Snow Crash (Bantam Books 1992).
18. Janet H. Murray, Hamlet on the Holodeck: The Future of Narrative in Cyberspace (Free Press 1997).
19. Thomas Richards, The Meaning of Star Trek 109 (Main Street Books 1997).
20. Michael Heim, Virtual Realism 99 (Oxford University Press 1998).
21. Castronova, Synthetic Worlds 285–294.
22. David Myers, The Nature of Computer Games (Peter Lang 2003).
23. Dibbell, My Tiny Life 52.
24. Peter P. Perla, The Art of Wargaming 17–34 (Naval Institute Press 1990).
25. Greg Lastowka, A Brief History of Wargames, December 3, 1999, available at: http://faculty.virginia.edu/setear/students/wargames/home.htm (last visited June 2009).
26. Perla, Wargaming 34–39.
27. Bill Slavicsek and Richard Baker, Dungeons & Dragons for Dummies 10 (Wiley Publishing 2005); Nick Monfort, Twisty Little Passages: An Approach to Interactive Fiction 74–76 (MIT Press 2005).
28. Espen Aarseth, Cybertext: Perspectives on Ergodic Literature 98 (John Hopkins University Press 1997).
29. Steve L. Kent, The Ultimate History of Video Games 21–26 (Prima 2001).
30. Kent, Ultimate History 16–21; Steven Levy, Hackers: Heroes of the Computer Revolution 56–66 (Penguin 2001).
31. D. J. Edwards & J. M. Graetz, PDP-1 Plays at Spacewar, 1 Decuscope 2 (April 1962), available at: http://www.wheels.org/spacewar/decuscope.html (last visited June 2009). For a discussion of the history of Spacewar, as well as its semiotic structure, see Myers, Computer Games 3–7.
32. Kent, Ultimate History 28–35.
33. Id. at 38–48.
34. Montfort, Twisty Little Passages 85–93.
35. Howard Rheingold, The Virtual Community: Homesteading on the Electronic Frontier 111 (MIT Press 2000); Bartle, Designing Virtual Worlds 17–18.
36. Bartle, Designing Virtual Worlds 4–7.
37. Turkle, Life on the Screen 177–254.
38. Bartle, Designing Virtual Worlds 47.
39. Lynn Cherny, Conversation and Community: Chat in a Virtual World 33–41 (Center for the Study of Language and Information 1999).
40. Bartle, Designing Virtual Worlds 9–10.

41. The most well-known account is Dibbell, My Tiny Life.
42. Cherny, Conversation and Community.
43. Kent, Ultimate History 186–189; Boellstorff, Coming of Age 48–49.
44. Benj Edwards, Woz Was Here—Steve Wozniak on His Gaming Past, Gamasutra, May 4, 2007, available at: http://www.gamasutra.com/features/20070504/edwards_03.shtml
45. Levy, Hackers 141.
46. Brenda Laurel, Computers as Theatre 3 (Addison-Wesley Professional 1993); Montfort, Twisty Little Passages 92.
47. Laurel, Computers as Theatre.
48. Turkle, Life on the Screen 34–43.
49. Bartle, Designing Virtual Worlds 18–19.
50. See Chip Morningstar & F. Randall Farmer, The Lessons of Lucasfilm's Habitat, available at: http://www.fudco.com/chip/lessons.html (last visited June 2009); Taylor, Play Between Worlds 24–25.
51. Morningstar & Farmer, Lessons.
52. Bartle, Designing Virtual Worlds 24–26.
53. For more information, see Ralph Schroeder, ed., The Social Life of Avatars (Springer 2002); Ralph Schroeder & Ann-Sofie Axelsson, eds., Avatars at Work and Play: Collaboration and Interaction in Shared Virtual Environments (Springer 2006).
54. Boellstorff, Coming of Age 128–131; Thomas M. Malaby, Making Virtual Worlds: Linden Lab and Second Life 17–20 (Cornell University Press 2009).
55. William J. Mitchell, City of Bits: Space, Place, and the Infobahn 118 (MIT Press 1996).
56. Rheingold, Virtual Community 169–172.
57. Nick Yee, The Daedalus Gateway: Gender-Bending, available at: http://www.nickyee.com/daedalus/gateway_genderbend.html (last visited June 2009).
58. See, e.g, comment of "Female Gamer" in PlayOn, On the Internet Everyone Knows You're Not Actually an Elf, September 13, 2006, available at: http://playon.parc.com/playon/archives/2006/09/lisa_nakamura_h.html (last visited June 2009).
59. Taylor, Play Between Worlds 93–124.
60. Edward Castronova, The Price of Bodies: A Hedonic Pricing Model of Avatar Attributes in a Synthetic World, 57 Kyklos 173 (2004).
61. Turkle, Life on the Screen.
62. For a range of stories about fluid avatar appearance, see, e.g., Wagner J. Au, The Making of Second Life: Notes from the New World 75–101 (Collins Business 2008); Boellstorff, Coming of Age 160–178; Dibbell, My Tiny Life 125–151; Rheingold, Virtual Community 169–172; Turkle, Life on the Screen 210–232. For an examination of the implications of this sort of fluid appearance for the law of defamation, see Bettina M. Chin, Regulating Your Second Life: Defamation in Virtual Worlds, 72 Brook. L. Rev. 1303 (2007).
63. Au, Making of Second Life 72–74; Tanner Higgin, Blackless Fantasy: The Disappearance of Race in Massively Multiplayer Online Role-Playing Games, 4 Game Studies 3–26 (2009); Jerry Kang, Cyber-race, 113 Harv. L. Rev. 1130

(2000); Lisa Nakamura, Digitizing Race: Visual Cultures of the Internet (University of Minnesota Press 2007).

CHAPTER 3: LANDSCAPE

1. Dal Yong Jin & Florence Chee, Age of New Media Empires: A Critical Interpretation of the Korean Online Game Industry, 3 Games & Culture 38–58 (2008).
2. Id.; Toh Mei Ling, Special Focus: Riding on Social Networking, The Edge Malaysia, May 21, 2007.
3. Mia Consalvo, Cheating: Gaining Advantage in Video Games 150 (MIT Press 2007).
4. Greg Howson, Home on PS3 Has 7 Million Users, Guardian Unlimited, June 26, 2009.
5. Chip Morningstar & F. Randall Farmer, The Lessons of Lucasfilm's Habitat, available at: http://www.fudco.com/chip/lessons.html (last visited June 2009).
6. See, e.g., Hilde G. Corneliussen & Jill W. Rettberg, eds., Digital Culture, Play, and Identity: A *World of Warcraft* Reader (MIT Press 2008).
7. Douglas Quenqua, To Harvest Squash, Click Here, New York Times, October 29, 2009, at E6.
8. Wagner James Au, Will Parents Pay $72 a Year for Virtual Barbies? Gigaom, June 8, 2008, available at: http://gigaom.com/2008/06/08/will-parents-pay-72-a-year-for-virtual-barbies/ (last visited June 2009); Toy Makers Expanding Online, Cutting Product Selection, Consumer Electronics Daily, February 19, 2009.
9. Jason Luciw, Welcome to Magic Kingdom North, Kelowna Capital News, June 21, 2009.
10. Evan Hessel and Peter C. Beller, Multiplayer Gaming Gold Mine, Forbes, July 13, 2009, at 86.
11. David McNeill, Woman Faces Jail for Hacking Her Virtual Husband to Death, Irish Times, October 25, 2008.
12. Victor Keegan, Virtual Worlds Are Getting a Second Life, Guardian Online, July 29, 2009, available at: http://www.guardian.co.uk/technology/2009/jul/29/virtual-worlds (last visited June 2009); Habbo Hotel—Where Else? available at: http://www.sulake.com/habbo (last visited June 2009).
13. See Vili Lehdonvirta, Virtual Consumption (PhD thesis, Turku School of Economics, 2009), available at: http://info.tse.fi/julkaisut/vk/Ae11_2009.pdf (last visited June 2009); Tameka Kee, Habbo Sold $60 Million in Virtual Goods in 2008, PaidContent.org, March 31, 2009, available at: http://paidcontent.org/article/419-habbos-virtual-goods-boom-worth-almost-60-million-in-2008/ (last visited June 2009).
14. See Greg Lastowka, Habbo Spending Cap, Terra Nova, September 5, 2008, available at: http://terranova.blogs.com/terra_nova/2008/09/habbo-spending.html (last visited June 2009).
15. Benjamin Duranske, Virtual Law: Navigating the Legal Landscape of Virtual Worlds 108 (American Bar Association 2008).
16. Live Gamer, True Games Interactive Signs Live Gamer as Exclusive Secondary Trading Partner, May 12, 2008, available at: http://www.livegamer.com/page_en/news.php?section=1&page=206 (last visited June 2009).

17. Richard A. Bartle, Hearts, Clubs, Diamonds, Spades: Players Who Suit MUDs, April 1996, available at: http://www.mud.co.uk/richard/hcds.htm (last visited June 2009).

18. For example, see Richard Bartle's comments in Timothy Burke, The Hidden Bartle Type, October 10, 2007, available at: http://terranova.blogs.com/terra_nova/2007/10/the-hidden-bart.html (last visited June 2009).

19. Greg Lastowka, Veblenesque Dorodango? Terra Nova, August 4, 2006, available at: http://terranova.blogs.com/terra_nova/2006/08/veblenesque_dor.html (last visited June 2009).

20. Thomas M. Malaby, Making Virtual Worlds: Linden Lab and Second Life 34–41 (Cornell University Press 2009); Tom Boellstorff, Coming of Age in Second Life: An Anthropologist Explores the Virtually Human 205–211 (Princeton University Press 2008).

21. Cory Ondrejka, Second Life: Collapsing Geography, 2 Innovations 27, 35 (2007).

22. Sean Percival, Second Life In-World Travel Guide (Que Publishing 2008).

23. BarbieGirls.com FAQs, http://www.barbiegirls.com/legal/faqs_text.html (last visited June 2009).

24. I have found the work of game studies researcher Sarah Grimes extremely helpful in understanding the landscape of virtual worlds targeted at children. See Sarah M. Grimes, Saturday Morning Cartoons Go MMOG, 126 Media International Australia 120–131 (2008); Sarah M. Grimes, Kids' Ad Play: Regulating Children's Advergames in the Converging Media Context, 8 International Journal of Communications Law and Policy 162–178 (2008).

25. Restatement (Second) of Contracts §12, 14 (American Law Institute 1982).

26. See, e.g., Children's Online Privacy Protection Act of 1998, 15 U.S.C. 6501–6506 (2000).

27. Virtual worlds designed for children raise a range of separate legal issues which deserve independent analysis. For some further thoughts on these issues, see David Naylor & Andrew Jaworski, Virtual Worlds: Children and Virtual Worlds, 10 Ecomm. L. & Pol'y (2008); Joshua A. T. Fairfield, Virtual Parentalism, 66 Wash. & Lee L. Rev. 1215 (2009).

CHAPTER 4: REGULATION

1. Lawrence Lessig, Free Culture 2–4 (Penguin 2004). For a fascinating historical account of aerial trespass, see Stuard Banner, Who Owns the Sky? The Struggle to Control Airspace from the Wright Brothers On (Harvard University Press 2008).

2. SMU Law Review Association, Journal of Air Law & Commerce Overview, available at: http://smu.edu/lra/Journals/JALC/Overview.asp (last visited June 2009).

3. Fred Howard, Wilbur and Orville: A Biography of the Wright Brothers 327 (Courier Dover Publications 1998).

4. Herbert A. Johnson, Wingless Eagle: U.S. Army Aviation through World War I 29 (UNC Press 2001).

5. Benjamin Cardozo, The Nature of the Judicial Process 61 (Yale University Press 1921).

6. Air Commerce Act of 1926, Pub. L. No. 69–254, 44 Stat. 568 (1926).

7. *United States v. Causby*, 328 U.S. 256 (1946); Lessig, Free Culture 1–3.
8. Lessig, Free Culture 2–4.
9. John Edward Cribbet, Concepts in Transition: The Search for a New Definition of Property, 1986 U. Ill. L. Rev. 1.
10. Julian Dibbell, A Taxpayer May Wonder, Terra Nova, January 24, 2009, available at: http://terranova.blogs.com/terra_nova/2009/01/index.html (last visited June 2009); Benjamin Duranske, Virtual Law: Navigating the Legal Landscape of Virtual Worlds 225–240 (American Bar Association 2008).
11. Greg Lastowka, Chinese Fatigue Regulations, Terra Nova, August 24, 2005, available at: http://terranova.blogs.com/terra_nova/2005/08/chinese_fatigue.html (last visited June 2009).
12. See Ung-gi Yoon, Real Money Trading in MMORPG Items from a Legal and Policy Perspective, December 13, 2004, available at: http://ssrn.com/abstract=1113327 (last visited June 2009).
13. Katie Hafner & Matthew Lyons, Where Wizards Stay Up Late: The Origins of the Internet (Simon and Schuster 2000).
14. Brian Winston, Media Technology and Society. A History: From the Telegraph to the Internet 166–167 (Routledge 1998).
15. Hafner & Lyon, Wizards.
16. David G. Post, In Search of Jefferson's Moose 31–32 (Oxford University Press 2009).
17. 18 U.S.C. § 1030 (2009).
18. 15 U.S.C. § 7701 (2009).
19. 47 U.S.C. § 231 (2009); 18 U.S.C. § 2510 (2009).
20. 15 U.S.C. § 1125(c) (2009).
21. 17 U.S.C. § 512 (2009).
22. 47 U.S.C. § 230 (2009).
23. 15 U.S.C. § 7001 (2009).
24. Duranske, Virtual Law 14; Michael L. Rustad, Internet Law in a Nutshell (West 2009). Rustad's nutshell summary of Internet law folds Second Life into the history of cyberlaw generally.

CHAPTER 5: JURISDICTION

1. See, e.g., Foreword, In the Twilight of the Nation-State: Subnational Constitutions in the New World Order, 39 Rutgers L.J. 801, 804–805 (2008).
2. John Locke, Two Treatises of Government (1698).
3. John Langbein, Renee Lettow Lerner, & Bruce P. Smith, History of the Common Law: The Development of Anglo-American Legal Institutions (Aspen 2009).
4. Daniel A. Farber & Philip P. Frickey, Law and Public Choice: A Critical Introduction (University of Chicago Press 1991).
5. This problem was pointed out in an early article by David Johnson & David Post, Law and Borders: The Rise of Law in Cyberspace, 48 Stan. L. Rev. 1367 (1996).
6. *Young v. New Haven Advocate*, 315 F.3d 256 (4th Cir. 2002).
7. Ung-gi Yoon, Real Money Trading in MMORPG Items from a Legal and Policy Perspective, December 13, 2004, available at: http://ssrn.com/abstract=1113327 (last visited June 2009).

8. Jack Goldsmith & Tim Wu, Who Controls the Internet? Illusions of a Border-less World (Oxford University Press 2006).

9. Julian Dibbell, A Rape in Cyberspace, The Village Voice, December 21, 1993.

10. Id.

11. Elizabeth Hess, Yib's Guide to Mooing: Getting the Most from Virtual Communities on the Internet 305 (Trafford Publishing 2003).

12. Julian Dibbell, My Tiny Life: Crime and Passion in a Virtual World 24 (Henry Holt 1998).

13. Jennifer L. Mnookin, Virtual(ly) Law: The Emergence of Law in LambdaMOO, reprinted in Crypto Anarchy, Cyberstates, and Pirate Utopias 245 (Peter Ludlow, ed., MIT Press 2001); Dibbell, My Tiny Life 195–228.

14. Mnookin, Virtual(ly) Law 264, 270.

15. Pavel Curtis, How LambdaMOO Came to Exist and What It Did to Get Back at Me, in High Wired: On the Design, Use, and Theory of Educational MOOs (eds. Cynthia Haynes & Jan Rune Holmevik, University of Michigan Press 1998).

16. Howard Rheingold, The Virtual Community: Homesteading on the Electronic Frontier (MIT Press 2000).

17. William J. Mitchell, City of Bits: Space, Place, and the Infobahn (MIT Press 1996).

18. Dan Hunter, Cyberspace as Place and the Tragedy of the Digital Anticommons, 91 Cal. L. Rev. 439, 453–454 (2003).

19. Mitchell, City of Bits 118–121; Rheingold, Virtual Community 149–180.

20. Julie E. Cohen, Cyberspace as/and Space, 107 Colum. L. Rev. 210, 255-56 (2007). Cohen's work on this issue responded to prior legal scholarship analyzing the role of spatial concepts in cyberlaw. Mark A. Lemley, Place and Cyberspace, 91 Calif. L. Rev. 521, 525–526 (2003); Hunter, Cyberspace as Place 442–444.

21. Alfred C. Yen, Western Frontier or Feudal Society? Metaphors and Perceptions of Cyberspace, 17 Berkeley Tech. L.J. 1207 (2002).

22. John Perry Barlow, Keynote Address, 1994 Ann. Surv. Am. L. 355. See also John Perry Barlow, Edited Comments Concerning Differentiating Action and Expression in a Virtual World, 1994 Ann. Surv. Am. L. 451.

23. Barlow Dec.

24. *Reno v. American Civil Liberties Union*, 521 U.S. 844 (1997).

25. William S. Byassee, Jurisdiction of Cyberspace: Applying Real World Precedent to the Virtual Community, 30 Wake Forest L. Rev. 197 (1995).

26. David R. Johnson & David Post, Law and Borders—The Rise of Law in Cyberspace, 48 Stan. L. Rev. 1367 (1996).

27. Jack L. Goldsmith, Against Cyberanarchy, 65 U. Chi. L. Rev. 4 (1998). For Post's response, see David G. Post, Against "Against Cyberanarchy," 17 Berkeley Tech. L.J. 1365 (2002).

28. David G. Post, In Search of Jefferson's Moose 168–169 (Oxford University Press 2009). I should note that both Johnson and Post are well aware that the evolution of contemporary virtual worlds provides support for their earlier claims. See David R. Johnson, How Online Games May Change the Law and Specifically Legal Institutions, 49 N.Y.L. SCH. L. REV. 51 (2004); Post, Jefferson's Moose 181–184.

29. Viktor Mayer-Schönberger, Napster's Second Life? The Regulatory Challenges of Virtual Worlds, 100 Nw. U. L. Rev. 1775 (2006).

30. Timothy Wu, Application-Centered Internet Analysis, 85 Va. L. Rev. 1163 (1999).

31. Raph Koster, Declaring the Rights of Players, August 27, 2000, available at: http://www.legendmud.org/raph/gaming/playerrights.html (last visited June 2009).

32. Jay M. Feinmann, Law 101, 191–193 (Oxford University Press 2000).

33. *ProCD, Inc. v. Zeidenberg*, 86 F.3d 1447 (7th Cir. 1996).

34. CNN.com, Terms, available at: http://www.cnn.com/interactive_legal.html (last visited June 2009).

35. Brian Stelter, Facebook's Users Ask Who Owns Information, New York Times, February 16, 2009, available at: http://www.nytimes.com/2009/02/17/technol ogy/internet/17facebook.html (last visited June 2009).

36. Andrew Jankowich, Eulaw: The Complex Web of Corporate Rule-Making in Virtual Worlds, 8 Tul. J. Tech. & Intell. Prop. (2006).

37. Second Life, Terms of Service, available at: http://secondlife.com/corporate/tos .php (last visited June 2009).

38. Joshua A. T. Fairfield, Anti-social Contracts: The Contractual Governance of Virtual Worlds, 53 McGill L.J. 427 (2008).

39. James Grimmelmann, Virtual Worlds as Comparative Law, 49 New York Law School Law Review 147 (2004).

40. Robert Ellickson, Order without Law: How Neighbors Settle Disputes (Harvard University Press 2005).

41. Club Penguin Rules, available at: http://support.clubpenguin.com/help/faq/ club_penguin_rules.htm (last visited June 2009).

42. Second Life, Community Standards, available at: http://secondlife.com/corpo rate/cs.php (last visited June 2009).

43. Wagner James Au, Crime Scene: In Linden Incident Reports, Content Theft Violations Hardly Register, New World Notes, September 30, 2009, available at: http://nwn.blogs.com/nwn/2009/09/crime-scene.html (last visited November 2009).

44. World of Warcraft Terms of Use Agreement, available at: http://www.world ofwarcraft.com/legal/termsofuse.html (last visited June 2009).

45. A similar organization of "player police officers" exists in Habbo Hotel. Mia Consalvo, Cheating: Gaining Advantage in Video Games 131 (MIT Press 2007).

46. This particular comment was found in a World of Warcraft forum, but there are posts similar to it that can be found in the online forums of many virtual worlds.

47. Second Life, Terms of Service, available at: http://secondlife.com/corporate/tos. php (last visited June 2009).

48. Consalvo, Cheating 142.

49. This possibility has been explored by Ethan Katsh, one of the original pioneers of cyberlaw. Ethan Katsh, Bringing Online Dispute Resolution to Virtual Worlds: Creating Processes Through Code, 1 N.Y.L. SCH. L. REV. 271 (2004). See also Farnaz Alemi, An Avatar's Day in Court: A Proposal for Obtaining

Relief and Resolving Disputes in Virtual World Games, 2007 UCLA J.L. & Tech. 6 (2007).

50. Compare Michael Risch, Virtual Third Parties, 25 Santa Clara Computer & High Tech. L.J. 415 (2008) (arguing that third parties may assert rights in some cases) with Joshua Fairfield, Third Party Beneficiaries and Other Fantastical Beasts in Virtual Worlds, Terra Nova, April 14, 2009, http://terranova.blogs .com/terra_nova/2009/04/third-party-beneficiaries-and-other-fantastical -beasts-in-virtual-worlds.html (last visited June 2009) (arguing that third parties generally will not be able to assert rights under standard virtual world agreements). See also Benjamin Duranske, Virtual Law: Navigating the Legal Landscape of Virtual Worlds 132–135 (American Bar Association 2008).

51. Benjamin Duranske, *Hernandez v. IGE* Settles, IGE U.S. Confirms It Will Not "Engage in the Selling of WoW Virtual Property or Currency" for Five Years; Class Action Still Possible, Virtually Blind, August 27, 2008, available at: http:// virtuallyblind.com/2008/08/27/hernandez-ige-settles/ (last visited June 2009). I should note that I consulted with the firm representing Hernandez in this case.

CHAPTER 6: GAMES

1. New York Times, August 17, 1920. For various and sometimes conflicting accounts of the Chapman tragedy, see Stanley H. Teitelbaum, Sports Heroes, Fallen Idols 199–200 (University of Nebraska Press 2008); Leigh Montville, The Big Bam: The Life and Times of Babe Ruth 116–118 (Random House 2007); Robert C. Cottrell, Blackball, the Black Sox, and the Babe: Baseball's Crucial 1920 Season 188–192 (McFarland 2002); Emile Rothe, The Day Ray Chapman Was Killed, Baseball Digest, August 1972, at 38–40.

2. Michael Walzer, Spheres of Justice: A Defense of Pluralism and Equality (Basic 1983).

3. For details, see the National Center for Catastrophic Injury Research web site, available at: http://www.unc.edu/depts/nccsi/ (last visited June 2009).

4. See Centers for Disease Control and Prevention, Sports-Related Injuries among High School Athletes—United States, 2005–06 School Year, Morbidity and Mortality Weekly Report, September 29, 2006, available at: http://www.cdc.gov/ mmwr/preview/mmwrhtml/mm5538a1.htm (last visited June 2009).

5. Jackson J. Benson, Hemingway: The Writer's Art of Self-Defense 73–74 (University of Minnesota Press 1969), quoted in Jeffrey O. Segrave, Sport as Escape, 24 Journal of Sport & Social Issues 61 (2000).

6. Along a similar vein, Jack Balkin has argued that virtual worlds need to be insulated as spaces where participants have freedom to design and play apart from the conventional legal order. Jack Balkin, Virtual Liberty: Freedom to Design and Freedom to Play in Virtual Worlds, 90 Va. L. Rev. 2043 (2004).

7. Johan Huizinga, Homo Ludens 46 (Beacon Press 1971).

8. For an extended mediation on the "gameness" of law, see Allan C. Hutchinson, It's All in the Game (Duke University Press 2000).

9. I Come before the Committee with No Agenda. I Have No Platform, New York Times, September 13, 2005, at A1.

10. Stephen G. Miller, Ancient Greek Athletics (Yale University Press 2004).

11. Jesse Dukeminier, James Krier, Gregory Alexander, and Michael Schill, Property (Aspen 6th ed. 2006).

12. Huizinga, Homo Ludens 13.

13. Roger Caillois, Man, Play, and Games 5 (University of Illinois Press 2001).

14. Bernard Suits, The Grasshopper: Games, Life and Utopia 34 (Broadview Press 2005).

15. Admittedly, there are many ways to think of the nature of human play. For a more careful and thorough investigation, see Brian Sutton-Smith, The Ambiguity of Play (Harvard University Press 2001).

16. *Georgia High School Assn. v. Waddell*, 285 S.E.2d 7 (Ga. Sup. Ct. 1981).

17. John Barnes, Sports and the Law in Canada 2 (Butterworths 1996).

18. *Hackbart v. Cincinnati Bengals, Inc.*, 435 F. Supp. 352 (D. Colo. 1977).

19. Id. at 358.

20. *Hackbart v. Cincinnati Bengals, Inc.*, 601 F.2d 516, 520 (10th Cir. 1979).

21. Id. at 521.

22. Id.

23. *Martin v. PGA Tour*, 984 F. Supp. 1320 (D. Or. 1998), affirmed by 204 F.3d 994 (9th Cir. 2000).

24. *PGA Tour, Inc. v. Martin*, 532 U.S. 661 (2001).

25. Id. at 685.

26. Id. at 700.

27. Huizinga, Homo Ludens 8.

28. A. Bartlett Giamatti, Take Time for Paradise: Americans and Their Games 70 (Summit Books 1991).

29. Mihaly Csikszentmihalyi, Creativity: Flow and the Psychology of Discovery and Invention 49 (Harper Perennial 1997).

30. Jesper Juul, Half-Real: Video Games between Real Rules and Fictional Worlds 92 (MIT Press 2005).

31. Thomas M. Malaby, Making Virtual Worlds: Linden Lab and Second Life 85 (Cornell University Press 2009).

32. John Stuart Mill, On Liberty and Other Essays 96 (Oxford University Press 1991).

33. Henry David Thoreau, Letter to Harrison Blake, November 16, 1857, found in The Writings of Henry David Thoreau, Volume 6 at 317 (eds. Bradford Torrey and Franklin Benjamin Sanborn, Houghton, Mifflin & Co. 1906).

34. Suits, The Grasshopper 172–178.

35. Thorstein Veblen, The Theory of the Leisure Class: An Economic Study of Institutions (B. W. Huebsch 1912).

36. McKenzie Wark, Gamer Theory 006 (Harvard University Press 2007).

37. Edward Castronova, The Right to Play, 49 N.Y.L. Sch. L. Rev. 185 (2004); Benjamin Duranske, Virtual Law: Navigating the Legal Landscape of Virtual Worlds 57–78 (American Bar Association 2008). In game studies circles, the "magic circle" terminology is alternately attacked and defended. The detractors seem slightly more numerous to me at the moment. See, e.g., Vili Lehdonvirta, Virtual Consumption 103–129 (PhD thesis, Turku School of Economics, 2009),

available at: http://info.tse.fi/julkaisut/vk/Ae11_2009.pdf (last visited June 2009).

38. Peter Johnson, Unravelling Foucault's "Different Spaces," 4 History of the Human Sciences 75, 75–76 (2006).

39. Wark, Gamer Theory 109.

40. Julie E. Cohen, Cyberspace as/and Space, 107 Colum. L. Rev. 210, 218, n.26 (2007).

41. Orin S. Kerr, Criminal Law in Virtual Worlds, 2008 U. Chi. Legal Forum 415 (2008). The cases Kerr cites are *Hernandez v. State*, 63 SW 320 (Tex. Crim. App. 1901); *Palmer v. State*, 160 SW 349 (Tex. Crim. App. 1913); and *Temple v. State*, 215 SW 965 (Tex. Crim. App. 1919).

42. I should note that much of my understanding of EVE comes from the work of Terra Nova author Nate Combs. Nate blogs at Scratchpad, http://scratchpad.roaringshrimp.com/ (last visited June 2009).

43. See Leigh Alexander, At Sixth Birthday, EVE Online Reaches 300,000 Users, Gamasutra, May 6, 2009, available at: http://www.gamasutra.com/php-bin/news_index.php?story=23502 (last visited June 2009).

44. Details as well as various legal readings of Cally's scam can be found in Hannah Yee Fen Lim, Who Monitors the Monitor? Virtual World Governance and the Failure of Contract Law Remedies in Virtual Worlds, 11 Vand. J. Ent. & Tech. L. 1053 (2009); Jason T. Kunze, Regulating Virtual Realms Optimally: The Model End User License Agreement, 7 Nw. J. Tech. & Intell. Prop. 102 (2008); Bobby Glushko, Tales of the (Virtual) City: Governing Property Disputes in Virtual Worlds, 22 Berkeley Tech. L.J. 507 (2007); Ethan E. White, Comment: Massively Multiplayer Online Fraud: Why the Introduction of Real World Law in a Virtual Context Is Good for Everyone, 6 Nw. J. Tech. & Intell. Prop. 228 (2008).

45. Ralphedelominius, CCP Speaks Out on the EIB Scam, Ten Ton Hammer, September 26, 2007, available at: http://www.tentonhammer.com/node/34217 (last visited June 2009).

46. Yee Fen Lim, Who Monitors.

47. See EVE Online, Terms of Service, available at: http://www.eveonline.com/pnp/terms.asp (emphasis added) (last visited June 2009).

48. Kunze, Regulating Optimally, citing Caroline McCarthy, Cons in the Virtual Gaming World, ZDNet News, August 31, 2006, citing Timo K., Biggest Scam in EVE Online History, QJ.Net, August 22, 2006, available at: http://mmorpg.qj.net/Biggest-scam-in-EVE-Online-history/pg/49/aid/62826 (last visited June 2009).

CHAPTER 7: PROPERTY

1. Arno R. Lodder, Conflict Resolution in Virtual Worlds: General Characteristics and the 2009 Dutch Convictions on Virtual Theft, in Virtual Worlds and Criminality (ed. Kai Cornelius, Springer 2010). As noted earlier, there is a growing literature concerning virtual crimes. Articles include: Andrea Vanina Arias, Life, Liberty and the Pursuit of Swords and Armor: Regulating the Theft of Virtual Goods, 57 Emory L.J. 1301 (2008); Susan W. Brenner, Fantasy Crime: The Role of Criminal Law in Virtual Worlds, 11 Vand. J. Ent. & Tech. L. 1, 58 (2008); Benjamin

Duranske, Virtual Law: Navigating the Legal Landscape of Virtual Worlds 197–206 (American Bar Association 2008); Orin S. Kerr, Criminal Law in Virtual Worlds, 2008 U. Chi. Legal Forum 415 (2008); F. Gregory Lastowka & Dan Hunter, Virtual Crimes, 49 N.Y.L.S. L. REV. 293 (2004).

2. Lodder, Conflict Resolution.

3. Ung-gi Yoon, Real Money Trading in MMORPG Items from a Legal and Policy Perspective, June 5, 2006, available at: http://ssrn.com/abstract=1113327 (last visited June 2009).

4. Id.

5. Complaint, *Bragg v. Linden Research, Inc.*, No. 06–08711 (Pa. Ct. Com. Pl. 2006).

6. See Yoon, Real Money Trading ("In-game items . . . are devoid of 'tangibility,' an essential attribute of property"), citing Civil Code of Korea, Art. 98 ("For the purposes of this Act, the term 'goods' means tangible entities and manageable natural energies, including electric power").

7. William Blackstone, Commentaries on the Laws of England, Volume 1, 713–714 (ed. Wiliam Carey Jones, Bancroft-Whitney 1915).

8. Id. at 707–708.

9. See *Intel Corp. v. Hamidi*, 30 Cal. 4th 1342 (2003) (establishing that the owner of an e-mail server has the right to technologically exclude unwanted interactions as well as use the law to enjoin unauthorized interactions that cause damage to the server).

10. Blackstone, Commentaries 737 ("Their existence is merely in idea and abstracted contemplation; though their effects and profits may be frequently objects of our bodily senses").

11. If you are curious about what kind of property interest Alice possesses, this particular creature is called a "springing executory interest" (provided the grantor is currently in possession of the estate).

12. See, e.g., *Landy v. Cahn*, 792 A.2d 544, 555 (N.J. App. Div. 2002).

13. Model Penal Code § 223.0(6).

14. Black's Law Dictionary 1095 (5th ed. West 1979).

15. *People v. Johnson*, 560 N.Y.S.2d 238 (Crim. Ct. 1990).

16. *People v. Molina*, 547 N.Y.S.2d 546 (N.Y. Crim. Ct. 1989). I thank Orin Kerr for calling these cases to my attention.

17. *Moore v. The Regents of the University of California*, 51 Cal. 3d 120 (1990).

18. *Simmons v. Simmons*, 244 Conn. 158 (1998); *Greenfield v. Greenfield*, 650 N.Y.S.2d 698 (1996).

19. John Locke, Two Treatises of Government § 28 (1698).

20. I should stress that the "law and economics" formulation I use here is not intended to encompass all legal scholarship that makes use of economic concepts and tools. It is a thumbnail portrait—perhaps even a slight caricature—of the "Chicago School."

21. Ronald H. Coase, The Problem of Social Cost, 3 Journal of Law & Economics 1 (1960).

22. Frank H. Easterbrook, Cyberspace and the Law of the Horse, 1996 U. Chi. Legal Forum 207.

23. Joshua Quittner, Billions Registered: Right Now There Are No Rules to Keep You from Owning a Bitchin' Corporate Name as Your Own Internet Address, Wired, October 1994, 50–51.

24. *Kremen v. Cohen*, 99 F. Supp. 2d 1168 (N.D. Cal. 2000).

25. *Kremen v. Cohen*, 337 F.3d 1024 (9th Cir. 2003).

26. See, e.g., Jason A. Archinaco, Virtual Worlds, Real Damages: The Odd Case of American Hero, the Greatest Horse that May Have Lived, 11 Gaming L. Rev. 21 (2007); Charles Blazer, The Five Indicia of Virtual Property, 5 Pierce L. Rev. 137 (2006); M. Scott Boone, Ubiquitous Computing, Virtual Worlds, and the Displacement of Property Rights, 4 ISJLP 91 (2008); M. Scott Boone, Virtual Property and Personhood, 24 Santa Clara Computer and High Tech. L.J. 749 (2008); Allen Chein, Note: A Practical Look at Virtual Property, 80 St. John's L. Rev. 1059 (2006); Duranske, Virtual Law 79–114; Bobby Glushko, Tales of the (Virtual) City: Governing Property Disputes in Virtual Worlds, 22 Berkeley Tech. L.J. 507 (2007); Steven J. Horowitz, Competing Lockean Claims to Virtual Property, 20 Harv. J. L. & Tech. 443 (2007); Steven J. Horowitz, Note: *Bragg v. Linden*'s Second Life: A Primer in Virtual World Justice, 34 Ohio N.U.L. Rev. 223 (2008); Kurt Hunt, Note: This Land Is Not Your Land: Second Life, CopyBot, and the Looming Question of Virtual Property Rights, 9 Tex. Rev. Ent. & Sports L. 141 (2007); Jamie J. Kayser, The New New-World: Virtual Property and the End User License Agreement, 27 Loy. L.A. Ent. L. Rev. 59 (2007); Andrew Jankowich, Property and Democracy in Virtual Worlds, 11 B.U. J. Sci. & Tech. L. 173 (2005); Dan E. Lawrence, It Really Is Just a Game: The Impracticability of Common Law Property Rights in Virtual Property, 47 Washburn L.J. 505 (2008); Michael Meehan, Virtual Property: Protecting Bits in Context, Rich. J. Global L. & Bus. (2006); Daniel C. Miller, Note: Determining Ownership in Virtual Worlds: Copyright and License Agreements, 22 Rev. Litig. 435 (2003); Juliet M. Moringiello, Towards a System of Estates in Virtual Property, Cyberlaw Security & Privacy (ed. Sylvia Mercado Kierkegaard, 2007), available at: http://ssrn.com/abstract=1070184; David Nelmark, Virtual Property: The Challenges of Regulating Intangible, Exclusionary Property Interests Such as Domain Names, 3 Nw. J. Tech. & Intell. Prop. 1 (2004); David P. Sheldon, Claiming Ownership, but Getting Owned: Contractual Limitations on Asserting Property Interests in Virtual Goods, 54 UCLA L. Rev. 751 (2007); Justin B. Slaughter, Virtual Worlds: Between Contract and Property (2008), available at: http://lsr.nellco.org/yale/student/papers/62 (last visited June 2009); Elizabeth Townsend Gard & Rachel Goda, Second Life, Virtual Property and a 1L Property Course, 24 Santa Clara Computer and High Tech. L.J. 915 (2008); Ryan G. Vacca, Viewing Virtual Property Ownership Through the Lens of Innovation, 76 Tenn. L. Rev. 33 (2008); Theodore J. Westbrook, Owned: Finding a Place for Virtual World Property Rights, 2006 Mich. St. L. Rev. 779 (2006).

27. See Nicolas Suzor, On the (Partially-)Inalienable Rights of Participants in Virtual Communities, 130 Media International Australia 90 (2009).

28. John Boudreau, Pondering New Puzzle: Who Inherits Digital Data, San Jose Mercury News, May 29, 2005, at 1; Tina Susman, Parental vs. Privacy Rights,

Newsday, January 30, 2005, at A8; Jennifer Chambers, Family Fights to See Soldier's Last Words, The Detroit News, December 21, 2004, at 1A.

29. For an in-depth discussion of post-mortem interests in online assets, see Deven R. Desai, Property, Persona, and Preservation, 81 Temple L. Rev. 67 (2009).

30. Robin Linden, Formerly Known as Telehubs, Second Life Blogs, November 28, 2005, available at: https://blogs.secondlife.com/community/features/blog/2005/11/28/formerly-known-as-telehubs (last visited June 2009); Second Life Wikia, Telehubs, available at: http://secondlife.wikia.com/wiki/Telehubs (last visited June 2009).

31. Tom Boellstorff, Coming of Age in Second Life: An Anthropologist Explores the Virtually Human 89–91 (Princeton University Press 2008); T. L. Taylor, Play Between Worlds: Exploring Online Game Culture 21–65 (MIT Press 2006).

32. *Kremen v. Cohen*, 337 F.3d 1024 (9th Cir. 2003).

CHAPTER 8: HACKERS

1. Mia Consalvo, Cheating: Gaining Advantage in Video Games 114 (MIT Press 2007).

2. Chip Morningstar & F. Randall Farmer, The Lessons of Lucasfilm's Habitat, available at: http://www.fudco.com/chip/lessons.html (last visited June 2009).

3. William J. Mitchell, City of Bits: Space, Place, and the Infobahn 111 (MIT Press 1996).

4. James Grimmelmann, Regulation by Software, 114 Yale L.J. 1719 (2005).

5. Tim Wu, When Code Isn't Law, 89 Virginia L. Rev. 679 (2003); Greg Lastowka, Decoding Cyberproperty, 40 Indiana L. Rev. 23 (2007).

6. Mitchell, City of Bits 112.

7. Joel R. Reidenberg, Governing Networks and Rule-Making in Cyberspace, 45 Emory L.J. 922 (1996); Joel R. Reidenberg, Lex Informatica: The Formulation of Information Policy Rules Through Technology, 76 Tex. L. Rev. 553 (1998).

8. James Boyle, Foucault in Cyberspace: Surveillance, Sovereignty, and Hardwired Sensors, U. Cinn. L. Rev. 177 (1997).

9. M. Ethan Katsh, Software Worlds and the First Amendment: Virtual Doorkeepers in Cyberspace, 1996 U. Chi. Legal F. 335; see also M. Ethan Katsh, Law in a Digital World (Oxford University Press 1995).

10. Lawrence Lessig, Foreword: Cyberspace and Privacy: A New Legal Paradigm? 52 Stan. L. Rev. 987, 990 (2000).

11. Thomas M. Malaby, Making Virtual Worlds: Linden Lab and Second Life 20 (Cornell University Press 2009).

12. Ren Reynolds, Hands Off My Avatar! available at: http://www.ren-reynolds.com/downloads/HandsOffMYavatar.htm (last visited June 2009).

13. Specific details about the nature of MapleStory marriage can be found in various places on the Internet, including the MapleStory web site, maplestory.nexon.net/, and Strategy Wiki, MapleStory/Towns/Amoria, available at: http://strategywiki.org/wiki/MapleStory/Towns/Amoria (last visited June 2009).

14. David McNeill, Woman Faces Jail for Hacking Her Virtual Husband to Death, The Irish Times, October 25, 2008, at 1.

15. World of Warcraft, Raid Groups, available at: http://www.worldofwarcraft .com/info/basics/raidgroups.html (last visited June 2009).

16. Same Gender Marriage for Maple Story Global Petition, available at: http:// www.petitiononline.com/SGMFMSGP/petition.html (last visited June 2009); Second Life Blogs, Marriage in SL, August 3, 2009, available at: https://blogs .secondlife.com/message/7120 (last visited November 2009) ("We've gotten requests from lovebirds . . .").

17. See, e.g., Joshua A. T. Fairfield, The God Paradox, 89 B.U.L. Rev. 1017 (2009).

18. Compare James Grimmelmann, Virtual World Feudalism, 118 Yale L.J. Pocket Part 126 (2009) with Fairfield, God Paradox (explaining and criticizing the "deity" approach); Richard Bartle, Virtual Worldliness, in The State of Play: Law, Games and Virtual Worlds 31, 37 (eds. Jack Balkin & Beth Noveck, New York University Press 2006) (stating that the administrators of virtual worlds need "absolute control over their world").

19. Morningstar & Farmer, Lessons.

20. T. L. Taylor, Play Between Worlds: Exploring Online Game Culture 32–36 (MIT Press 2006).

21. Id.

22. Dave Myers, Play and Punishment: The Sad and Curious Case of Twixt (2008), available at: http://www.masscomm.loyno.edu/~dmyers/F99%20classes/Myers_ PlayPunishment_031508.doc (last visited June 2009).

23. Eric S. Raymond, The Cathedral and the Bazaar, available at: http://catb.org/ esr/writings/cathedral-bazaar/cathedral-bazaar/index.html (last visited June 2009).

24. E. Gabriella Coleman, The Social Construction of Freedom in Free and Open Source Software: Hackers, Ethics, and the Liberal Tradition (unpublished PhD dissertation, University of Chicago, August 2005, on file with author); Douglas Thomas, Hacker Culture 10–11 (University of Minnesota Press 2002); Steven Levy, Hackers: Heroes of the Computer Revolution 23–35 (Penguin 2001).

25. Timothy Burke, Rubicite Breastplate Priced to Move, Cheap: How Virtual Economies Become Real Simulations (June 2002), available at: http://www.swarthmore .edu/SocSci/tburke1/Rubicite%20Breastplate.pdf (last visited June 2009).

26. See EQ2, The Dog Days of Duping Cont . . . , Plaguelands, August 2005, available at: http://plaguelands.com/eq2-dogs-duping-days-cont/ (last visited June 2009). I should note that Sony Online reportedly disputed some of the facts in the account.

27. Tim Guest, Second Lives 63–69 (Random House 2007).

28. Id. at 70.

29. Julian Dibbell, Play Money (Basic Books 2006).

30. Edward Castronova, Synthetic Worlds: The Business and Culture of Online Games 237 (University of Chicago Press 2005).

31. Bragg v. Linden Research, Inc., Defendant's Answer & 1st Amended Counterclaims, Case No. 06–4925 (E.D. Pa. Aug. 17, 2007).

32. 18 U.S.C. § 1030 (2009).

33. United States v. Morris, 928 F.2d 504 (2d Cir. 1991) (stating that Morris was testing security); Jonathan Zittrain, The Future of the Internet—And How to Stop

It 36–40 (Yale University Press 2008) (stating that Morris was counting the number of computers on the Internet).

34. *United States v. Morris*, 928 F.2d 504 (2d Cir. 1991).
35. Toby Green, The Information, The Independent, November 7, 2009, at 46.
36. Matt McCormack, Taterf—All Your Drives Are Belong to Me!!!1!one!, June 20, 2006, available at: http://blogs.technet.com/mmpc/archive/2008/06/20/taterf -all-your-drives-are-belong-to-me-1-one.aspx (last visited June 2009). (If you cannot translate this article, you will need to speak to someone who plays World of Warcraft.)
37. *United States v. Drew*, 259 F.R.D. 449 (C.D. Cal. 2009).
38. Id. at 466.

CHAPTER 9: COPYRIGHT

1. See Complaint, *Marvel Enterprises, Inc. v. NCSoft Corp.*, No. 04CV9253 (C.D. Ca. Nov. 11, 2004), available at: http://www.eff.org/IP/Marvel_v_NC-Soft/20041115_Marvel_NCSoft.pdf (last visited June 2009).
2. *Atari, Inc. v. N. Am. Philips Consumer Elecs. Corp.*, 672 F.2d 607, 619–20 (7th Cir. 1982); Jon Festinger, Video Game Law 53–55 (LexisNexis Publishers 2004). As Festinger's book makes clear, video games have often been at the forefront of computer technology and intellectual property laws.
3. See Doc. No. 124, Civil Minutes—General, *Marvel Enterprises, Inc. vs. NCSoft Corp.*, No. 04CV9253 (C.D. Ca. Aug. 22, 2005).
4. *Marvel Enters. v. NCSoft Corp.*, 2005 U.S. Dist. LEXIS 8448 (C.D. Cal. Mar. 9, 2005).
5. Mark A. Lemley, Property, Intellectual Property, and Free Riding, 83 Texas Law Review 1031 (2005); Richard M. Stallman, Did You Say "Intellectual Property"? It's a Seductive Mirage, http://www.gnu.org/philosophy/not-ipr.html (last visited June 2009).
6. Concerning trademark law and virtual worlds, see Candidus Dougherty & Greg Lastowka, Virtual Trademarks, 24 Santa Clara Computer and High Tech. L.J. 749 (2008); David Naylor & Andrew Jaworski, The Tangled Web of Virtual Marks, Trademark World (June 2007), available at: http://www.ffw.com/publi cations/all/articles/the-tangled-web-of-virtual-mar.aspx (last visited June 2009).
7. For discussions of the privacy implications of virtual worlds, see Tal Z. Zarsky, Information Privacy in Virtual Worlds: Identifying Unique Concerns Beyond the Online and Offline Worlds, 1 N.Y.L. Sch. L. Rev. 231 (2004); Jonathon W. Penney, Privacy and the New Virtualism, 10 Yale J. L. & Tech. 194 (2007).
8. For in-depth examinations of the early evolution of copyright, see generally Lyman Ray Patterson, Copyright in Historical Perspective 28–32 (Vanderbilt University Press 1968); Mark Rose, Authors and Owners: The Invention of Copyright (Harvard University Press 1993); Joseph Loewenstein, The Author's Due (University of Chicago Press 2002).
9. United States Constitution, article 1, § 8.
10. The Statute of Anne, 8 Anne c. 19 (1710).
11. Jessica Litman, Digital Copyright: Protecting Intellectual Property on the Internet (Prometheus Books 2000).
12. *Sony Corp. of America v. Universal City Studios*, 464 U.S. 417 (1984).

13. Jessica Litman, War Stories, 20 Cardozo Arts & Ent. L. J. 337 (2002).
14. The Digital Millennium Copyright Act of 1998 (DMCA), Pub. L. No. 105–304, 112 Stat. 2863 (1998).
15. 17 U.S.C. § 512.
16. Brad Stone, Amazon Faces a Fight Over Its E-Books, The New York Times, July 27, 2009 at B3; Miguel Helft, Amazon Offers to Replace Orwell Books It Deleted, The New York Times, September 5, 2009 at B2.
17. *MAI Systems Corp. v. Peak Computer, Inc.*, 991 F.2d 511 (9th Cir. 1993).
18. The facts of the case recounted here are summarized from the legal pleadings and numerous opinions. *MDY Indus., LLC v. Blizzard Entm't, Inc.*, 616 F. Supp. 2d 958 (D. Ariz. Jan. 28, 2009); 2008 U.S. Dist. LEXIS 53988 (July 14, 2008); 2009 U.S. Dist. LEXIS 24151 (March 10, 2009); 2009 U.S. Dist. LEXIS 25650 (March 25, 2009); 2009 U.S. Dist. LEXIS 38260 (April 1, 2009); 2009 U.S. Dist. LEXIS 65089 (July 16, 2009).
19. *MDY Indus., LLC v. Blizzard Entm't, Inc.*, 616 F. Supp. 2d 958, 966 (D. Ariz. Jan. 28, 2009).
20. Mia Consalvo, Cheating: Gaining Advantage in Video Games 164–166 (MIT Press 2007).
21. Though this distinction is important, the notion of reader passivity should not be overstated. Audiences have always been critically and imaginatively engaged, and often creatively engaged, with popular authorial works. The Internet has simply made it much easier for audiences to share "fan" creativity with each other. See generally Henry Jenkins, Textual Poachers: Television Fans and Participatory Culture (Routledge 1992); Julie E. Cohen, The Place of the User in Copyright Law, 74 Fordham L. Rev. 347 (2005); Clay Shirky, Here Comes Everybody: The Power of Organizing Without Organizations (Penguin 2008).
22. Sal Humphreys, Norrath—New Forms, Old Institutions, 9 Games Studies (April 2009), available at: http://gamestudies.org/0901/articles/humphreys (last visited June 2009).
23. *Williams Electronics, Inc. v. Arctic International, Inc.*, 685 F.2d 870 (3d Cir. 1982).
24. Id.
25. Espen Aarseth, Cybertext: Perspectives on Ergodic Literature (Johns Hopkins University Press 1997).
26. Torill Mortensen, Playing with Players: Potential Methodologies for MUDs, 2 Game Studies 1, available at: http://www.gamestudies.org/0102/mortensen/ (last visited June 2009).
27. Ryan, Narrative as Virtual Reality 310–312.
28. Lisbeth Klastrup, A Poetics of Virtual Worlds, in Proceedings of the Fifth International Digital Arts and Culture Conference (2003), available at: http://hypertext.rmit.edu.au/dac/papers/Klastrup.pdf (last visited June 2009).
29. Yochai Benkler, The Wealth of Networks 74 (Yale University Press 2006).
30. Shirky, Here Comes Everybody (discussing "mass amateurization").
31. Mira Burri-Nenova has explored the various policy implications of this shift with regard to virtual worlds. Mira Burri-Nenova, User Created Content in Virtual Worlds and Cultural Diversity (December 18, 2008), available at: http://ssrn.com/abstract=1316847 (last visited June 2009).

32. Lord of the Rings Online, End User License Agreement, available at: http://www .lotro.com/support/policies/218-eula (last visited June 2009).

33. Fred Broson, The Billboard Book of Number 1 Hits (Billboard Books 2003).

34. Katie Dean, Music Muffled in Star Wars Game, Wired.com, available at: http://www.wired.com/entertainment/music/news/2005/06/67720?currentPage =all (last visited June 2009).

35. Mike Musgrove, Shooting a Movie in a Fantasy World Is Not All Fun and Game, Washington Post, October 14, 2007, at F1.

36. World of Warcraft, Machinima, available at: http://www.worldofwarcraft.com/ community/machinima/ (last visited June 2009).

37. For further reading on virtual world copyright issues, see John Baldrica, Mod as Heck: Frameworks for Examining Ownership Rights in User-Contributed Content to Videogames, and a More Principled Evaluation of Expressive Appropriation in User-Modified Videogame Projects, 8 Minn. J.L. Sci. & Tech. 681 (2007); Woodrow Barfield, Intellectual Property Rights in Virtual Environments: Considering the Rights of Owners, Programmers and Virtual Avatars, 39 Akron L. Rev. 649 (2006); Mia Garlick, Player, Pirate or Conducer? A Consideration of the Rights of Online Gamers, 7 Yale J. L. & Tech. 422 (2005); Andrea W. M. Louie, Designing Avatars in Virtual Worlds: How Free Are We to Play Superman? 11 J. Internet L. 5:3 (2007); Todd David Marcus, Note: Fostering Creativity in Virtual Worlds: Easing the Restrictiveness of Copyright for User-Created Content, 52 N.Y.L. Sch. L. Rev. 67 (2007); W. Joss Nichols, Painting Through Pixels: The Case for a Copyright in Videogame Play, 30 Colum. J.L. & Arts 101 (2007); Erez Reuveni, Authorship in the Age of the Conducer, 54 J. Copyright Soc'y U.S.A. 285 (2007); Erez Reuveni, On Virtual Worlds: Copyright and Contract Law at the Dawn of the Virtual Age, 82 Ind. L.J. 261 (2007); Molly Stephens, Note: Sales of In-Game Assets: An Illustration of the Continuing Failure of Intellectual Property Law to Protect Digital-Content Creators, 80 Tex. L. Rev. 1513 (2002).

38. Sarah E. Galbraith, Second Life Strife: A Proposal for Resolution of In-World Fashion Disputes, 2008 B.C. Intell. Prop. & Tech. F. 90803. Second Life's strategic embrace of user-generated content owes much to Cory Ondrejka, the former Chief Technology Officer of Linden Lab, who passionately and thoughtfully pursued the vision of a user-generated metaverse. See Cory Ondrejka, Escaping the Gilded Cage: User Created Content and Building the Metaverse, 1 N.Y.L. Sch. L. Rev. 81 (2004–2005).

39. Second Life FAQ, http://secondlife.com/whatis/faq.php (last visited June 2009).

40. Elaine Silvestrini, Entrepreneurs Sue to Protect Virtual Sales, Tampa Tribune, October 17, 2009, at B1.

41. For more details about the case, see Melissa Ung, Comment: Trademark Law and the Repercussions of Virtual Property (IRL), 17 CommLaw Conspectus 679 (2009); Harris Weems Henderson, Note: Through the Looking Glass: Copyright Protection in the Virtual Reality of Second Life, 16 J. Intell. Prop. L. 165 (2008).

42. Wagner James Au, The Heartbreak of Second Life Content Theft, New World Notes, November 6, 2009, available at: http://nwn.blogs.com/nwn/2009/11/ the-heartbreak-of-content-theft.html (last visited November 2009).

43. Silvestrini, Entrepreneurs.
44. Cf. Sal Humphreys, Discursive Constructions of MMOGs and Some Implications for Policy and Regulation, 130 Media International Australia 53 (2009) (arguing that the productive and creative labor of individuals "need to be thought about alongside those of corporate publishers"); Nicolas Suzor, On the (Partially-)Inalienable Rights of Participants in Virtual Communities, 130 Media International Australia 90 (2009) (arguing that public values can and should inform the structure of governance in the "private" spaces of virtual worlds).

CONCLUSION

1. Nicolas Suzor, On the (Partially-)Inalienable Rights of Participants in Virtual Communities, 130 Media International Australia 97 (2009).
2. What the law ultimately makes of virtual worlds depends on how we choose, collectively, to speak of their nature. There are multiple ways of framing that discourse. See Sal Humphreys, Discursive Constructions of MMOGs and Some Implications for Policy and Regulation, 130 Media International Australia 53 (2009).
3. Torill Elvira Mortensen, Flow, seduction, and mutual pleasures, in Proceedings of the Other Players Conference, Copenhagen, December 6–8, 2004, available at: http://itu.dk/op/papers/mortensen.pdf (last visited November 2009).

INDEX